W9-CHB-915

The International Computer Industry

The International Computer Industry

Innovation and Comparative Advantage

Alvin J. Harman

Harvard University Press
Cambridge, Massachusetts
1971

091010

© Copyright 1971 by The Rand Corporation
All rights reserved
Distributed in Great Britain by Oxford University Press, London
Library of Congress Catalog Card Number 79–133211
SBN 674–45830–3
Printed in the United States of America

To Karen

Preface

A degree of stability is coming to the computer industry. The number of computer manufacturers in the United States is no longer changing dramatically—the dilettantes have departed and the virtuosos are approaching profitability. Although the technology itself is still fluid, new entry into the industry is discouraged by the growing cost of significant advancements. There is continuing debate abroad among firms and governments over the extent of their future involvement in computer technology. This debate is motivated in part by the recognition that computers are now fundamental to the information systems vital to overall technological development and economic growth. The time is ripe for a closer look at the process of innovation within computer firms and at the comparative advantage between countries with respect to the computer industry.

In this book I develop a model for analyzing international comparative advantage that accounts for the effects of innovation. It classifies industries in general into two groups: "new" and "standard." An industry in which technical knowledge is limited to only a few nations is defined as "new." Research and development may lead to innovations by firms in such an industry; a comparative advantage is gained by the nation with the most innovative firms. An industry becomes "standard" when for various reasons technology is no longer limited internationally. The relative abundance of factors of production then becomes the dominant influence. I specifically formulate the part of the model pertinent to new industries and apply it to the computer industry, a prime example of the limited availability of an industrial technology.

This approach also lends itself to a consideration of the implications of the "technological gap" in the international computer industry. However, rather than try to evaluate the essentially political and philosophical problems posed to various governments by this gap, I have confined the work mainly to a display of empirical results which those responsible for making such evaluations may find useful.

An important requirement for the evaluation of empirical results is a knowledge of the underlying data. The quantitative data are presented here by permission of the following journal sources: *Automatic Data Processing Newsletter, Computers and Automation,* and *Datamation*. Special thanks are due to my former colleague at the Massachusetts Institute of Technology, Nelson Hanover, for furnishing me with refined versions of some of these data. My knowledge of corporate operations and intertwinings in the computer industry originates almost entirely in the sources listed in the bibliography. As is evident from that listing, I am greatly indebted to the *Economist* and to the trenchant articles by William D. Smith of the *New York Times*.

The research was undertaken mainly as part of a doctoral dissertation supported by a National Science Foundation Graduate Fellowship and submitted to the Economics department of the Massachusetts Institute of Technology in 1968. I am especially grateful to my thesis committee—Professors Charles P. Kindleberger, Franklin M. Fisher, and Robert M. Solow—for their guidance and encouragement during that period. Aided by further constructive reviews from Professor Raymond Vernon and from my colleague at The Rand Corporation, Kent P. Anderson, I have, in the present text, expanded the scope, refined the logic, and further interpreted the outcomes of the thesis research.

I am pleased to acknowledge that support for this synthesis was undertaken by The Rand Corporation as a part of its study program for the United States Air Force in the area of research and development planning. My efforts in preparing the final manuscript were greatly aided by the editorial suggestions and guidance of Helen B. Turin and Malcolm A. Palmatier, and the accurate and indefatigable secretarial support of Johanna Staehling. Needless to say, I am responsible for any remaining errors or inadequacies.

Undoubtedly the most fundamental contribution to the completion of this work was made by my wife, Karen, to whom I dedicate this book.

Alvin J. Harman

Santa Monica, Calif.
February 1970

Contents

091010

Tables

Figures

The International Computer Industry

1

Introduction: Comparative Advantage and the Technological Gap

Technology has become an important determinant of international comparative advantage. For the econometric analysis of trade patterns, this fact demands consideration.

This book uses a model for analyzing comparative advantage that accounts for the effects of innovation. There are now several theories directed toward the elaboration of a framework embodying the effect of technology on international trade. But until these recent developments, the Heckscher-Ohlin theory was fairly universally accepted as the primary description of trade patterns resulting from comparative advantage. This theory states that, under a number of assumptions, a country will export a good that is produced by a process intensive in the factor of production that that country has in relative abundance. For example, when wiring transistorized radios was a labor-intensive operation, and after the technology spread beyond the borders of the United States, Japan became a leading exporter because of its relative abundance of labor. One of the assumptions needed to arrive at the Heckscher-Ohlin conclusion is that production processes are the same in all countries, that technical knowledge is available everywhere. This theory is still applied to trade in primary products and raw material-intensive manufactured goods, where land or a particular natural resource is the factor in relative abundance in particular countries. But for many industrial products the universal technology assumption may not hold, especially during the early developments in an industry.

As new technologies have become increasingly important economically, their advancement in various countries has become a matter of deep political concern. In the past few years, the debate has intensified among economists and social scientists over the existence and size of a "technological gap" between Europe and the United States. Servan-Schreiber's recent book, *The American Challenge*, which has been useful in widely circulating a discussion of the issues involved, places emphasis on the role of computers in the growth of the gap.[1]

Some have observed a technological gap but have emphasized that

1. J. J. Servan-Schreiber, *The American Challenge*, New York, Atheneum (trans. R. Steel), 1968. Some specific recommendations have been advanced by C. Layton in *European Advanced Technology: A Programme for Integration*, London, Allen & Unwin, 1969.

it is not new.[2] Others point to deficiencies in the sophistication of management techniques as the "real" gap between Europe and the United States.[3] Regardless of the cause, the argument has been raised that any such gap should not evoke concern, since it is strictly another manifestation of comparative advantage. According to this last tack, it is merely good economics for Europe to benefit by allowing the United States to continue to predominate in the provision of advanced, technology-based products.

But there *is* concern. And it is really quite common and appropriate that for essentially political questions—involving national security, political or cultural autonomy, or even prestige—economic arguments are not always decisive. Thus, economists must be expected not only to present cogent arguments for the most economically efficient policy, but also to delineate the costs of the alternatives.

The objectives of developing an empirically relevant modification to the usual theory of comparative advantage and evaluating the extent of a technological gap converge if the analysis is performed for particular industries. This method has occasionally been used in trade theory, for example, by Douglass, Hufbauer, Hirsch, and Stobaugh.[4] But until recently, most studies of the technological gap considered data, such as research and development activity, for entire national economies.[5] Even the United States government, often identified as the prime financier of the American dominance in technology, has become interested in the research competence of other countries in individual fields in the hopes of getting better

2. J. B. Quinn, "Technological Competition: Europe vs. U.S.," *Harvard Business Review* 44, no. 4, July–Aug. 1966, pp. 113–130; R. R. Nelson, "The Technology Gap: Analysis and Appraisal," presented at a conference in Turin, Italy, November 1967; also P-3694-1, The Rand Corporation, December 1967. See also his "Big Technology, the Technology Gap, and a Dangerous Policy Pitfall," P-3795, The Rand Corporation, March 1968; and T. Suranyi-Unger, Jr., "What Is the Technology Gap?" *Interplay* 2, no. 1, June–July 1968, pp. 22–25.

3. A. T. Knoppers, "The 'Technostructure' Gap," *Interplay* 1, no. 9, Apr. 1968, pp. 26–34; "The Technology Gap," *Time*, Jan. 13, 1967, pp. 18–19.

4. G. K. Douglass, "Product Variation and International Trade in Motion Pictures," Ph.D. thesis, Department of Economics, Massachusetts Institute of Technology, 1963; G. C. Hufbauer, *Synthetic Materials and the Theory of International Trade*, London, Duckworth, 1965; S. Hirsch, *Location of Industry and International Competitiveness*, London, Oxford University Press, 1967; R. B. Stobaugh, Jr., "The Product Life Cycle, U.S. Exports, and International Investment," D.B.A. thesis, Graduate School of Business Administration, Harvard University, 1968. Recent analyses of the effects of technology on trade at the national level have been reported by W. Gruber, D. Mehta, and R. Vernon, "The R & D Factor in International Trade and International Investment of United States Industries," *Journal of Political Economy* 75, Feb. 1967, pp. 20–37.

5. See the recent reports by the Organization for Economic Cooperation and Development, *Gaps in Technology: General Report*, especially *Gaps in Technology: Electronic Computers* (Paris, OECD, 1968 and 1969).

returns from its research dollar on some projects by contracting for them abroad.

This study has been designed to take into account the importance of technological developments in different fields on comparative advantages within different industries. The analysis to follow is based on the identification of industries within one of two groups: "new" and "standard." Those in which technical knowledge is limited internationally are classified as "new." Here, research and development leads to innovations by *firms* in an industry. Such considerations as the size of the (potential) domestic market, the availability of technology and research funds, and the rate of innovation of the nation's firms may be crucial in determining comparative advantage for the country *in that industry.* When these special circumstances have been fully exploited and technology is no longer limited in its international availability, the industry can be classified as "standard." Then relative factor abundance within the Heckscher-Ohlin framework becomes the dominant influence.

The historical support for this dichotomy within a theory of comparative advantage has been presented elsewhere. Based on a number of surveys of international trade, several pertinent facts concerning trade patterns were identified.[6] Of primary importance, relatively few countries provide the exports in the industries with the most rapidly expanding exports.[7] The stable and declining categories of exports have had more widely dispersed origins. In particular, the United States has concentrated on exports in the relatively expanding category. Since this category of trade has included those goods

6. A. J. Harman, "Innovations, Technology, and the Pure Theory of International Trade, Ph.D. thesis, Massachusetts Institute of Technology, 1968, Chapter 2. See also F. Hilgerdt, *Industrialization and Foreign Trade*, Geneva, League of Nations, 1945; A. O. Hirschman, *National Power and the Structure of Foreign Trade*, Berkeley, University of California Press, 1945; H. Tyszynski, "World Trade in Manufactured Commodities, 1899–1950," *Manchester School of Economics and Social Studies* 19, 1951, pp. 272–304; I. Svennilson, *Growth and Stagnation in the European Economy*, Geneva, United Nations, 1954; A. K. Cairncross, "World Trade in Manufactures since 1900," *Economia Internazionale* 8, Nov. 1955, pp. 715–738; W. A. Lewis, "International Competition in Manufactures," *American Economic Review, Supplement*, 47, May 1957, pp. 578–587; R. E. Baldwin, "The Commodity Composition of Trade: Selected Industrial Countries, 1900–1954," *Review of Economics and Statistics*, 40, Supplement, February 1958, pp. 50–71; F. H. Awad, "The Structure of World Export Trade, 1926–1953," *Yorkshire Bulletin* 11, July 1959, pp. 19–37; P. L. Yates, *Forty Years of Foreign Trade*, London, Allen & Unwin, 1959; E. Devons, "World Trade in Invisibles," *Lloyd's Bank Review* 60, Apr. 1961, pp. 37–50; A. Maizels, *Industrial Growth and World Trade*, Cambridge, Cambridge University Press, 1963; and S. Kuznets, *Modern Economic Growth: Rate, Structure and Spread*, New Haven, Yale University Press, 1966.

7. In this discussion, I am speaking of export expansion as a proportion of total world trade.

produced in newer innovative industries, these past patterns of exports fit in very well with the new industry portion of the theory.[8] A recent feature of comparative advantage in a "new" industry is direct investment, leading to local production in foreign countries.

The above description of a theoretical basis for comparative advantage is brief and general; the specific objective of this study is to formulate the new industry portion of the theory and to apply it to the computer industry, which is widely regarded as an example of a new industry *par excellence*. International availability of technology is clearly limited to a few countries, making application of the Heckscher-Ohlin theory inappropriate.

Also, within the technological-gap evaluation, the role of information systems is already a crucial feature of technological development and economic growth and is likely to become even more vital in the future. A fundamental building block for these systems is the computer.[9] Design and production capabilities, as well as knowledge of the needs of computer customers, can be important assets in acquiring the ability to use computers creatively.[10] Thus, aside from political considerations, the long-term objective of computer-use competence provides an economic argument for bridging any gap in this area of technical capability. The investigation of a gap between foreign countries and the United States in this industry will include both managerial and technological deficiencies; within the latter, this study will consider the relative abilities to explore problems in the latest technology, as well as the outcomes of these explorations.

Chapter 2 briefly reviews the history of computer technology and then describes the activities of firms in the industry. There is some evidence of the managerial gap and support for the theoretical underpinnings of a new industry's international activities.

Chapter 3 deals with a "new industry" in general, rather than with the computer industry explicitly. It begins with an elaboration of the international features of the new industry model. Then the analysis

8. It also supports the point made by Nelson, "The Technology Gap" that a technological gap between the United States and Europe is not new.

9. This proposition is also a cornerstone of Servan-Schreiber's analysis (*The American Challenge*, pp. 277–278) and of the Group of Experts on electronic computers (*Gaps in Technology: Electronic Computers*, pp. 24–29).

10. William Knox, then a special assistant in the White House Office of Science and Technology, asserted that "perhaps the largest barrier to achieving the potential benefits of the new information-processing technologies will prove to be a lack of understanding about its possibilities" (quoted from Servan-Schreiber, *The American Challenge*, pp. 97–98). Part of the awareness of these possibilities can come from an understanding of the design and logic features of the equipment, as well as from an up-to-date knowledge of applications undertaken by other computer users.

is directed to the dynamic behavior of an individual firm in such an industry. Criteria for identifying an industry as "new" are also discussed.

In Chapter 4, the focus returns to the computer industry. The model of firm behavior is respecified in an appropriate form for econometric analysis and is explored using data for American firms. The estimation of parameter values is undertaken for the innovation and demand functions for these firms.

The analysis is extended in Chapter 5 to consideration of possibilities for American and European firms in the future. Projections of innovative achievements by 1980 are made for the U.S. firms, and also (under explicitly stated assumptions) for two important European efforts: Compagnie Internationale de l'Informatique, created at the end of 1966 by France's *Plan Calcul*, and International Computers, Ltd., which resulted from the 1968 merger in Britain's industry. The possibility (and concomitant cost) of bridging the technological gap in computers is thereby revealed. Benefits to computer firms from a more fully integrated Europe are also explored.

The book concludes with an evaluation of the modified theory of comparative advantage and a prognosis for non-American firms in the computer industry.

2
The Computer Industry in an International Setting

Understanding the classification of the computer industry as "new" involves an appreciation of the developments that have been made in computer technology. Even more important than the scientific work, however, are the innovative efforts of firms in the industry. The discussion below reveals that there are Europeans and Japanese who have been involved with the technology for many years, but firms in the United States emerge in the dominant position as innovators.[1]

Computer History and Characteristics

In the late 1930s automatic calculators with electromechanical relays were being developed by Friedrich Zuse in Berlin, Howard H. Aiken of Harvard University, and George R. Stibitz of the Bell Telephone Laboratories. Zuse, with his colleague, Dr. H. Schreyer, was also first to begin work on electronic machines very early in the 1940s; the efforts were suspended when Schreyer was drafted and official support for the project was refused. The first U.S. design based on the vacuum tube was the ENIAC, developed by J. Presper Eckert and John W. Mauchly of the University of Pennsylvania beginning in 1942. A British group was actually using an automatic calculator as early as 1943 for analyses of wartime problems; Germany, at one time during the war, had two such machines in operation.

The term "computer" as now used implies the ability of the machine to store a program (set of operating instructions) in its own memory.[2] Eckert and Mauchly developed the first practical proposal for such a machine during the war and produced the first commercial computer within a company they formed. This was the Eckert-Mauchly UNIVAC I, which was first delivered early in 1951. As

1. This book is concerned with developments in the noncommunist world; only in Chapter 6 will there be discussion of the possible pertinence of the Soviet Bloc countries to the considerations previously discussed.

2. J. McCarthy, "Information," *Scientific American* 215, Sept. 1966, pp. 65–72. Much of the historical information comes from articles in this issue of *Scientific American* (especially one by D. Evans, "Computer Logic and Memory," pp. 75–85), as well as from C. Freeman's discussion of the computer industry in his "Research and Development in Electronic Capital Goods" (*National Institute Economic Review* 34, Nov. 1965, pp. 40–91) and the OECD report *Gaps in Technology: Electronic Computers*. A detailed listing of sources of information for this chapter is given in the "computer industry" section at the end of the bibliography.

with many of the companies involved in early computer development, the Eckert-Mauchly Company had financial troubles throughout its short life; it was absorbed in 1950 by Remington Rand, which was itself joined by Sperry Gyroscope Corporation to form Sperry Rand in 1955.

This is a typical example of the evolution of many firms in the computer industry. After a brief outline of the development of computers in general, I shall discuss the firms in the United States, Japan, and Europe.

Under the heading "computer industry," this book will explore activities related to general purpose digital computers.[3] The broadest market for computers has developed in this area, and much of the innovative activity has been focused on the inhibiting frontiers of this technology.[4] These machines have several basic functions: input, output, and processing of information, and storage of information and subordinate calculations in a form convenient to the processor. This last function is customarily performed by the "memory" of the machine, the processing is accomplished in the "central processor," and the input and output require the use of what has become a vast array of "peripheral equipment"—card readers and punchers, magnetic tape units and drums, disk storage devices, typewriters and line printers, as well as video display units, light pens, and pressure-sensitive input tablets. The frontiers of each of these functions have been expanded enormously since the beginning of the 1950s.

The computer has been described most broadly as having developed through three generations—from vacuum tube circuitry to transistors to integrated circuits; it is heading toward a fourth generation —large-scale integration. This description usually deals with the central processor function and has been dated with the first UNIVAC

3. All computers can be categorized as either digital or analog (or hybrids of the two). The digital computer works with actual numbers in the binary system and is programmed to operate step by step; the analog computer uses as its fundamental element an "operational amplifier" and processes information continuously through variations in electrical voltages. The latter are gaining wide acceptance in industry now, particularly in process control, but they still form a minor share of the value of all sales of computers. See R. Vichnevetsky, "For Easy Rapport Between Man and Machine There's Nothing Quite Like an Analog Computer," *New York Times*, Jan. 9, 1967, p. 140.

Within the digital computer segment, "general purpose" computers are the main section, distinguished from special one-of-a-kind computers, usually needed for military or specialized experimental purposes.

4. The Value Line survey has reported that industry shipments of general purpose digital computers totalled $3.7 billion in 1966 and was projected as increasing to $12 billion per year by the mid-1970s, implying a fivefold increase in total value of electronic data processing equipment to $100 billion in under 10 years. See "E.D.P. Industry," *Value Line Selection and Opinion* 23, no. 12, Jan. 5, 1968, p. 164.

I in 1950 for the first generation, the PHILCO 2000 in 1958 for the second.[5] The third generation technology was known widely in the early 1960s and was first implemented by the Radio Corporation of America and the United Kingdom's English Electric in 1965.[6] The OECD Group of Experts identify the above changes as essentially *component* technology, and admit that until the third generation of *computer* technology the two technologies changed together.[7] The generation concept is itself an enormous simplification; thus the dating of first implementations is of little significance.

Memory design also played a big role in improvement of the machine. "For most of the period during which computers have evolved, the limiting factor in their design and cost has been memory capacity. The speed of computers has been restricted by the time required to store and retrieve information."[8] Mercury delay lines were used in some of the earliest computers. Magnetic core memories, made up of thousands of very small doughnut-shaped ferrite cores in arrays, have been used extensively as a form of "random access" memory in which the storage and retrieval time is independent of the sequence in which the information is stored. Other random access devices have been developed that use thin metallic films, which have the property that large arrays of elements can be stably magnetized in either of two directions. It is anticipated that big improvements will be made in this area in the near future, as well as in memory devices using integrated circuits, high resolution photography with laser scanners, and color coding.

5. Burroughs and Sperry Rand also claim to have had the first operational second-generation machine.

6. "RCA's Spectra 70 Series was the first major computer series to incorporate integrated circuits as basic components," "Impact of Integrated Circuits on the Computer Field," *Computers and Automation* 14, July 1965, p. 9. See "Who Leads Computers," *Economist* 216, Sept. 25, 1965, p. 1228, on "System 4" of English Electric. It was the first to introduce a line of computers extending to the smaller ranges which had microelectronic features. The article indicates that there had been a few earlier introductions of integrated circuits in the United States in larger computer models. This combination of initial introductions is not surprising, since RCA and English Electric have arrangements to exchange technology. These arrangements between firms in the industry will be dealt with extensively later in this chapter.

For a discussion of possible future improvements in computers along these same lines, see, for example, G. M. and L. D. Amdahl, "Fourth Generation Hardware, A View from the Third," *Datamation* 13, Jan. 1967, pp. 25–26.

7. "Computer technology" is identified as follows: "first generation machines were operated through programs written in machine language, whereas the second generation computers used higher-level languages. Third generation computers have a multiprogramming capability and limited time-sharing, and the fourth generation computers can be expected to have telecommunications capability." See OECD, *Gaps in Technology; Electronic Computers*, p. 70, as well as the discussion of it in Chart 6.

8. D. Evans, "Computer Logic and Memory," p. 78.

In studying developments in computers still further, one finds that not all the improvements resulted from the physical components, nor were the research activities in the industry devoted entirely to this work. Some of the major work for general purpose systems has been devoted to the more efficient use of the physical components. The coordination of a mercury delay line, fast access memory with a magnetic tape availability for large capacity of storage is an example from the late 1940s and the Eckert-Mauchly Corporation. Index registers and concurrent processing and input-output operations via buffer storage registers provide other examples. More recent examples of efforts of manufacturers in the improvement of their systems are modularity of computer design (allowing for expansion of computer capabilities by adding further modules), and software packages (computer compilers and assemblers that allow the user to write instructions symbolically in a language of English and algebraic statements, from which the computer develops—compiles—its own set of machine instructions to perform the operations).

The United States Industry

By far the most important country in the computer industry is the United States. Although the initial breakthroughs and even implementation have not always come from American firms, these firms have most consistently been leaders in the industry. Many of the firms that have shown at least serious efforts to enter the industry will be discussed below (see Table 2.1).

To understand what factors contribute to success in this industry, it is important to consider firms that have been in it and have not been independently successful.[9] Underwood Corporation and El-Tronics are interesting examples of such firms. The small size of these companies and their apparent inability to innovate were probably decisive factors in their exit from the industry. Underwood (assets in 1958 of $63 million) acquired the assets of Electronic Computer Corporation in 1952 and was in the market with ELCOM 100 by December; it had quietly dropped out of the industry by about 1959 or 1960. El-Tronics (assets in 1958 of $3.5 million) was a bit more dramatic, having acquired the computer division of Alwac Corporation (which had produced computers at least since 1952) in

9. Much of the information on companies in this discussion was obtained from various *Moody's Industrial Manual* histories; from comments included with J. Diebold and Associates, *Automatic Data Processing Service Newsletter* computer censuses; from Chapter 6 of W. F. Sharpe, *The Economics of Computers*, Columbia University Press, New York, 1969; and from the OECD report, *Gaps in Technology: Electronic Computers*.

Table 2.1. United States Firms in the Computer Industry

Active in 1969

Bunker-Ramo Corp.
Burroughs Corp.[a]
Business Information Technology, Inc.
Computer Automation, Inc.
Computer Development Corp.
Control Data Corp.[a]
Data General Corp.
Datacraft Corp.
Data Mate Computer Systems, Inc.
Decade Computer Corp.
Digiac Corp.
Digital Equipment Corp.[a]
Electronic Associates
EMR Computer
General Automation, Inc.
General Electric Co.[b]
Hewlett-Packard Co.
Honeywell, Inc.[b]
Hughes Aircraft Co.
IBM Corp.[a]
Interdata, Inc.
Litton Industries
Lockheed Electronics Co.
Motorola Instrumentation & Control, Inc.
National Cash Register Co.[a]
Pacific Data Systems
Potter Instrument Co.
Raytheon Co.
RCA Corp.[b]
Redcor Corp.
Scientific Control Corp.
Scientific Data Systems[c]
Sperry Rand Corp.[a]
Standard Computer Corp.
Systems Engineering Laboratories
Tempo Computers, Inc.
Varian Associates
Westinghouse Electric Corp.
Wilkinson Computer Sciences, Inc.

Not independently active[d]

Addressograph-Multigraph
Advanced Scientific Instruments
Alwac Corp.
Autonetics
Bailey Meter Co.
Bendix Corp.[b]
Budd Electronics
Clary Multiplier
Computer Control Corp.
Computer Research Corp.
Corbin Corp.
Cubic Corp.
Eckert-Mauchly Corp.
Electrodata Corp.
Electronic Computer Corp.
El-Tronics, Inc.
Engineering Research Associates
Friden
General Intellitronics
General Mills
General Precision Equipment Corp.[b]
Hampshire Engineering
Hogan Labs
HRB Singer
H-W Electronics
International Telephone and Telegraph
J. B. Rea Co.
Laboratory for Electronics
Marchant Calculators
Monroe-Calculating Machine Co.[b]
Mountain Systems
Northrop Aircraft
Packard-Bell
Philco Corp.
Royal McBee
Sylvania Electric
TRW, Inc.
Underwood Corp.
United Aircraft

Sources: Compiled in part from *Business Automation*, "Reference Issue" 16, no. 9, Sept. 1969; *Computers and Automation* 18, nos. 7 and 13, June 30 and Dec. 1969; and *Automatic Data Processing Newsletter*, "Diebold Semi-Annual Computer Census" 13, no. 15, Feb. 24, 1969.

Notes: This list includes all the participants in the "computer industry" as defined in this study: producers of general purpose digital computers.

[a] Data pertaining to the corporation are used in both demand and innovation analyses in Chapter 4.

[b] Data are used in the demand analysis in Chapter 4.

[c] Data are used in the innovation analysis in Chapter 4.

[d] These are firms that have dropped out of the industry, have been absorbed by other firms, or are primarily special purpose digital computer manufacturers.

March of 1958 and reorganized under the Pennsylvania Bankruptcy Act by November of 1960.

Philco Corporation made its entry into the industry in 1958 by being the first to introduce a second-generation (all transistor) computer. It continued to develop new models for a time but no longer makes general-purpose computers. The main emphasis of its R&D has been in the area of computer peripherals. The company was quite widely diversified even before it became a member of the Ford Motor Company group in 1961.

The history surrounding the machines marketed by General Precision Equipment Corporation and Royal McBee is also quite revealing. One of the computers, LGP 30 (number 92 in Table 4.9), was brought into the Royal McBee marketing structure through the joint venture it undertook with the General Precision Corporation in 1956—the Royal Precision joint subsidiary. This computer had been designed by a scientist, Stanley P. Frankel, at the California Institute of Technology; the rights to develop and produce the machine were obtained by the Librascope Group of General Precision. Royal McBee had no experience in research on computers before its joint venture with General Precision; its involvement in the industry began with what proved to be an extremely successful first-generation computer (introduced in 1956, there were still over 100 installations in operation in the United States in 1966, and over 30 in West Germany). Royal McBee (with assets of $69.1 million at the time) apparently had second thoughts about the research end of the computer industry by 1962, when it sold its 50 percent interest in Royal Precision to General Precision for $5 million, taking a nearly $7 million loss. General Precision continued to develop and manufacture computers in the United States for a while; a subsidiary in West Germany, Eurocomp, handled marketing there. In 1965 Control Data Corporation (CDC) bought out the Commercial Computer Division (of the Librascope Group) of General Precision (assets at the end of the year were $152.6 million). This computer division thereby followed the route of the computer division of the Bendix Corporation (assets at the time of $436.5 million), which was acquired by the Control Data Corporation in 1963. Royal McBee became associated with the computer industry again in 1965 when it merged into Litton Industries, which had acquired the Monroe Calculating Machine Company in early 1958. The Monroe subsidiary still represents Litton's only venture in the computer industry; even though it has been in the industry since at least 1955 (with assets of about $30 million before its merger), it is not as successful as many of the other companies listed as "active" in Table 2.1.

In most of these cases in which the computer industry was abandoned or the corporation was acquired by a larger firm or more successful computer specialist, the firms involved were reasonably small. Probably more important, the computer endeavors were not their original field of interest nor were they a source of current profit. Although the data for these firms simply are not available, their size and other interests suggest a relatively small independent research effort in computer technology as a reasonable conjecture.

Even among the main firms now in the industry, only one has been showing large profits from computer operations for any length of time: IBM Corporation (formerly International Business Machines Corporation). It was one of the originators of the digital computer as manufacturer of the Harvard Mark I in 1944, which it viewed at the time as a showpiece of IBM's engineering talent and as a gift to science and education. In fact, the company was slow to appreciate the commercial possibilities of computers; IBM's machines did not begin to outsell Sperry Rand's UNIVACs until 1956.

By 1968 IBM held about 70 percent of the computer market and achieved a one-third *increase* in profits over 1967—to $871 million. As is well known, it is a huge corporation (assets of $4.6 billion in 1966), the largest in the industry, and has contributed to the development of computer technology throughout the life of the industry. Even after its decision to produce computers commercially, IBM was not always the leader in innovations. In the early 1960s its research department carried the development of a second-generation "8000" series for quite a while before finally eliminating it in favor of the more advanced hybrid circuitry in the System 360 designs.[10] The company's efforts are now largely in the computer and closely related fields, rather than widely diversified; more than three-fourths of annual sales are accounted for by sales, service, and rentals of punch-card accounting and electronic data processing machines and systems. Its policies of leasing its equipment and of not changing the rental price of individual systems from year to year after their

10. For a thorough discussion of the decisions during this period, see T. Wise, "I: IBM's $5,000,000,000 Gamble" and "II: The Rocky Road to the Marketplace," *Fortune* 74, nos. 4 and 5, Sept. and Oct. 1966, pp. 118ff, 138ff. Even after rejecting the second generation circuitry, IBM still used a hybrid integrated circuitry in which passive (connections and resistors) and active (transistors) components are kept separate and manufactured in distinct stages rather than in one continuous production process. Their claim was that "if and when monolithic (integrated) circuitry ever did prove to have decisive advantages over IBM's hybrid circuitry, ... the computers themselves and three-quarters of the component manufacturing equipment could be adapted fairly inexpensively to monolithics," ibid. (II), p. 206. However, IBM was undoubtedly committed to these hybrid circuits for at least three or four years.

introduction have formed a pattern for the industry. It took a consent decree resulting from the 1956 antitrust suit against IBM to require the company to sell as well as rent its machines. Two of IBM's competitors filed suits late in 1968 for alleged monopolistic practices.[11] And early in 1969, the Justice Department filed an antitrust suit alleging violation of the Sherman Act. Although it is unlikely that these actions will drastically change IBM's structure or position, they may provide a temporary opportunity or incentive for other firms to increase their participation in this rapidly growing industry.

The Sperry Rand Corporation, second in sales in recent years, has been making profits from its computer operations only since 1965. Part of its history in the computer field was noted at the beginning of this chapter. The Remington Rand Corporation took over the Eckert-Mauchly Corporation in 1950 and Engineering Research Associates, another important early firm in electronic computing, in 1952. These two acquisitions were maintained as separate divisions until Remington's 1955 merger with Sperry Gyroscope. UNIVAC, Remington Rand's line of computers, was a name virtually synonymous with "computer" in the early 1950s. But Sperry Rand lost its position as the commercial market leader to IBM in 1956.

In contrast with IBM, Sperry Rand does not at the present time have a substantial majority of its endeavors in the computer industry. It had just over one-third of gross sales in 1966 in its business equipment division, which includes business machines and equipment (office equipment produced by the Remington Rand Division as well as electronic data processing equipment produced by the UNIVAC Division). It had about the same proportion of sales generated from its instrumentation and controls division, and slightly under one-third of sales came from its hydraulic and farm equipment division.

Nearly surpassing Sperry Rand in computer sales by 1967 was Honeywell, whose computer business had just become profitable in 1966. Its operations are also diversified, with the automatic controls business contributing 28 percent to sales, and the computer business 20 percent (in 1966). Honeywell had entered the industry in 1955 when it joined (with 60 percent interest) Raytheon Manufacturing Company, forming Datamatic Corporation, to make and sell computers. It subsequently bought out the minority interest and proceeded to develop in this industry on its own. It attained an important

11. One suit is concerned with IBM's policy for provision of software and was filed by Data Processing and Financial General Corp., software specialists. The other is being pursued by Control Data Corp.; see below and A. Pantages, "Control Data Puts Legal Money Where Its Mouth Was ... Sues IBM," *Datamation* 15, no. 1, Jan. 1969, pp. 78–79.

position only late in 1963, when it introduced a new generation of data processing machines (the H-200 line) that were compatible with IBM machines. Honeywell enlarged its product line further in 1966 with the acquisition of Computer Control Corporation, a designer of small computers for use in scientific projects. The company further revised its organizational structure by early 1969 to begin providing computer services (including time-sharing) within its computer and communication group.

Control Data Corporation was one of the few other firms in the industry showing a profit on computer operations in 1967. But this position of profitability was recaptured only after a year of unprofitable performance. It was the first firm after IBM to become profitable, even though the company was only formed in 1957. Its appearance of newness is a bit deceptive, however. The company was formed by a group that had been together even prior to the formation of Engineering Research Associates (in 1947) and finally struck out on its own from Sperry Rand's UNIVAC Division (a lawsuit over this departure was decided in favor of CDC's right to exist). Thus, although the company was small and new in the industry, it was devoted exclusively to computer technology and had experience in this field antedating the company's inception. Since that time it has grown rapidly by continuous acquisitions including, as noted earlier, the computer operations of Bendix in 1963 and of General Precision in 1966. CDC has already established a leading position in the rapidly growing market for very large computers; its traditional strength has been in computers for scientific uses. The main cause of the company's financial problems in 1966 seems to have been in developing computer software—the means by which users can communicate conveniently with the machines and use one machine to solve different types of problems.[12] This may have been a factor in CDC's decision to acquire the computer service and consulting company CEIR in late 1967. As noted above, CDC preceded the U.S. Justice Department by filing suit against IBM late in 1968 for alleged violations of U.S. antitrust laws. Its principal concern in pursuing the case seems to be competition in very large computers—in particular, it accused IBM of premature announcement of the 360/91 to capture potential

12. J. Western, in a feature article in the *National Observer* ("With Computers, Sales Pitch Is for 'Software'," Feb. 6, 1967, pp. 1, 20), noted that software, which formerly was supplied free to customers of a firm's hardware, is increasingly growing into a business of its own. Both hardware manufacturers and exclusively software specialists are vying for this rapidly growing market.

Commercial prospects in this field were given a big boost in 1968 when the United States Court of Customs and Patent Appeals ruled that "truly novel" computer programs are to be considered as inventions and are therefore patentable.

customers for CDC's 6600 in 1964. IBM's machine was then late in delivery and discontinued after very few were produced. With CDC introducing its latest giant, the 7600, just two weeks before filing suit, it clearly was taking precautions against repeating that 1964 experience.

The Burroughs Corporation is another of the " old timers " in the industry, having been a participant since the early 1950s. In 1949, as Eckert and Mauchly were forming their own company, Burroughs was hiring a member of their ENIAC development team, Irven Travis, to lead its research laboratory. The company has made only one acquisition of independent computer talent since entering the industry. This was Electrodata Corporation (assets of $3.3 million in 1955), which was acquired in 1956 with the consent of the controlling stockholder, Consolidated Electro-Dynamics (formerly Consolidated Engineering, with assets of about $16 million in 1955). However, the acquisition was not effectively integrated into Burroughs until the early 1960s.

Although Burroughs has a long-established reputation for fine hardware and has even been a supplier of memory modules to other manufacturers, it has only recently begun to demonstrate increasing abilities in software, servicing, and other customer-support efforts. It is similar to IBM in being concentrated in the business data processing area but has concentrated much more heavily in the adding and accounting machine fields, as well as in business supplies. For the first time in 1968 the company began to show a " modest profit " from its computer operations; it is directing its participation in the industry toward medium and large computer systems.

Most of the remaining firms are not yet achieving profits from their computer efforts. National Cash Register has also been designing computers since the early 1950s; it purchased the Computer Research Corporation shortly after the latter introduced the CRC-102 in 1952. In the late 1950s it had an agreement with General Electric whereby systems designed by NCR are manufactured by GE. It has concentrated in the past on developing business in the financial and retailing parts of the computer market. Its operations in this area are not yet profitable, but company spokesmen have expressed the view that they are moving toward a profitable position as planned. This sentiment seems to be verified by their actions, which included a massive worldwide series of demonstrations in 1968 of a new, broader line of machines, their third-generation Century series of computers. Orders for this new computer family by the end of that year gave the company its largest data processing backlog in its history. However, NCR clearly has its largest involvement outside the computer industry, with only about one-tenth of total revenue coming from computer operations.

RCA Corporation (formerly Radio Corporation of America) is in the same category as National Cash Register—a widely diversified company that has made a genuine effort to succeed in profitable computer operations. It entered the industry in the early 1950s and was showing a profit on its operations from 1963 to 1965. Although it built up its sales force drastically in 1965 and achieved a 40 percent increase in sales in 1966, higher costs attributed to R&D eliminated profitability; by the end of 1968 the company was still "moving as planned" back to a profitable position (expected in the early 1970s). Following the highly successful route taken by Honeywell, its latest series—Spectra 70, which embodies fully integrated circuitry—has been designed to be compatible with IBM's System 360. Latest models of this series, introduced in 1969, have been designed to achieve the company's entry into the large-scale and time-sharing markets. The RCA Information Systems Division manufactures, as well as designs, develops, and merchandises, its systems; RCA Laboratories conducts research in computer technology as one of its areas of interest. Although widely diversified, the company has expressed its intention to make electronic data processing the dominant segment of its business.

General Electric might be thought of as being in this same category. It entered the industry in the early 1950s also and has been reported as having "more computers in use in the early days than any other company," although the figures in Tables 4.9 and 4.11 below do not verify this assertion.[13] GE really is not in this category, however, in the sense that its operations in general purpose digital computers have been distinctly less successful than have those of the other two companies. It has never shown a profit in these computer operations, even though some observers in the past had considered GE the greatest potential threat to IBM's dominant position in the industry. Its former chairman attributed their lack of success to lack of interest within the corporation; he emphasized that the company chose to

13. *New York Times*, "Former G.E. Chief Tells How IBM Won on Computers," Oct. 14, 1967, pp. 31, 36. This discrepancy may reflect the possible uneven coverage (across companies) of the Knight selection of computers discussed in the Appendix to Chapter 4. Part of the optimistic view of GE's future in computers in the early days undoubtedly came from its victory over 29 competitors in a $55 million dollar contract, "Erma," from the Bank of America; see "GE's Computer Troubles—How They Happened," *Forbes* 99, Apr. 1, 1967, p. 23.

concentrate its talent in other areas where it has been successful.[14] In 1966, GE's sales were about one-third derived from computer operations (up from just over one-quarter in 1961); its other spheres of interest are broadly heavy capital goods, consumer goods, and aerospace and defense work. By the end of 1966 it had experienced so much software difficulty that it had to lay off manufacturing personnel. Even by the end of 1968 the best estimate from the company was that its computer business should become profitable by the early 1970s.

The last two entries of Table 2.1 to be described here are among the smallest significant firms in the computer industry, both of which specialize in the industry. Digital Equipment Corporation, with assets of $21 million by June 1967,[15] has made it an explicit company policy since its formation in 1957 to sell computers outright, leasing only in special situations. This is contrary to the dominant practice of other firms of leasing their equipment. DEC has also made a policy of retaining all earnings and devoting a large measure of these to R&D; it was making a profit on its operations in 1968.

Scientific Data Systems was formed only in 1961, but it ranked third in dollar-per-share profits behind IBM and CDC by 1965.[16] During this period, it chose to concentrate on small- to medium-sized computers for scientific, government, and industrial markets, to the exclusion of business applications. By 1966, profits had increased another 26 percent over 1965 results (and have continued to grow rapidly through 1968); in that year the firm also introduced its now highly successful third-generation Sigma series. In the spring of 1969, the merger of SDS into Xerox Corporation, the technologically oriented copier/duplicator manufacturer, was approved and the company became Xerox Data Systems.[17] This combination could allow computer operations of the joint corporation to become more diversified and expand even more rapidly into large-scale computer systems.

14. "Former G.E. Chief," p. 36. The interview was with Ralph J. Cordiner, chairman of GE until 1963.

15. Its assets were still under $4 million in 1962.

16. The OECD mentions SDS as "an offshoot of Packard-Bell"; *Gaps in Technology; Electronic Components*, Paris, OECD, 1968, p. 75. "Involuntary spinoff" might be a better description, since several key members of Packard-Bell, including Max Palevsky (president of SDS), left the company to form their own. Packard-Bell's activities in computers essentially ended at that time; it was subsequently acquired by Raytheon.

17. Throughout this book, reference will be made to SDS rather than XDS since the period of analysis of its operations was prior to the merger. Some of the possible effects of the merger are mentioned below.

In summary, then, many of the potentially if not yet actually successful computer firms operate in other industries as well. The smaller firms are all in the computer industry exclusively. All firms conform to the basic scheme to be used in the theoretical model: they seek to maximize profits over an extended time horizon. They all recognize the importance of research to success in the industry, and research has been the stumbling block for several firms that have now departed. Retained earnings have also been kept high by most companies to finance their future development efforts; many have expressly aimed these efforts at large-scale systems.

Europe and Japan

In the discussion of other countries with firms undertaking operations in the computer industry, consideration will be given to the foreign arrangements of U.S. firms and the operations of foreign firms. In reviewing the operations of these firms, it will be important to note the extent to which their behavior fits the pattern elaborated by Linder, Kravis, and Posner—that is, to what extent is development of computers geared to local market considerations, and to what extent do foreign firms imitate developments made by U.S. firms?[18] It will also be of interest to note the extent of, and motive for, direct investment by these firms abroad.[19]

Before considering the firms in detail, however, it may be useful to put the countries involved in the investigation into proper perspective.[20] The United States is far and away the largest user of computers. Although measures vary, the United States has from 12 to 18 times the number (or value) of computers as the country in second place. In terms of the number of machines in use, West Germany, Japan, and the United Kingdom hold second position (the ordering

18. S. Burenstam Linder, *An Essay on Trade and Transformation*, Stockholm, Almquist and Wiksells, 1961; I. B. Kravis, "'Availability' and Other Influences on the Commodity Composition of Trade," *Journal of Political Economy* 64, no. 2, Apr. 1956, pp. 143–155; M. V. Posner, "International Trade and Technical Change," *Oxford Economic Papers* 13 (N.S.), Oct.1961, pp. 323–341. For a more detailed discussion of these theories, see Chapter 3. Their theories were applied to entire national economies, rather than to individual firms, as will be done in the new-industry theoretical framework.

19. The assumption in considering direct investment is that this is a useful method available to the firm to keep closest guard on its own technological developments. See S. H. Hymer, "The International Operations of National Firms, A Study of Direct Foreign Investment," Ph.D. thesis, Massachusetts Institute of Technology, 1960.

20. For surveys of the industry see "Computers: Europe Fights Back," *Economist* 219, June 11, 1966, pp. 1209–1210; "Where the Brains are," *Newsweek*, Jan. 29, 1968, p. 57; OECD, *Gaps in Technology; Electronic Computers*; or the Diebold *Automatic Data Processing Newsletter* computer censuses.

varies from one source of information to the next). France is not very far behind these countries; its projected rate of acquisition of additional machines is higher than for any other country, so that it is projected to be second only to the United States by the early 1970s. When the comparison is made by value of computers, Japan falls sharply to fifth position, indicative of the Japanese market's heavier reliance on small computers. By either measure Italy is next. It shares sixth position with Canada in number of machines but is decidedly ahead in value.[21] Benelux is eighth, with less than two percent of the number of computers that are in use in the United States. Scandinavia is behind the Benelux countries. Switzerland has a smaller number of computers but has nearly one-third as many as the United States relative to the size of each country's nonagricultural labor force— approximately double the relative number available in France. Israel is in a similar position.

American firms account for about 95 percent of the world computer market and upward of 90 percent of the European market, in which the most significant non-American competition exists. The broad outline of the Posner hypothesis[22] is certainly verified by the national experiences in this industry—the innovating U.S. industry commands essentially its *entire* home market and not less than half of any other country's market (see Figure 1). Since IBM alone accounts for about 80 percent of the world market and over half of the European, it is quite appropriate that the discussion should begin with this firm.

Only about 4 percent of IBM's shares are owned outside of the United States. Still, this firm is quite close to being truly international both in organization and objectives. It was one of the first firms to enter the European market. As a result, it not only held 70 percent of the U.S. computer market in 1966 but also had 73 percent of West Germany's, 50 percent of Britain's, 74 percent of France's, 40 percent of Japan's (but 60 percent by value of sales), and 80 percent of Italy's. IBM's fundamental advantage over all its competitors is the excellent marketing and servicing network it has established throughout the world. Its machines are good, but so are those of most of its

21. Canada is not considered further in this survey, since its computer market is essentially an extension of the U.S. market. See G. S. Slinski, "Computing in Canada," *Datamation* 11, no. 5, May 1965, pp. 38–39; and OECD, *Gaps in Technology; Electronic Computers*, p. 35.

22. Posner, "International Trade." For a more thorough discussion of the imitation lag behind the innovating country, which leads to a period during which the innovator exports, see the discussion of the innovation/imitation model in Chapter 3.

010180

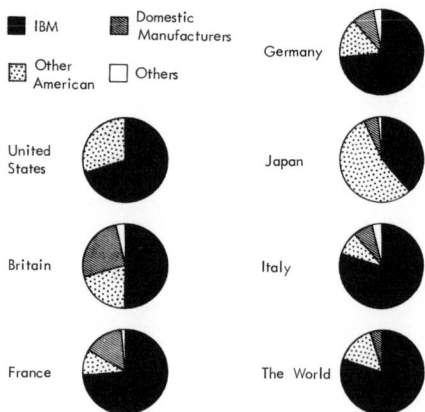

Fig. 1. How the market is split.

The total is minus "vintage" computers plus orders before May 1966. (Reproduced with permission from "Computers: Europe Fights Back," *Economist* 219, June 11, 1966, 1210.)

competitors; the repair of problems and provision of useful software for the users' needs have therefore been crucial to IBM's success.

Not only is IBM organized internationally for marketing, its manufacturing operations are similarly widespread. Of the gross revenue from non-U.S. operations, roughly 70 percent is attributable to European plant sales. Rather than produce a large part of the product line in a plant in each country, manufacturing plants in Europe are specialized and the part of the product line produced in each follows closely the probable main demand of each country.[23] In Vimercate, Italy, the smallest of the 360 system series is manufactured (the model 20); in Mainz, West Germany, the 360/30; and in Montpellier, France, the 360/40. The 1130 scientific computer, as well as teleprocessing networks, are manufactured at the plant in Greenock, United Kingdom. Even the manufacture of peripheral equipment is specialized: equipment for the 360 series is made in Stockholm, Sweden; disks are made near Stuttgart, West Germany; punch-card machines are made in Berlin. A separate plant in Brussels, Belgium, is set up solely to recondition older computers (mainly German machines), which are then shipped primarily to developing countries.

23. Also according to major sources of demand, all of the company's really big machines are still manufactured only in America; see T. Dakin, "Marketing: Computer Colossus Expands in Europe," *British Industry Week*, Oct. 1967, pp. 14–16. Dakin notes that rental of machines in a country that does not produce that model is accomplished by importing the machine from the foreign plant in which it is produced and subsequently renting it to the user by the local IBM subsidiary.

091010

Specialization in production has combined with the large volume of production to make vertical integration to the electronic components field feasible. In an area where there are important economies of scale that make nearly all foreign firms as well as many U.S. firms dependent on U.S. suppliers (for example, Fairchild, Texas Instruments, Motorola) for their electronic components, IBM's volume has enabled it to set up six plants—four in the United States (in New York and Vermont), one in Sindelfingen, West Germany, and one in Corbeil-Essones, France—to manufacture its own hybrid integrated circuits for the 360 systems. Again, in components, the plants are specialized: the French plant makes the "Solid Logic Technique Modules" for all IBM computers in Europe, as well as some for the United States; the German plant makes all the cards to mount them on.

IBM research and development laboratories are also diffused throughout Europe. This has the advantage of enabling the company to keep in close contact with many nations' related scientific research (and thereby protect its market position, or the length of the "trading period" in the terminology of the Posner model), but there could easily be disadvantages from fractionizing research efforts. These disadvantages are reputed to be minimized by a system of interconnected computers that exchange engineering and manufacturing information in both directions between the United States and European plants and laboratories on a daily basis. Thus, when the Boeblingen, West Germany, R&D laboratory was designing the System 360/20, it was in communication with the Sindelfingen plant, which later became the product manager of the model; when other manufacturing plants such as one in San Jose, California, began producing the Model 20, prompt information on production and engineering improvements in the machine was received through these rapid communication channels.

The firm has had some problems in recent years, especially during the development of the System 360 and the hybrid integrated circuit it used, as well as with the software required for these systems. But these problems have now clearly been overcome and the series is quite successful. As a reflection of the self-sufficiency of the European subsidiaries, the Italian and German subsidiaries set a corporate precedent in May 1966, "by shipping a new product—the System 360/20—even before U.S. plants got them off the line."[24]

The international aspects of IBM's objectives are exemplified by

24. N. McInnes, "No Monopoly on Brains; Competition Has Sharpened in the Fast-Growing Foreign Market for Computers," *Barrons* 46, Oct. 31, 1966, p. 9.

two main phenomena. First, there has been an increasing emphasis on placing non-American executives in top (nonfigurehead) positions in the foreign subsidiaries. For example, in 1967 George R. S. Baring, the third Earl of Cromer and former governor of the Bank of England, was named chairman of IBM-U.K. Holding, the British producing and marketing arm of the IBM World Trade Corporation. The other phenomenon is the nationalistic attitudes of its foreign subsidiaries. In particular, as noted by McInnes:

"IBM-France's product line has played a vital part in making the Fifth French Republic into the world's fourth nuclear power . . . According to the subsidiary's latest report: 'Our military division is an autonomous organization, subject to national security requirements . . . It is pursuing its efforts to endow the national defense with the most modern arms systems.' In both cases, of course, when IBM-France says 'national' it means French."[25]

There is a growing feeling both in Europe and in Japan that a genuinely national entry in the computer industry must be maintained. It is therefore not terribly surprising (nor, perhaps, revealing) to find IBM adopting appearances of a national firm of the country;[26] it is particularly important for IBM's French subsidiary in the face of former President de Gaulle's *Plan Calcul*, which created the "all French" Compagnie Internationale de l'Informatique as an important competitor for France's *force de frappe* and space business.[27] IBM's Japanese subsidiary has been in operation since 1963 and is the only foreign firm actually producing computers in Japan. It has also been trying to look like a Japanese company because of increasing government restrictions on direct investment and requirements for Japanese material content of computers.

Clearly, none of the other firms in the industry has the international breadth of operations of IBM. Only one other American firm had its own international *network* of production facilities—General Electric. It accomplished this feat by acquisitions; but by 1968, four years after establishing its "beachhead" in Europe, GE's facilities were still far from being a coordinated network of operations.

General Electric gained control of Compagnie des Machines Bull

25. *Ibid.*
26. See, for example, C. Tugendhat, "IBM's World-Wide Research Organization: Wary Eye on the Problems of National Pride," *Financial Times*, Jan. 3, 1969, p. 14.
27. This last totally French-owned computer company, only a part of the results of implementing the *Plan Calcul*, is described later in this chapter.

in the summer of 1964. This largest of the French computer manufacturers was relinquished by the French government to American control under a 50-50 ownership agreement for $43 million only after it had concluded that the financial problems of Bull were so severe that a *solution française* was impractical.[28] After continuing to lose money on its operations, in May 1967 the French partner of Bull-GE agreed to give GE clearer control by a 66-34 joint ownership. In return, GE was to put up an additional $30 million; return to half ownership could be obtained again by Machines Bull by repayment within three years of $15 million to GE.

Acquisition of 75 percent interest in the small electronic data processing division of Italy's Olivetti was accomplished just after the Bull-GE venture began. This division had been losing money up to the time control was relinquished for $12 million (during rescue operations after the death of the firm's founder, Adriano Olivetti), and has not yet been made profitable. The Olivetti company had undergone sizable difficulties in its own takeover of the American firm, Underwood; but even as the latter became profitable in 1965, the drain from the Olivetti-GE joint venture continued. Finally, in April 1968, Olivetti sold its remaining 25 percent holding to GE (valued still at about $4 million) and withdrew its name from the joint venture. Thus GE has no further "nationalistic cloak" in Italy; its operation there became General Electric Information Systems Italia. Olivetti, on the other hand, may have gained some additional expertise in electronics that could find application in its activities in the desk office equipment market.

Two other holdings complete GE interests in Europe. In the fall of 1966, it added 25 percent holding in stock to the 50 percent holding which Bull had had since 1959 in its joint venture in Britain, De La Rue Bull Machines, a firm with computer marketing operations in the United Kingdom. It had been described by the *Economist*, before the increase in stockholding by GE, as "little more than a satellite

28. Bull was among the earliest of the European entries into the industry; its first "computer," Gamma 3, was essentially a powerful calculator and was introduced in 1953. See P. Reveillon, "A Comparison of the Approach to E.D.P. Systems in America and in Europe," in OECD, *Integrated Data Processing and Computers*, Paris, E.P.A. Project (6/02B), 1961; and OECD, *Gaps in Technology: Electronic Computers*, pp. 102–104.

The agreement with GE transformed Compagnie des Machines Bull into a holding company and formed two operational units: Societe Industrielle Bull General Electric (49 percent owned by GE), which makes the computers, and Compagnie Bull General Electric (51 percent owned by GE), which markets them. N. McInnes, "No Monopoly on Brains," p. 9.

of Paris headquarters and does not offer the sort of base General Electric wants."[29] The other holding is, for the present at least, essentially a portfolio investment: 10 percent holding in West Germany's Allgemeine Elektrizitäts-Ges. (AEG) whose subsidiary, Telefunken, makes computers for scientific and engineering applications.

Thus GE had the same approach as IBM—it is entering the European computer industry by direct investment.[30] In all detailed respects, however, these entries are quite different. The company realized even in 1964 that there would be duplication in both computer lines and development activities between the domestic U.S. operations in Phoenix, Arizona; Sunnyvale, California; and the French and Italian operations. But the duplication, concomitant costs, and political intricacies of coordinating this acquired world network were grossly underestimated. After four years the company has not yet been able to bring about specialization in its plants to reap the economies of scale secured by IBM. Its development programs have overlapped flagrantly, as described by the head of GE's computer engineering: "Line printers are a good concrete example. Bull developed a new line printer. Olivetti developed a new line printer. GE continued and expanded using the Anelex line printer, and GE even went off and picked up a new little business to make nonimpact printers."[31]

In actual computers they have fared no better. The status at the time of the GE takeovers was as follows: Olivetti had two designs for small computers and Bull had two (designed with some help from De La Rue Bull Machines). But each computer from one research laboratory was nearly the same in price-performance characteristics as the one from the other laboratory. Both were, however, smaller than the present GE line contained. GE gave the

29. "Computers: Here Comes GE," *Economist* 220, July 16, 1966, p. 283. GE also has had an arrangement with England's Associated Electrical Industries to distribute its GE/PAC 4000 series; Computer Consultants Ltd., *British Commercial Computer Digest 1966*, Enfield, England, 1966.

30. GE's activities in Japan have been limited to a license agreement with Tokyo Shibaura Electric Co. (Toshiba, see below) in which it has only about 10 percent interest. These two firms and Mitsubishi Electric of Japan (which is a joint venture with the American Company, Bunker Ramo) deadlocked in 1967 in an effort to establish a joint computer concern. Problems preventing agreement appear to have involved the Japanese government's insistence on restricting the import of GE computer components and certain financial arrangements proposed by GE. Indicative of the portfolio nature of GE's minority holding, Toshiba is reported to have led opposition to the GE terms ("GE, Japanese Firms Deadlocked on Plans for Computer Concern," *Wall Street Journal*, Aug. 24, 1967, p. 18).

31. *Forbes*, "GE's Computer Troubles ...," pp. 25–26.

go-ahead to one Olivetti design, designated the GE-115, and scrapped the other, while having the duplicate French system redesigned to fill the gap between this small 115 and the lower end of the GE-Phoenix-designed 400 series; this was to be the Gamma 140. The other French design was to be brought out as the Gamma 55, a very small desk-size computer. As part of the integration of the product line, the GE-115 and Gamma 140 were to be completely compatible, so that programming for one could be used for the other. When Bull-GE had finally tooled up for production in late 1966, it turned out that the Gamma 140 line was incompatible; within a few months (and one vice-president later) the 140 line was canceled by GE.[32] Layoffs at home and abroad and complete elimination of computer research in the Sunnyvale Computer Research Laboratories have been among the further efforts to coordinate present corporate facilities. Plans for vertical integration, to begin production of its own integrated circuits, have been mentioned but must certainly be among the company's long-range goals. GE has experienced some success, notably with the Italian designed GE-115, which has found wide acceptance in Europe and was successfully introduced in the U.S. market in early 1968.

IBM and GE have become classic examples in the computer industry of the success and failure of direct investment in Europe. In fact, in the spring of 1970 GE sold its foreign and domestic computer operations to Honeywell. The only firms whose foreign operations are making significant contributions to earnings are those that made the earliest serious entry into the European market—IBM, Sperry Rand, and NCR.

By contrast with IBM's operations, the National Cash Register Company had entered Europe by an agreement with Britain's Elliott Automation, whereby Elliott manufactures NCR machines (mainly the 315 systems) for destinations outside North America.[33] The agreement also calls for NCR to market Elliott equipment in the data processing field in the United States and for both to share any software developments with each other. NCR's success in Europe has come mainly since 1965. In Japan NCR has captured 3 percent of the market through exports.

The Sperry Rand Corporation has also made a profit from foreign

32. A license agreement for manufacturing the Gamma 140 and 141 has been concluded by Bull-GE with a Czechoslovak company; OECD, *Gaps in Technology: Electronic Computers*, p. 47.

33. With its traditional product line, NCR has long had extensive operations abroad through foreign subsidiaries. See E. A. McCreary, *The Americanization of Europe*, Garden City, N.J., Doubleday, 1964, Chapter 21.

operations but only since the mid-1960s. Unlike most of the other American firms it has not formed any license agreements or associations with European firms; its UNIVAC division does business with Europe by exporting. In Japan it does have a joint venture, Oki Electric, and has second position in the market with about 16 percent of sales. In early 1965 when other companies were committing themselves to various forms of third-generation technology, Sperry Rand adopted a "wait and see" attitude; after arriving at a design in the new technology, the company now feels that it has sufficient volume to begin making plans for vertical integration into integrated circuitry production.

The only other American computer manufacturer to contemplate this step of vertical integration is the Radio Corporation of America. Rather than adopt the direct investment or strictly export route to foreign markets, RCA has the most extensive set of licensing agreements of any U.S. firm in the industry. In the United Kingdom, it has had links with English Electric, which enabled the latter to be an early developer of a series of computers, System 4, embodying integrated circuits. The manufacture of the very successful RCA 301 was licensed to English Electric and France's Machines Bull. In what was apparently a premature show of corporate loyalty, Bull-GE paid RCA $8.5 million in 1965 to terminate this license. GE's indirect affiliate in West Germany, Telefunken, still had a license agreement with RCA in 1967. West Germany's largest computer firm, Siemens, also has a licensing agreement and is currently producing RCA's Spectra 70. In the Netherlands the giant firm, Philips, is linked in the same way; in Japan the license agreement is with Hitachi. Although this method of entering foreign markets has been used successfully by RCA until now, it does not seem to be a good long-term solution; more and more of its associates, who have gained experience in the industry through their association, are now choosing to expand their commitment to computers on their own.[34]

Honeywell is using direct investment, as well as licensing agreements, to develop its overseas position, which became profitable in 1968. It has been setting up branch offices in various countries, with major computer manufacturing plants at Newhouse, Scotland; and Frankfurt, West Germany. These are basically European manufacturing operations in the sense that 90 percent of components are either manufactured or purchased locally. Aside from its own sales abroad, Honeywell has licensing agreements with Saab in Sweden

34. See English Electric and Siemens below.

and Nippon Electric in Japan. As mentioned above, it took on the job of integrating GE's operations with its own in the spring of 1970.

Although it has had facilities in Britain and has been marketing in Europe since the nineteenth century, Burroughs is still actually manufacturing only calculators abroad. By the end of 1966 it had expressed the intention to add computers to its extensive line of office machinery manufactured and sold by its many branch offices throughout Europe. But the company still relies mainly on exports from U.S. manufacturing plants; its wholly owned British subsidiary, Burroughs Machines, was still *planning* a large computer plant at Glenrothes, Scotland, at the end of 1968.

Some of the other U.S. computer specialist firms have also made moves into foreign markets. Control Data Corporation exports its computers, some of which are among the largest available. It has, however, started branch offices for sales and maintenance support in some countries. By exporting, it is still vulnerable, as the widely publicized temporary shipment prohibition to France[35] emphasizes, to future U.S. State Department stop-go. Digital Equipment Corporation has been exporting for only a few years and has been quite successful in providing computers for local nuclear physics laboratories in Britain, as well as in marketing in West Germany and the Benelux countries.

In 1965 Scientific Data Systems established licensing agreements with the British firm, General Electric Company (GEC), to market its Series 90 and Sigma 7 systems. GEC had an agreement with the French Compagnie pour l'Informatique et les Techniques Electroniques de Controle (CITEC), both for research and to market SDS machines—GEC covered the European Free Trade Area markets and CITEC the European Economic Community. After considerable rationalization of the British and French industries (which will be described in detail below), there is now only one major domestic firm in each country: International Computers, Ltd. (ICL) in the United Kingdom and Compagnie Internationale de l'Informatique (CII) in France. Early in 1968 the license with GEC for distribution in non-EEC countries was terminated by SDS and, by midyear, SDS had set up an office in London for its activities in these

35. In October 1966, the ban on the shipment of two CDC giant machines, the 6600s, was lifted. See R. Mooney, " U.S. to Drop Ban on Sale of Computers to France," *New York Times*, Oct. 22, 1966, pp. 37, 47.

By contrast, IBM with a manufacturing subsidiary in France could have relatively easily bypassed this type of restriction on a similar order for a giant 360/91; IBM executives claim to have no such plan for manufacturing the largest of their line in France.

countries. CII, despite its mandate from former President de Gaulle to be an all-French computer manufacturer, has maintained its agreement for joint research as well as distribution of SDS machines; in early 1969 this agreement was extended through 1975.[36] Plans were completed late in 1968 for the formation of a joint venture by SDS, the Discount Bank Investment Corporation of Israel, and the small Israeli firm, Elron-Elbit Computers. They established SDS Israel to develop peripheral equipment and components to serve the European markets.

Thus American firms have used basically three approaches to foreign markets. Direct investment appears to be the best long-run method of securing these markets—it does, in fact, provide a way of protecting technological developments as Hymer has suggested.[37] It may also be attractive for computer companies by contributing to the volume of production that makes vertical integration feasible. The Linder thesis, that domestic market considerations have an important influence on the innovative process, seems to be well established in the computer industry; notable examples are the small computers designed by IBM's West German subsidiary (the System 360/20) and by Olivetti-GE in Italy (the GE-115). Licensing agreements with local companies in foreign countries seem to be a useful method for entering a foreign market; they help to overcome what Posner and Douglass have called the foreign " demand lag." But they seem to be short-run solutions for the licensor, in the sense that they may help the licensee to learn how to imitate the innovations.[38]

With this considerable activity by American firms in Europe and Japan, what place is there for independent competition from firms in these other countries? The remainder of this section will deal with foreign firms (see Table 2.2)—the activities that have taken place already and the attempts to nurture independent competition (Chapter 5 will deal with evaluating the potential of these attempts).

In Japan there are seven domestic producers to compete with IBM and NCR machines. These " home " producers accounted for 38 percent of the market in 1966. Five of them actually have licensing ties with U.S. designers: Hitachi with RCA, Nippon Electric with Honeywell, Tokyo Shibaura Electric (Toshiba) with GE, Oki Electric

36. For more information on the results of this license arrangement, see the discussion of CII below.

37. S. H. Hymer, "The International Operations of National Firms."

38. These relationships between innovator and imitator form the basis for the international aspects of the theory of comparative advantage described in detail in Chapter 3.

Table 2.2. Non-United States Firms in the Computer Industry

United Kingdom
International Computers, Ltd.[a] (formerly International Computers and Tabulators, including Ferranti; and English Electric-Leo-Marconi including Elliott Automation and British General Electric)

France
Compagnie Internationale de l'Informatique[a] (formerly Compagnie Européene d'Automatisme Electronique and Société Européene d'Automatisme)

West Germany
Allgemeine Elektrizitäts-Ges. (subsidiary is Telefunken, A.G.)
Diehl, GmbH.
Nixdorf, GmbH.
Siemag Feinmechanische Werke, GmbH.
Siemens and Halske AG. (including Zuse, k, G.)

Japan
Fuji Communication Apparatus Manufacturing Co., Ltd.
Hitachi Ltd.
Matsushita Electric Industrial Co., Ltd.
Mitsubishi Electric Manufacturing Co., Ltd.
Nippon Electric Co., Ltd.
Oki Electric Industry Co., Ltd.
Tokyo Shibaura Electric Co., Ltd.

Other
A/S Norsk Data Elektronikk (Norway)
A/S Regnecentralen (Denmark)
Elron-Elbit Computers (Israel)
Olivetti S. p. A. (Italy)
Philips N. V. (The Netherlands, including Electrologica N.V.)
Saab Aktiebolag (Sweden)

Note: [a]ICL and CII are analyzed quantitatively in Chapter 5.

with Sperry Rand, and Mitsubishi Electric with Bunker Ramo.[39] Only Fuji Communication Apparatus (Fujitsu), one of the biggest, makes computers that are entirely Japanese in design and materials. Most of the firms are widely diversified. Fujitsu has begun to manufacture

39. Japan has relied heavily on licensing for technological acquisition; see T. Ozawa, "Imitation, Innovation, and Trade: A Study of Foreign Licensing Operations in Japan," Ph.D. thesis, Columbia University, 1966. The survey by OECD applauds Japan's success in adopting new techniques (*Gaps in Technology: General Report*, OECD, 1968, p. 28).

However, Hitachi started research in analog computers in 1951 and began serious research on digital computers in 1956. It was only in May 1961 that the technical agreement with RCA was concluded, and Hitachi does have some independently designed machines on the market. This is also true of some of the other companies with U.S. ties; see J. Diebold and Assoc., "Japanese Computers—A Threat?" *Automatic Data Processing Newsletter* 8, no. 3, July 8, 1963. As of 1965, Hitachi also had a licensing agreement with Britain's ICT.

integrated circuits and has a line of machines, Facom 230, that is subdivided (as with the IBM System 360) from 10 to 80. The 230-40 and the larger 230-60 were the first to implement the integrated circuitry. Fujitsu has hopes of developing an export market for its machines, a possibility excluded from the other firms by their license agreements. This company has already licensed a Bulgarian firm to manufacture one of its models.

The Japanese government favors machines of Japanese " content " through the Japanese Electronic Computer Company. It buys approved machines (required to have 20 percent Japanese material in 1966, and eventually to be raised to 50 percent) from manufacturers, and rents them to the 80 percent of domestic users who do not purchase their equipment.[40] Several of the companies (Hitachi, Nippon Electric, and Fujitsu) also have taken steps to make domestic machines competitive by setting up, in October 1966, the Japan Soft Ware Company, which develops software and provides consulting services for the domestic electronic computer companies.

In Europe, Denmark and the Netherlands each has a small designer-manufacturer that has established a market for itself. Regnecentralen, the Danish Institute of Computing Machinery in Copenhagen, manufactures scientific machines. It is a nonprofit, independent institute, so although it seeks customers for its Gier systems and its software packages, it actually operates "more like a university research and development centre with a very sensitive commercial antenna than like a manufacturing organization."[41] Many of the 200-member staff also participate directly in other business enterprises.

Electrologica is located in The Hague, and is quite similar to Regnecentralen in that it has established a place for itself in scientific-computer markets in the Benelux countries, and in West Germany and France as well. In 1966, the *Economist* believed that the Dutch electrical giant Philips N. V. did not have the resources to enter significantly into the computer industry,[42] but this company had already acquired Electrologica in 1965; it also obtained a 40 percent holding of a small German firm, Siemag. Even before these acquisitions, Philips and its subsidiaries were main suppliers of core storage

40. This firm bought an estimated $1.6 billion in computers in fiscal 1969 (beginning Apr. 1, 1968) and is projected to purchase another $2 billion for fiscal 1970.
41. C. White, " European EDP, the View from England," *Datamation* 12, no. 9, Sept. 1966, p. 23.
42. Special emphasis was directed toward large-scale computers; see " European Computers; The Money Runs Out on Philips," *Economist* 220, Sept. 10, 1966, p. 1048.

and electronic components to other computer makers. They had also developed a family of integrated circuit processors for process control that were projected to be marketed by late 1966. One of the subsidiaries, Philips Industries of France, brought out its first general and scientific computer in 1965. By June 1968, Philips had announced a new "1000" series of computers. It plans to produce models of three basic types—1100s, 1200s, and 1400s—to compete with the IBM system 360/30s, 40s, and 50s.

Siemens and Halske, in West Germany, was reported in 1966 to be spending $125 million to establish a place in the computer industry independent of RCA, with which it had only recently established license agreements. It had begun deliveries of computers in 1958; along with its present production of the RCA Spectra 70 machines (under the Siemens 4004 label), Siemens has gained experience with installations of its own 3003 design, which handles reservations. The company's intention is to move from 5 percent to 15 or 20 percent of the German market. With the activation of additional production facilities in 1966, the import content of Spectra 70 production was to be reduced to 25 percent. In addition to these plants, in early 1967, Siemens acquired 70 percent interest in the German company, Zuse, which had been purchased by the Swiss firm, Brown Boveri, only in 1964. Zuse contributes competence to Siemens in machines for process control, as well as its long experience in the technology, dating from Friedrick Zuse's original designs and extending through the company's first- and second-generation machines developed between 1953 and 1961. The combined operations puts Siemens second only to IBM in the West German market by the end of 1968.

Among the other West German computer firms is the "reasonably independent"[43] AEG subsidiary, Telefunken, which was mentioned above as an RCA licensee and indirectly partially owned by GE. It has been described as the manufacturer of "a few large, specialized machines (not the kind that make money)."[44] There are also several small companies: Siemag was mentioned earlier as partially owned by Philips; Diehl is a privately owned firm that entered the industry in the mid-1960s with a very small machine designed by the same American whose LGP 30 design contributed to General Precision's earlier participation in the industry; and Nixdorf specializes exclusively in small computers and was projected to have sales of only

43. See S. Gee-Smith, "Computer Companies Fight for EEC Market," *European Community*, no. 97, Oct. 1966, p. 12.
44. "Aux Armes Citoyens," *Economist* 218, Mar. 19, 1966, p. 1151.

about $25 million for 1968. Beginning in 1966 the German government has increasingly supported domestic efforts by purchasing German-made hardware.

Perhaps the most widely known government support for its home industry exists in the United Kingdom. A " 25 percent rule " has been established, whereby British machines not more than 25 percent more expensive than a comparable American system are preferred (or at least allowable) purchases for government agencies, which are clearly the single most important category of purchasers. Although computers have been commercially developed in Britain since the early 1950s, government encouragement has come only since 1965.[45] As shown in Figure 1 the minimum penetration of American firms in another country's market was 70 percent in 1966; this was the share held by American firms (or through license agreements with British firms) in the United Kingdom. IBM's minimum penetration of a market is also here; it held about 50 percent in 1966 but dropped below 40 percent by the end of 1968. When these facts are combined with the long-standing participation of British scientists in computer technology, dating from World War II, one must conclude that Great Britain has the ingredients for a viable home industry independent of and (at least for the immediate future) second only to the American one.

In 1968 the two separate firms remaining in the industry (after considerable past consolidation) combined their commercial and scientific computer businesses to form International Computers, Ltd., the fourth largest computer firm in the industry and the largest non-American one. Prior to the merger, International Computers and Tabulators was the dominant British manufacturer, having the same share (about 40 percent) of the market as IBM. Until 1949, ICT (then called British Tabulating Machinery Company) had a long-standing exclusive franchise for IBM products in Britain. Later, it was a licensee of RCA, as well as a distributor of some Sperry Rand UNIVACs. During the first half of the 1950s ICT designed and developed a small computer, the Hollerith HEC; its efforts during the second half of the decade were directed through a joint venture with the British General Electric Company in 1956.[46]

More recently completely independent, the company has grown through several mergers: adopting the name ICT after its merger with

45. Most companies involved in the computer industry in 1956—British Tabulating Machine, Elliott Brothers, Ferranti, and Power-Samas—were still looking to the future for their first delivery; see P. Reveillon, "A Comparison of the Approaches to E.D.P. Systems," p. 294.

46. Detailed history of British efforts can be found in C. Freeman, " Research and Development," p. 61.

Powers-Samas Accounting Machine Company in 1959, acquiring the data processing activities of the EMI Electronics subsidiary of Electric and Musical Industries in 1962, and taking over the computer department of Ferranti in 1963. This last company has been the market leader among British firms in integrated circuit production and brought out a line of military and process control computers using this latest technology.

ICT began to make a profit in 1966, largely owing to the success of its latest 1900 series (which is competitive with IBM's System 360) and probably also to massive efforts in software provisions to back up its new hardware. In research ICT has benefited from grants and credit from the British government, but these funds are still not on a scale comparable to what some of the larger American firms devote to research. In marketing, ICT has made significant progress abroad, exporting about one-third of its machines. It has established small bases in Europe, with ICT-France, Germany, and Scandinavia (its Italian operation was dropped in 1966), and had been named as a possible partner to undertake a joint venture with Olivetti.[47]

A review of the history of ICT reveals some of the problems plaguing the entire industry. C. Freeman has emphasized an important distinction for understanding British developments:

The distinction between the "scientific" and the commercial "EDP" markets is important. Sometimes they may use the same machine, although with different configurations and peripherals. But, whereas the "scientific" customer usually knows a good deal about the machine and can do a lot of his own "software" and maintenance, the "commercial" customer usually needs a great deal of training, advice and assistance from the manufacturer. The field force in the EDP market must be much larger, and firms which are successful in one market will not necessarily be successful in the other.

British development work lagged behind in "software" and in the peripherals for commercial users. The heavy costs of successive new developments, and still more the cost of selling and maintaining equipment and training staff, in relation to the relatively small sales achieved, have made it an unprofitable venture [as of 1965] for the firms involved.[48]

This distinction between customers is primarily relevant to the "managerial gap" rather than a "technological gap," in computer-design ability. To the extent that British firms have regarded EDP customers as if they were "scientific" customers, their sales efforts have been misdirected. ICT's history suggests that any shortcomings

---

47. Although Olivetti has released its past computer works to GE, it has retained the right to do future R&D in software and peripheral equipment.
48. C. Freeman, "Research and Development," p. 61.

in managerial behavior present in the 1950s and early 1960s has now been completely overcome.

The English Electric Company is the other firm involved in the 1968 merger. As has already been mentioned, it has had license agreements with RCA that contributed to its ability to be among the first to bring out its System 4 computers with integrated circuitry. Until 1964, its computer and automation group had been known as English Electric-Leo-Marconi, emphasizing its mergers with the small computer manufacturer, LEO,[49] and with the components (including integrated circuits) and process-control computer manufacturer, Marconi. English Electric has prided itself on not being dependent on government assistance for research funds, but it did allow itself to be prodded into acquiring Elliott Automation in 1967 by a £15 million loan from the Industrial Reorganisation Corporation. Elliott had had the range of smaller computers virtually to itself as late as 1965 and had bought out the British General Electric's computer operations, which were mainly in process control, just before its own merger into English Electric. Elliott had also been making a significant entry into integrated circuitry production, with the help of a know-how agreement with one of the three main U.S. producers, Fairchild. In marketing, English Electric (without Elliott) had concentrated on its home market, with "footholds" in South African, South American, and Eastern European markets, while Elliott Automation had concentrated its nondomestic efforts in Eastern Europe. Even combined, their scale of exports was not nearly as great as ICT's.

The point of this elaboration of acquisitions is that the combined firm, ICL, has potential competence in every major area of computer and components activity.[50] Properly integrated, this firm could be as fully vertically integrated and as widely diversified in computer production as IBM. The actual computer group that was formed in 1968 is somewhat more limited in objectives. It is essentially a takeover by ICT of English Electric's computer operations, except "its business and defense systems . . . [and] process control" activities.[51]

49. Actually, LEO (Lyons Electronic Office) started as a food chain and designed its own computer, in collaboration with Cambridge University, for accounting and payroll operations. In 1958, five years after the completion of LEO I, the firm decided to try to manufacture the machine commercially. OECD, *Gaps in Technology: Electronic Computers*, pp. 101–102.

50. For comments on 1967 developments by these companies in peripheral equipment, see M. Gunton, "Peripheral Trends in the U.K.," *Electronic News*, Nov. 13, 1967, sec. 2, p. 52.

51. "Britain's New Computer Group," *Economist* 226, Mar. 30, 1968, pp. 72–75.

Even an integration of this portion of their operations will take some time, since the ICT 1900 systems and the English Electric System 4 are not compatible. A new series of machines is not likely to be developed by the joint venture before the 1970s, but it has already been determined that compatibility of the present 1900 series, System 4, and a new line will be feasible. There has been speculation that the combined effort in ICL may be sufficient to produce a large scientific computer of the sort that is now being produced only in the United States.[52]

The final participant in the merger, Plessey Company, is a producer of electronic components and telecommunications equipment. It did not join the ICL operations directly but owns 18 percent of the stock and will participate (with a 60 percent holding) in a joint development company to explore "the convergence between computer and communications activities."[53] English Electric also has an 18 percent interest in ICL, while ICT (including Ferranti) stockholders have the majority interest of 53.5 percent. The government has contributed to this venture both through research and development grants and through a 10.5 percent stock ownership. By the end of 1968, ICL had an estimated 45 percent of the British market, whereas IBM had under 40 percent. An official of the company has spoken of technical cooperation with Siemens, Telefunken, and Philips in developing future machines and establishing cross-licensing of peripheral equipment.[54] It continues to be the major exporter to Eastern Europe; an order in early 1969 for $6 million in System 4 medium and large systems brings the total value of sales in recent years to the Soviet Bloc to about $40 million.

Another widely publicized merger took place in France with the encouragement of the government in 1966. This merging of the remaining French computer firms in the industry is only a part of former President de Gaulle's *Plan Calcul*.[55]

The timing of two events involving computers seems to have had a decisive influence on the final formulation and direction of the *Plan*. Three years before its adoption, and reportedly with the intervention of de Gaulle himself, the other French computer companies were pressured into investing in Machines Bull in an effort to prevent GE

52. "Computers: World's Fourth," *Economist* 226, Feb. 3, 1968, pp. 56–58. The plausibility and cost of such an objective will be explored in Chapter 5.

53. "Britain's New Computer Group," *Economist*, p. 73.

54. These sentiments were expressed by Brian Murphy of ICL in a speech before the European Parliament. See C. H. Farnsworth, "Computer Builders in Europe Pressed to Challenge IBM," *New York Times*, Feb. 1, 1969, pp. 37, 41.

55. The main computer firms in France are, of course, IBM France (with about 50 percent of the market) and Bull-GE (with about 20 percent).

from gaining a 20 percent interest. One of the companies, Compagnie pour l'Informatique et les Techniques Electroniques de Controle, was even encouraged to take over Bull, but it declined.[56] By then, Bull's condition had further deteriorated and half ownership was approved for GE by the government.[57] With the leading two firms in the French industry controlled by American firms, the government then had to decide what future it should encourage for the remaining firms: whether or not they should merge; and whether to concentrate their production of medium-sized machines, or process control computers, or perhaps even to abandon computer production and concentrate on development of peripheral equipment. Then, in early 1966, the U.S. State Department refused an export license for CDC 6600 computers, thereby seriously threatening the future of de Gaulle's *force de frappe*.[58] By August, agreement between the firms and the government on the main ingredients of the *Plan Calcul* was completed, and remained unaltered even after the State Department in Washington relented on the CDC order in October. Thus, in large measure the *Plan Calcul* was politically motivated—the chances for its success based on past performance of the companies involved is therefore not really relevant. Of primary importance are the content of the Plan and the financial resources that are being raised to make its future successful.

The one all-French firm that was created at the end of 1966, Compagnie Internationale de l'Informatique, is the result of a merger of Compagnie Europeene d'Automatisme Electronique, the computer division of CITEC; and Société Européene d'Automatisme, a subsidiary of Jeumont-Schneider.[59] Each of these firms has had experience in computer development. CAE, the larger of the two, has developed

56. CITEC is a holding company formed by Compagnie Genérale de Télégraphie Sans Fil (CSF) and Compagnie Genérale d'Électricité (CGE).

57. See the discussion of GE's foreign operations for further development in Bull-GE.

58. J. Diebold and Assoc., "The French National Computer Effort," *Automatic Data Processing Service Newsletter* 11, no. 25, May 15, 1967, p. 2. For a discussion of the *force de frappe* concept, also known by the appellation "*force de dissuasion*," see A. Buchan, "Battening Down Vauban's Hatches," *Interplay* 1, no. 10, May 1968, p. 5.

59. As of 1966 these two firms combined held about 15 percent of the computer market; see "£40 m for French Computers," *Economist* 220, Aug. 13, 1966, pp. 659–662. One of the parent companies of CITEC, CSF, had such serious financial difficulties, (mainly from its early commitments to help save Machines Bull and from its endeavors in French color television development) that it merged into Compagnie Française Thomson-Houston-Hotchkiss-Brandt, a leading French electronic equipment manufacturer, during the fall of 1967. Jeumont-Schneider was exploring the possibility of allowing the U.S.'s Westinghouse to achieve a majority holding (60 percent) in late 1968; as expected, this prospect was strenuously opposed by President de Gaulle.

teleprocessing facilities and had a research agreement with the British GEC and research and marketing agreements with the American firm, SDS. One of its new computers in 1966 was the CAE 10070, which was based on SDS's Sigma 7. SEA has experience in scientific research and, at the time of the merger, was working on the development of some new peripheral equipment, for example, a new high speed optical character reader. Combined sales for these firms were only $34 million in 1966 and were expected to be $44 million for 1967.

The primary emphasis of CII has been the development of a range of four scientific computers (PO-P3), medium-sized at first but to be capable of being extended later into large scientific machines.[60] At the time of CII's formation, it was expected that the new line of machines would not be available before 1969. This schedule was met as the first machine to be developed, the P1, was scheduled in 1968 for delivery in 1969. The licensing agreement between SDS and CAE has been maintained since CII was formed; thus, some of the technical know-how for this "all French" series of machines is still based on American expertise. This should remain true for the P3— the heart of the French effort, with a capability of handling nuclear and space calculations—which will undoubtedly resemble the larger of SDS's Sigma series; in early 1969 the agreement with SDS was extended through 1975. The company has stated the objective of recapturing 30 percent of the market from the American-controlled companies, but as the 1970s approach it is not yet a serious threat. International commercial efforts by CII resemble ICL's in seeking out Eastern European customers. These include the early 1969 negotiations with the Hungarian government over a licensing agreement for CII's 10010 computer (which is also based on SDS technology).

Financially CII was to receive $80 million in research contracts and another $8 million in development aid from the government over a five year period beginning in 1966. It was anticipated that the firm would spend an additional $98 million of its own in developing the

---

60. It was reported in early 1967 that talks had begun with Britain's ICT and English Electric over the possibility of a joint project to build a large scientific machine (similar talks had broken down two years earlier); "Computers: Green Light for Plan Calcul," *Economist* 223, Apr. 22, 1967, p. 379. But by March 1968, it was still being reported that the formation of Britain's ICL "sparked fresh talk of bringing the British into a joint European effort." L. Garrison, "France Is Alarmed over the Inroads of U.S. Computers," *New York Times*, Mar. 30, 1968, p. 43. Thus the prospect of such cooperation does not seem too great, nor does the prediction of some observers of "a revival of Franco-German discussions to join hands in face of both the American and now the British threat." Ibid., p. 53.

new computer line. The government might have considered extending further grants for this project, as amounts of around $200 million had been mentioned in early discussions of the *Plan*; but the May 1968 upheaval in France and subsequent postponement of nuclear development undoubtedly also affected the *Plan Calcul* priority. Evaluation of the attempt to develop a large computer within this budget will be undertaken in Chapter 5.

The final elements of *Plan Calcul* include the establishment of a *Délégation Générale à l'Informatique* to oversee the expenditure of government funds and the direction of the firm's activities. It also was to coordinate government purchases of computers, although the *Délégate Générale* was not to insist that CII products be purchased unless they were really competitive. The government also encouraged the formation of Systèmes et Péripheriques Associés aux Calculateurs (a new company to develop peripheral equipment[61] realized by the merger of appropriate subsidiaries of Thomson-Houston and Compagnie des Compteurs), the creation of the Institute de Recherche d'Informatique et d'Automatique (an institute for research in computer technology), and was thought to be likely to establish a training center for computer specialists.

Thus the Japanese and European computer industries are nearly completely dependent on U.S. technology. At this relatively early stage in their development, the firms of most countries are just learning how to imitate the innovative successes of American firms. Only Japan's Fujitsu and even more clearly Britain's ICL are sufficiently technologically advanced in the field to be considered reasonably independent participants (with the American firms) in the international industry. France's CII may achieve this status, but prospects for RCA's German protégé, Siemens, and for Holland's Philips are in the much more distant future and are dependent on such "ifs" as the possibility of joint operations with other European firms, and the speed and degree of economic integration that the European Economic Community can achieve.[62]

61. Even with this new company, it was expected that CII would have to rely heavily on American technology for peripheral equipment, as it would for electronic components (including especially integrated circuits). See R. F. Fairchild, "French EDP Independence Leans Heavily on U.S. Support," *Electronic News* 11, Dec. 26, 1966, p. 29.

62. See Chapter 5 for an evaluation of the benefits to participants in the computer industry from a more fully integrated Europe—that is, with the United Kingdom in the European Economic Community.

3

Theoretical Model of a New Industry

The basic ideas of the theoretical model go back at least to David Hume, who pointed out in his essay "Of Money" that advantages from innovations (his examples came from textiles and iron manufactures) may be temporary: "Manufactures . . . generally shift their places, leaving those countries and provinces which they have already enriched, and flying to others, whither they are allured by the cheapness of provisions and labour."[1]

The theoretical basis of comparative advantage to be developed here involves a dichotomy of industries into "new" and "standard" categories.[2] This dichotomy emphasizes that in new industries technical knowledge is not freely available in all countries. The distribution of technical knowledge is important in determining the directions of international trade. As technical knowledge becomes more widely available, the industry becomes standard, and the Heckscher-Ohlin theory—that each country tends to export goods that intensively use the factors of production the country has in relative abundance—delineates the basic influences on the direction of trade.[3] In this

1. D. Hume, "Of Money," in T. H. Green and T. H. Grose (eds.), *Essays: Moral, Political, and Literary*, London, Longman's, Green & Co., 1875, p. 311.

2. A similar distinction has been suggested by C. P. Kindleberger, "Anciens et Nouveaux Produits en Commerce International," *Economie Appliquée* 7, no. 3, 1954, pp. 281–297.

3. See E. Heckscher, "The Effect of Foreign Trade on the Distribution of Income," *Ekonomisk Tidskrift* 21, 1919, pp. 497–512. (Reprinted in translation in *Readings in the Theory of International Trade*, Philadelphia, Blakiston Press, 1949); and B. Ohlin, *Interregional and International Trade*, Cambridge, Mass., Harvard University Press, 1933, See also reviews by S. Mookerjee, *Factor Endowments and International Trade; A Statement and Appraisal of the Heckscher-Ohlin Theory*, New Delhi, Asia Publishing House, 1958; R. E. Caves, *Trade and Economic Structure, Models and Methods*, Cambridge, Mass., Harvard University Press, 1960; and J. S. Chipman, "A Survey of the Theory of International Trade: Part 2—the neo-classical theory, Part 3—the modern theory," *Econometrica* 33, no. 4, Oct. 1965, pp. 685–760; 34, no. 1, Jan. 1966, pp. 18–76. Admittedly, I have characterized the Heckscher-Ohlin theory in rather less generality than recent trade literature has developed it. For example, some variation in the level of technology can be accommodated within the model; see, for example, R. W. Jones, "The Role of Technology in the Theory of International Trade," presented at the Conference on Technology and Competition in International Trade, Oct. 11–12, 1968, in Universities–National Bureau of Economic Research, forthcoming.

theoretical development, attention will be directed toward new industries.[4]

International Framework of the Theory

The theory to be developed here is intended to emphasize that technological information is not universally available.[5] Therefore production functions are not identical in all countries. Indeed, the aggregate output (over firms) concept for these new industries, required by an industry production function approach, does not seem appropriate. The theory, therefore, is based primarily on the developments made by Hicks, Kravis, Posner, and Douglass on an innovation/imitation approach to trade theory, which has been applied to motion pictures by Douglass and to synthetic materials by Hufbauer.[6] The theoretical basis for trade patterns will also involve elements of the product cycle approach.[7] It is, of course, very

4. See A. J. Harman, "Innovations, Technology, and the Pure Theory of International Trade," Ph.D. thesis, Department of Economics, Massachusetts Institute of Technology, 1968, for a theoretical and empirical exploration of the Heckscher–Ohlin theory for some "standard" industries. How one might identify an industry as "new" is discussed later in this chapter.

5. This is a cornerstone of I. B. Kravis' approach in his "'Availability' and Other Influences on the Commodity Composition of Trade," *Journal of Political Economy* 64, no. 2, Apr. 1956, pp. 143–155.

6. See J. R. Hicks, "An Inaugural Lecture," *Oxford Economic Papers*, N.S. 5, June 1953, pp. 117–135; I. B. Kravis, "'Availability' and Other Influences"; M. V. Posner, "International Trade and Technical Change," *Oxford Economic Papers*, N.S. 13, Oct. 1961, pp. 323–341; G. K. Douglass, "Product Variation and International Trade in Motion Pictures," Ph.D. thesis, Department of Economics, Massachusetts Institute of Technology, 1963; and G. C. Hufbauer, *Synthetic Materials and the Theory of International Trade*, London, Duckworth, 1965.

7. The product cycle was identified by S. Kuznets, *Economic Change*, New York, W. W. Norton & Company, 1953; and studied by R. Vernon, "International Investment and International Trade in the Product Cycle," *Quarterly Journal of Economics* 80, no. 2, May 1966, pp. 190–207; S. Hirsch, *Location of Industry and International Competitiveness*, London, Oxford University Press, 1967, and "The United States Electronics Industry in International Trade," *National Institute Economic Review* 34, Nov. 1965, pp. 92–97; L. T Wells, Jr., "Product Innovation and Directions of International Trade," Doctoral thesis, Harvard Business School, 1966; and R. B. Stobaugh, Jr., "The Product Life Cycle, U.S. Exports, and International Investment," D.B.A. thesis, Graduate School of Business Administration, Harvard University, 1968. See also E. Hoffmeyer, *Dollar Shortage and the Structure of the U.S. Foreign Trade*, Amsterdam, North-Holland Publishing Company, 1958; D. MacDougall, *The World Dollar Problem*, London, Macmillan, 1957; C. P. Kindleberger, "Anciens et Nouveaux Produits," and *Foreign Trade and the National Economy*, New Haven, Yale University Press, 1962; and J. Polk, I. W. Meister, and L. A. Veit, *U.S. Production Abroad and the Balance of Payments*, New York, National Industries Conference Board, 1966. An empirical comparison of some of the different theories explaining trade is given by G. C. Hufbauer, "The Commodity Composition of Trade in Manufactured Goods," presented at the Conference on Technology and Competition in International Trade, October 11–12, 1968; in Universities-National Bureau of Economic Research, forthcoming.

difficult to identify and credit the intellectual debt owed to previous authors for the developments that will be presented. I have attempted, however, to identify major characteristics of previous theory with their authors.

Before elaborating the theory, let me make explicit the definition of "innovation" that I intend to use: An innovation is the introduction of a new or significantly improved product into an economy or the implementation of a new or significantly improved production process.[8] In the model of firm behavior to be presented later in this chapter, the emphasis will be on product innovations. There is some justification for this, since studies have found that businessmen consider their research and development effort to have as major objectives new products rather than cost reduction.[9] Of course, there have been important cases of process innovations influencing trade patterns—for example, in iron and textiles in the early part of the industrial revolution, and high speed mechanization in textiles more recently. It is extremely difficult to separate product and process innovations in any case, so that a certain amount of judgment about what constitutes an innovation in a particular industry for the present model is inescapable. Judgment is, of course, also required for the modifier "significantly improved."

The main features of the innovation/imitation approach are displayed in Figure 2. This theory assumes that there is some country (or at most a very limited number of countries) successfully producing a new product for its home market when the time sequence begins. Domestic market considerations—size of market, affluence of consumers, tastes, and so on—are usually considered important to the original development of the product.[10] The "decision period" for

8. See, for example, R. E. Johnston, "Technical Progress and Innovation," *Oxford Economic Papers* 18, no. 2, July 1966, p. 160. A product in this context might refer to a service in the case of invisible trade; for example, the certificate of deposit in the banking industry was an American innovation.

9. See, for example, R. E. Johnston, "Technical Progress," p. 164; or W. E. Gustafson, "Research and Development, New Products, and Productivity Change," *American Economic Review, Papers and Proceedings* 52, no. 2, May 1962, pp. 177–185.

10. This domestic market emphasis is basic to the Linder approach in *An Essay on Trade and Transformation*, Stockholm, Almquist and Wiksells, 1961. However, it appears in the literature at least as early as Adam Smith's *Wealth of Nations*.

In modern times it is becoming a less essential feature. Although smaller-market countries cannot be innovators in all industries, they can selectively specialize and concentrate their research in one or two in which the initial market may not be exclusively domestic. The development in Britain of the Harrier VTOL aircraft is a good example of this specialization.

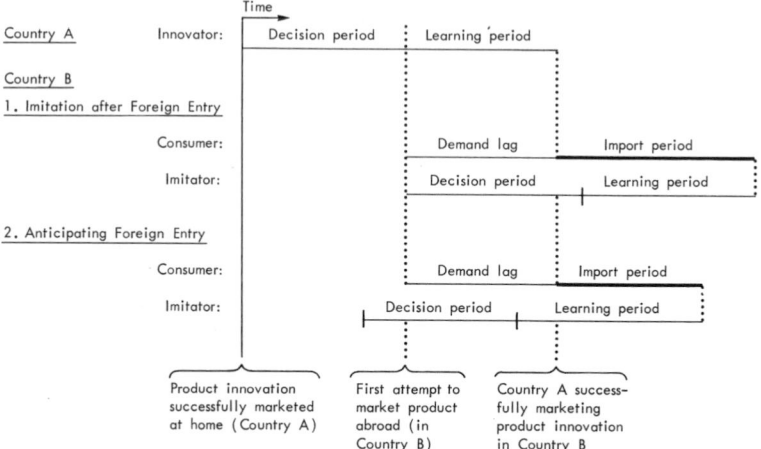

Fig. 2. Innovation/Imitation approach to international trade.

the innovator[11] is the period during which the innovator contemplates beginning foreign sales of the new product. This delay before exporting may be due to imperfect knowledge about foreign market opportunities (knowledge of those same factors that caused the innovator to develop his product for home consumption in the first place). If the producer finds a small domestic market for his product, he is likely to make the decision to proceed with entry into foreign markets quickly so as to reap further economies of scale in production. On the other hand, he may hesitate to introduce his product abroad if he has no previous export experience and therefore anticipates that some time and expense may be needed before he can develop a foreign market.

In considering how long it will take him to develop this foreign market, the innovator is considering how long his " learning period " will be. He may need time to learn the language and customs,[12] to set up a local distribution facility in the foreign country, to make the product known through advertising, thereby perhaps overcoming prejudice against foreign-produced goods or preference for domestic brands, or to emphasize fully the advantages of the innovation. From the point of view of the consumer in the foreign country, this period is the " demand lag " between the product's first introduction and its commercial acceptance.

Finally, foreign producers will notice that the new import might

11. The periods in Figure 2 are essentially those identified by M. V. Posner, "International Trade," and used by G. K. Douglass, *Product Variation.*

12. This is emphasized by C. Layton, *Trans-Atlantic Investments*, Foulogne-sur-Seine, France, The Atlantic Institute, 1966, especially with regard to foreign subsidiaries.

prove to be competition for their existing product line when the new product appears in their domestic market or very shortly thereafter. They must then decide whether or not to try to meet the competition by imitation—this is their "decision period." The closeness of substitutability of the new product, as well as the degree of industry protection, will influence the speed with which foreign producers must decide to imitate the new product. Once the decision is taken, the foreign producers must learn how to imitate the new product. This will depend on the character and complexity of the new product, the magnitude of the innovational changes, the frequency with which firms are forced to imitate, and the freedom of access to specialized engineering information in the industry.[13] The length of the import period is thus determined by the end of the foreign "demand lag" and the end of the imitators' "learning period."[14]

Information on new products may be sufficiently widespread that foreign producers could begin anticipating competition in their domestic markets before the new products were even introduced there. This anticipation is represented in the second type of reaction by country B in Figure 2, on the assumption that producers have a decision period of some standard length in viewing domestic innovations. This anticipation shortens the potential trading period for the innovator.

The basic lines of this innovation/imitation formulation will be followed in the present consideration of new industries, but there are several aspects of the approach that are not very appealing. The first is that trade ceases, according to the above model, at the end of the imitators' learning period. This makes continuous trade in *new* industries dependent on what Douglass calls "technical correlation," the tendency for innovations to cluster in particular industries (for example, because of accumulated expertise or larger research budgets).[15] A second major discomfort comes from the structure that implies that each new product will require decision and learning

13. Much of this discussion is based on a similar discussion by G. K. Douglass, *Product Variation*, especially Chapter 2. On this last point see J. Yance, "Investment Behavior in the Railroad Industry," Ph.D. thesis, Harvard University, 1955; and E. Mansfield, "Technical Change and the Rate of Imitation," *Econometrica* 29, no. 4, Oct. 1961, pp. 741–766.

14. It should be pointed out that the discussion here is emphasizing innovations as *the* basis for trade. Actually, trade may not end with international ability to produce the innovative product. This is one of the main features in viewing an industry as "new" at one time, and as "standard" at another. It is also an important distinction in the product cycle approach, in which the product goes through "new," "growth," and "mature" phases; see S. Hirsch, *Location of Industry*; and R. B. Stobaugh, Jr., *The Product Life Cycle*.

15. Douglass, *Product Variation*, pp. 46–50.

periods and will encounter demand lags: the entrepreneurs and consumers do not *learn* from experience with previous new products. And finally, the scheme does not identify a mechanism that produces the innovation, the driving force of the entire model.

These objections can be eliminated if the corporation, rather than the individual product, is taken as the focal point of the analysis of new products. The corporation may have a continuous flow of exports of new products over time without continuing to export each new product. Corporate research facilities not only have a large part in channeling company resources toward innovation; they also provide continuity for the innovative process. Furthermore, management may learn about new markets from one product; subsequent products can immediately enter these markets.[16] The corporation may even forestall foreign competition in these foreign markets by direct investment—foreign subsidiaries within which they can maintain technological leadership while using factors of production that have, perhaps, more favorable relative prices for the particular production process of the new products.[17]

Dynamic Structure of a Firm in a New Industry

Preliminary Considerations

The basic feature determining the ability of a country to participate in exports in a new industry is the availability of technology in that country. I shall assume that the countries producing in a particular new industry do not change; this is obviously a simplification.[18] The emphasis in the development to follow will be on *product* innovations —each product will be characterized by a certain level of "innovative content." Therefore a new industry has no meaningful measure of its

16. Aspects of the "learning by doing" approach may be appropriate to the theory. See K. Arrow, "The Economic Implications of Learning by Doing," *Review of Economic Studies* 29, 1962, pp. 155–173.

17. This is an important aspect in the work of S. H. Hymer, "The International Operations of National Firms, A Study of Direct Foreign Investment," Doctoral thesis, Massachusetts Institute of Technology, 1960. Stobaugh has found a preference for ownership over licensing of foreign operations in the *early* stages of the product cycle in the chemical industry; see his "Product Life Cycle." This finding lends some support to the expectation of such foreign operations in the "new" part of the present new/standard industries dichotomy.

18. It is useful nonetheless because (1) the question of which countries enter production largely depends on the characteristics of the industry and innovations involved, and (2) it is a longer term phenomenon than those considered here and may therefore be accounted for by the industry's becoming "standard." How the industry arose in the first place is not considered; see R. R. Nelson, "The Link Between Science and Invention: The Case of the Transistor," in Universities-National Bureau of Economic Research, *The Rate and Direction of Inventive Activity: Economic and Social Factors*, Princeton, Princeton University Press, 1962, pp. 549–587.

aggregate output; analysis using an aggregate production function for the industry is thereby precluded.

Even the operations of a firm in such an industry cannot be usefully represented merely by a production function. Research and development leading to innovations, highly trained nonhomogeneous personnel, management techniques, and so on make this type of representation an oversimplification. Instead, increases in output of the country will be distinguished by two phenomena: internal growth of firms and increase in the number of firms. Some very useful theoretical and empirical groundwork for this type of approach has been laid by Mansfield in studies of domestic industries of the United States.[19] The theoretical development below is in part an extension of his work into an international context. Other research that has been directly influenced includes a theoretical model presented by Ruff, which incorporates employment in research activities as a control variable in an optimal growth framework, and an analysis of demand for computers undertaken by Chow.[20]

My main emphasis will be on the analysis of growth of existing firms in a new industry. One pertinent aspect is the propensity of various firms in the industry to innovate. Johnston has summarized the main influences affecting a firm's ability to innovate:[21]

1. Research and development activity.
2. Purchase and flow of knowledge.
3. Talent.
4. Economic and market structure.
5. Investment and financial capability.

Researchers have studied research and development activity widely. Although it does have an influence on innovations, the results so far have not uncovered a definite relationship between R&D and any

19. Mansfield's studies of particular relevance include "Entry, Gibrat's Law, Innovation, and the Growth of Firms," *American Economic Review* 52, Dec. 1962, pp. 1023–1051; "Size of Firm, Market Structure, and Innovation," *Journal of Political Economy* 71, no. 6, Dec. 1963, pp. 556–576; "Technical Change and the Rate of Imitation," *Econometrica* 29, no. 4, Oct. 1961, pp. 741–766. See also his summary volumes *The Economics of Technological Change*, New York, Norton, 1968; and *Industrial Research and Technological Innovation*, New York, Norton, 1968.

20. L. E. Ruff, "The Optimal Program of Research and its Achievement in a Cournot Economy," a paper presented at the Econometric Society meetings, Dec. 1967; and G. C. Chow, "Technological Change and the Demand for Computers," *American Economic Review* 57, no. 5, Dec. 1967, pp. 1117–1130.

21. Johnston, "Technical Progress."

index of firm or industry performance.[22] A Department of Commerce study points out explicitly that research itself is not the *only* cost for successful innovations and that it is not even the main cost.[23]

The flow of knowledge as a factor is very hard to measure. Between countries it can be seen in part in the technological balance of payments that reflects payments for purchase of patents and licenses. But a large part of the flow of knowledge through domestic trade in patents and licenses, transfer and consulting of technical personnel, and flow between parent firm and foreign subsidiary goes unmeasured. Part of this flow may also be accounted for by the sale of capital equipment.

Talent can be broken down into several modes of influence: the supply of scientific and engineering personnel, their distribution and function in the firm and industry (research, production, management), and the attitude and general education of labor and management. The supply of scientific and engineering personnel has been measured only very crudely; nor are there consistent detailed descriptions of this allocation for many countries. It has been determined that small firms generally neither perform research nor use research associations. No thorough examination of labor and management's attitudes toward innovation or of the influence of education has been performed.

One aspect of economic and market structure that has been explicitly studied is the relationship between competition within an industry and the size of its firms. Mansfield has uncovered evidence suggesting that the largest firms of an industry tend to have a greater than proportional share of innovations when the following conditions prevail: the required investment for participation in the industry is large; the minimum size of firm that can use the industry's innovations is large; and the average size of the largest firms is very much greater than the average size of all firms that could use the innovations.[24] It should be emphasized, however, that innovation is often undertaken with a large element of ignorance about its precise outcome and commercial desirability. Thus participation in an innovative industry requiring large investment is still fundamentally

22. See also D. Hamberg, *R&D: Essays on the Economics of Research and Development*, New York, Random House, 1966. One of his main conclusions is that "each industry should be treated as an individual entity" in considering the effects of R & D activity (p. 67).

23. U.S. Department of Commerce, *Technological Innovation: Its Environment and Management*, Washington, D.C., 1967, p. 9.

24. E. Mansfield, "Size of Firm, Market Structure, and Innovation," *Journal of Political Economy* 71, no. 6, Dec. 1963, pp. 556–576.

different from activity in a capital-intensive industry. Mansfield also found that, in industries characterized by small firms, imitation tended to be undertaken as rapidly as among industries with large firms, but original innovation was not as rapid. Neither competition nor market control seems to be absolutely necessary for innovations. Several studies have considered the extent of economies of scale for research but no general conclusions have been reached. Very few other market or economic factors have been explored. It is thought that stable economic growth would be the best environment for the innovative process; Mansfield has suggested that neither cyclical troughs (with meager profits and future uncertainty) nor peaks (with lack of unutilized capacity) are likely times for introduction of innovations or imitating others.

As for the final influences affecting a firm's ability to innovate, investment and financial capability, it is thought that unexploited innovations may be needed to observe investment increasing from innovation. On the other hand, some innovations may be capital-saving and thereby result in lower investment rates in the future. Furthermore, R&D can be viewed as a form of investment, competitive with current investment in capital goods.[25] The lack of financing may, of course, slow or stop the flow of innovations. Smaller firms may therefore be least likely to innovate.

Model for a Firm

A fundamental aspect of the model characterizing a firm in a new industry will be the allocation of resources between efforts to innovate and other investment possibilities. The complete environment of the firm involves its technical capabilities, its productive capabilities, and the demand conditions it faces. Through its R&D budget, the trade-off in the allocation of remaining net profits, the allocation of its factors of production over its product line, and its price structure, the firm will maximize profits over a time horizon. Table 3.1 summarizes the notation to be used below.[26]

Let us turn first to the firm's technical capabilities: the ability to produce products (machines) having a certain level of innovative

25. See, for example, Hamberg, *R&D: Essays on the Economics of Research and Development*, p. 126. As noted above, this competition for investable resources within the firm is not on a strictly comparable basis; there are much larger elements of ignorance and risk in innovative activity than in capital goods acquisition.

26. I am indebted to Kent Anderson for many invaluable discussions of this general formulation of the model. In Chapter 4, I present a discrete time representation of this model with specific functional forms and explore it empirically.

Table 3.1   Notation for the Model of a Firm in a New Industry

α	Precautionary factor in firm's administration of R&D results
$C(t)$	Net cash flow
d	Proportion of net cash flow distributed as dividends
δ	Exponential rate of depreciation of capital goods
γ	Adjustment factor in a country's demand for the firm's machines
g	Proportion of net cash flow retained
$g_R(t)$	Proportion of retained cash flow devoted to innovative activity
$g_K(t)$	Proportion of retained cash flow devoted to investment in capital goods
$I_k(t)$	Industrial production of country k
$K(t)$	Total capital stock of the firm
$K(m, t)$	Capital devoted to producing machines of the mth type
k	Index of countries
$L(m, t)$	Labor devoted to producing machines of the mth type
M	Number of types (models) of machines in firm's product line
m	Index of machine models
ν	Exponential rate of depreciation through use of machines
$p(m, t)$	Price of a model m machine
$r(t)$	Cost of capital services in the industry
R	Research and development expenditure budget of the firm
ρ	Discount rate with which the firm views the future
$\sigma(m)$	Proportionality constant relating innovative content of mth model to the maximum
T	Time horizon relevant to the firm
τ	Period during which past expenditure on R&D remains useful
t	Index of time
$V(T)$	Present discounted value of the firm's profits over the time horizon
$w(t)$	Wage rate of production line labor in the industry
$\Xi^*(t)$	Potential cumulative value of innovations for the firm
$\Xi(t)$	Maximum value of implemented innovations up to the year t
$\Xi(m, t)$	Level of innovative content of model m.
$Y_k(m, t)$	Stock to time t of machines of type m installed in country k
$Z(m, t)$	Production of machines of model m, up to time t

---

content or level of performance. A quality index of the cumulative innovative content of machine m at time t is denoted $\Xi(m, t)$; the price of the machine is $p(m, t)$. Although this new industry discussion is intended to be general, rather than applicable only to the computer industry, it will probably be helpful to mention what types of characteristics Ξ might represent. In the computer industry, operations per second of particular functions (multiplications, additions, input from particular devices, outputs) and memory capacity have been widely recognized as computer characteristics that technological efforts have been used to improve. Although Ξ could be considered as a vector, the model will be developed here for a single "quality" index; in fact, the empirical investigation will use a single index of the above computer characteristics.[27]

Several assumptions are needed to simplify the innovative representation of the firm. First, the number of machines in the product line, M, is taken to be fixed. Thus the firm does not create any wholly new machines but rather continuously improves its existing line. The assumption is not really very severe, since the firm could choose not to produce some machines for some lengths of time and the industry is already in existence (by assumption) when the action starts.

The second assumption deals with the ordering of the product line. Since differences in machines are characterized entirely by $\Xi(m, t)$, there is no further loss in generality by assuming that

$$\Xi(m + 1, t) > \Xi(m, t), \qquad m = 1, \ldots, M - 1 \qquad (3.1)$$

and that the change in these characteristics through time maintains this ordering; that is,

$$\dot{\Xi}(m + 1, t) \geq \dot{\Xi}(m, t), \qquad m = 1, \ldots, M - 1. \qquad (3.2)$$

The simplifying restriction that is employed for this model is that

$$\dot{\Xi}(m + 1, t) = \dot{\Xi}(m, t), \qquad m = 1, \ldots, M - 1. \qquad (3.3)$$

The innovative content of a machine is changed through the firm's R&D effort; this assumption is therefore equivalent to the admittedly somewhat artificial hypothesis that R&D is "atmospheric"—it

27. To mention one other example of Ξ for a different industry, one might view miles per hour for commercially built automobiles as a suitable index in the early stages of automobile development. Or, since this may not have been pushed very far at first because of poor road networks, one could use miles per gallon. However, "miles per gallon" benefited from innovations in the petroleum industry. Similarly, "operations per second" may have benefited from innovations in electronic components. This possible externality is not really adequately reflected in this model, except insofar as the firm in question also conducts its research in these related areas (a plausible situation in the case of computer manufacturers, so further elaboration of this equation for the present application is not necessary).

The use of a variable such as Ξ, "cumulative innovative content" is a deliberate effort to sidestep the inherent assumption in Mansfield's work (counting innovations) that each innovation is of the same importance and their values are additive. This assumption is rather untenable as implied by G. S. Maddala and P. T. Knight ("International Diffusion of Technical Change—A Case Study of the Oxygen Steel Making Process," *Economic Journal* 77, no. 307, Sept. 1967, p. 550) when they noted that "if there is a wave of innovations it does not necessarily follow that every innovation will be adopted by every firm. It would be rational on the part of a firm to skip some intermediate innovations . . . ."

affects all of the firm's products uniformly.[28] Thus, with the definition

$$\Xi(t) \equiv \Xi(M, t), \tag{3.4}$$

then

$$\Xi(m, t) = \sigma(m)\Xi(t), \qquad m = 1, \ldots, M \tag{3.5}$$

with

$$0 < \sigma(1) < \cdots < \sigma(m) < \cdots < \sigma(M - 1) < \sigma(M) \equiv 1.$$

Thus the $\sigma(m)$ are proportionality constants characterizing the firm's product line over time; that is, if $\sigma(m) = .5$, the mth machine is always half as powerful as the most powerful of the line.[29]

The firm's *innovation implementation frontier* can now be characterized by potential and actual innovative behavior according to the following relations:

$$\Xi^*(t) = f^{11}\left[\int_{t-\tau}^{t} [R + g_R(\iota)C(\iota)]\, d\iota\right], \qquad f^{11'} > 0 \tag{3.6}$$

$$\dot{\Xi}(t) = f^{12}[\Xi^*(t), \Xi(t); \alpha] \qquad \begin{cases} f_1^{12} > 0 \\ f_2^{12} < 0, f_3^{12} > 0 \end{cases} \tag{3.7}$$

The first of these portrays the potential level of innovative advancement as a function of the total expenditure on R&D over a past period of length τ. Thus R&D is not expected to produce results immediately and only for the present year; it is a form of investment for the firm. The relevant past period may be to the beginning of the firm's efforts in this (or related) industry's technological development or it may be later, the research effort prior to such a period being considered to be completely redundant in calculating its effects on the total value of potential innovations. Within the relevant period, however, there is assumed to be no diminishing value of older research on present innovative improvements.

The total R&D expenditure is made up of two components. The variable R is the fixed amount budgeted by the firm continually. Thus the firm realizes that research endeavors cannot be turned on and off frequently and remain effective; it may also recognize a certain

28. Although completely "atmospheric" R&D is not an accurate description of the computer industry, there is a certain amount of fallout from technological breakthroughs on particular computers to those in different parts of the product line. This is particularly true of changeovers from one generation of machines to another. Also, very rapid improvements in performance of some of the machines leading to crossovers in performance within the line could be viewed as less rapid change in all machines with no crossovers as in equation (3.1).

29. The increased generality of equation (3.2) over (3.3) could be achieved by allowing the σs to vary with time as additional firm control variables.

threshold minimum level of R&D expenditure that is essential to participation in the industry.[30] However, there are additional gains in $\Xi^*(t)$ to be achieved by additional expenditure on R&D. Thus a second term which can vary from time to time is present.

A component of this term, $C(t)$, represents net cash flow to the firm—total revenue less labor costs less the fixed budget R&D:[31]

$$C(t) = \sum_{m=1}^{M} [p(m, t)\dot{Y}_k(m, t) - w(t)L(m, t)] - R \qquad (3.8)$$

I am assuming in this formulation that the firm's only source of financing of investment alternatives is internal resources.[32] It can allocate a certain proportion of its resources to research and development $[g_R(t)]$, another proportion to capital goods accumulation $[g_K(t)]$, and the remainder to distribution as dividends (d).[33] Also by assumption, the firm always retains a fixed proportion (g) of its net cash flow and distributes the rest.[34] These considerations yield

$$g + d = 1 \qquad (3.9)$$

and

$$g_R(t) + g_K(t) = g. \qquad (3.10)$$

If the assumption that internal financing is essential to investment by the firm is not accurate, it would be necessary to reinterpret $C(t)$

---

30. There is some evidence of a threshold in the computer industry; C. Freeman, "Research and Development in Electronic Capital Goods," *National Institute Economic Review* 34, Nov. 1965, p. 69.

31. The realized demand at time t, $\dot{Y}_k(m, t)$, is described below. Throughout the theoretical development of the model, k is used to subscript the Y variable to represent demand from country k. However, only one country is assumed to exist to simplify the notation (i.e., only aggregate demand for each machine is considered). Features of individual countries are explored in Chapter 4.

32. For the plausibility of this supposition in the computer industry, see Chapter 4.

33. I should note a further relevant alternative, expenditure on sales effort and organization. Thus, while $g_R(t)$ affects innovative activity in equation (3.7), and $g_K(t)$ affects production through equation (3.13), an additional $g_s(t)$ could influence the demand characterization (3.16). The concept of alternatives to capital goods investment is captured by the presence of $g_R(t)$; this further alternative has been ignored to simplify the mathematical investigation of the model. It does appear in the empirical analysis of Chapter 4 as one of the influences causing γ to vary between firms. I am indebted to Raymond Vernon for identifying this omission of the theoretical model.

34. This assumption of g and d fixed leaves the amount of dividends $[dC(t)]$ as the residual; it is opposite from the policy usually thought to be maintained by a firm—the reluctance to modify the amount of the dividend. However, it may not be too unrealistic for firms that are rapidly innovating. Such firms characteristically keep dividend distributions very small and thus maintain g reasonably stable and close to one. For the accuracy of this expected high g in the computer industry, see Chapter 4.

as the total investable resources available at time t from whatever source: current operations, debt or equity financing.[35] The proportions $g_R(t)$ and $g_K(t)$ would then apply to the new $C(t)$ and presumably g would be higher than before, since dividends would come out of current operations only.

In viewing the term $g_R(t)C(t)$ in equation (3.6), one must also keep in mind that a firm can implement innovations that it has not discovered, that is, the firm can also imitate. In this case, its capacity to implement innovations is strictly a function of its ability to finance development efforts for the innovation—to achieve the capacity to use the innovation. The need for this financing will undoubtedly vary through time as the opportunities for imitation arise.

The other equation (3.7) of the innovation implementation frontier is intended to embody the precautionary motive of the firm in implementing advances in its product line. It states that the rate of change in the maximum level of actually implemented innovations depends on the relationship between this level $[\Xi(t)]$ and the potential maximum $[\Xi^*(t)]$. The α is a precautionary factor characteristic of the firm. Since the firm faces uncertainty both in the demand for products close to its innovative frontier and in the possible outcome of further research, which may make attainment of the current level of $\Xi^*(t)$ in the future much less costly, it is unlikely that the firm will want to implement all innovations immediately.[36]

The firm's productive capabilities will be represented in the model by a set of production functions, one for each model in the firm's product line:

$$\dot{Z}(m, t) = f^{2m}[L(m, t), K(m, t); Z(m, t)], \qquad m = 1, \ldots, M. \qquad (3.11)$$

Including total production within the function is intended to suggest the possibility of shifts in the function through "learning by doing." Assuming that capital goods are the same for producing all models of machines, we define

$$K(t) \equiv \sum_{m=1}^{M} K(m, t). \qquad (3.12)$$

35. It should be noted that equity financing cannot be undertaken independently of some of the other variables in the system. Such variables as current profits and, for an innovative industry, amount of research expenditure would have a definite influence on the ability of the company to float new shares. Thus, if this reinterpretation of $C(t)$ were used, the model interrelations would have to be reformulated also.

36. This α will become a lagged adjustment parameter in the actual equation to be explored empirically. It should be noted that α could have been considered to be another control variable of the firm. From time to time events and research reports might indicate that management ought to be more or less cautious in introducing further innovations in its product line. However, in this formulation α is treated as an unchanging characteristic of the firm.

Then, an increase in the firm's capital stock will arise from

$$\dot{K}(t) = g_K(t)C(t) - \delta K(t), \tag{3.13}$$

where δ is the exponential rate of depreciation of the capital stock.

The final aspect of the firm's environment is the set of demand conditions for its product line. It is assumed that the industry includes relatively few firms,[37] and that each faces demand curves of finite elasticity. The static demand relation for each model of machine, m, is viewed at the country level:

$$Y_k^*(m, t) = f^{3m}[p(m, t), \Xi(m, t), I_k(t), t], \qquad m = 1, \ldots, M$$

$$\begin{cases} f_1^{3m} < 0 \\ f_3^{3m} > 0, f_4^{3m} \gtrless 0, \end{cases} \tag{3.14}$$

which, from equation (3.5) becomes

$$Y_k^*(m, t) = f^{3m}[p(m, t), \sigma(m)\Xi(t), I_k(t), t]. \tag{3.15}$$

Here $Y_k^*(m, t)$ represents a stock of machines; the firm is assumed to sell capital goods that will be used over a period of time by the purchaser. Factors entering into the decision to purchase the machine are essentially price and income variables: $p(m, t)$ is the price of machine m of "quality" $\Xi(m, t)$, and I_k is the industrial production of country k. The influence of $\Xi(m, t)$ in this relation could be in either direction depending on the characteristics of the industry and innovations.

In Chow's formulation,[38] gross national product is entered as an influence on the optimal stock of computers demanded. The reasoning given is that demand for an input to a production process is related to the volume of output of that process. The present formulation follows this reasoning but views industrial production as the relevant "volume of output" to which demand for computer systems is related. This is an especially important distinction in a cross-sectional analysis where the proportion of GNP accounted for by I varies significantly (as it does, for example, between the United Kingdom and Italy). Thus I_k does have this other interpretation, beside its appearance in the demand function as an "income" variable.

37. The existence of few firms seems a reasonable assumption since technical knowledge is limited—which is one of the defining characteristics of a "new" industry. C. Freeman points out that in electronic capital goods the typical market situation is oligopoly, with between three and a dozen firms in world markets in each product. See "Research and Development," p. 68.

38. Chow, "Technological Change and the Demand for Computers," pp. 1120, 1129–1130.

Competition of one firm's machine with other firm's models of similar characteristics is treated here simply as increasing through time, while a trend through time in demand for the firm's machines may be positive or negative. Competition between machines of similar characteristics within one firm's product line could appear, in this formulation, as reduced levels of each of the demand functions for these models. Similarly, selling and other efforts at product differentiation between firms could influence the relative heights of the demand functions, as well as the price elasticities of demand faced by each of the firms in the industry.[39]

So far this model accounts only for the equilibrium number of machines for a country to possess; a dynamic adjustment is assumed to prevail in a country's attempt to acquire this equilibrium number of a firm's machines:

$$\dot{Y}_k(m, t) = f^{4m}[Y_k^*(m, t), (1 - v)Y_k(m, t); \gamma], \qquad m = 1, .., M$$

$$\begin{cases} f_1^{4m} > 0 \\ f_2^{4m} < 0, f_3^{4m} > 0. \end{cases} \qquad (3.16)$$

This formulation is similar to equation (3.7); the rate of change in the stock of machines is related to the equilibrium and the actual (after depreciation through use at the rate v) stock of machines. The adjustment factor, γ, reflects several influences. It should reflect the hesitancy of purchasers to commit themselves to machines of the present state of technology. Different γ's applied to the rate of acquisition of different firms' machines could also be a reflection of relative effectiveness of selling efforts by the firms. It is certainly conceivable that γ could vary by country also, or even by country but not by firm. This last possibility seems least likely if there is any difference in selling effort to create brand preference.[40]

This environment, within which the firm operates, is summarized graphically in Figure 3. Beginning with total revenue, the firm hires labor and budgets its fixed R&D expenditure. With the remaining net cash flow, it either distributes dividends or invests in capital goods or additional research, as indicated by equations (3.9) and (3.10) of

39. It is assumed that this is the only way in which the various firms take account of each other's activity in the industry. Thus, a combination of Cournot and Bertrand-Edgeworth behavior on the supply side is assumed. That is, each firm makes decisions concerning production independently of the decisions of its competitors and each sets its price structure independently. The outcome for each firm is a certain combination of sales and changes in inventories.
40. In the case of computers, brand preference can be developed through a very important aspect, the service network for the firm's machines in the particular country. This provision seems almost certainly sufficient to make γ differ among firms.

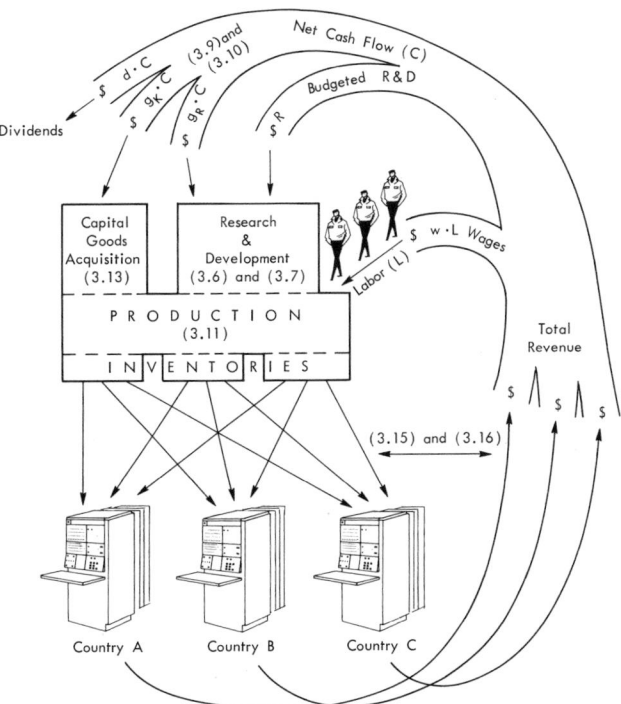

Fig. 3. Static view of the firm's environment.

the model. With this allocation of resources, it produces its line of machines and either sells them directly to users in the various countries [when $\dot{Z}(m, t) = \dot{Y}(m, t)$] or accumulates or uses up inventories. Proceeds from the sales complete the cycle.

Subject to this environment, profit maximization is assumed to be the basic driving force of the firm. Since it must expect to be successful (positive profits) only after some initial period of innovative efforts, the relevant maximization will be the present discounted value of profits over the time horizon (T) that the firm in question views as relevant. The discount rate (ρ) is also assumed to be one the firm feels is relevant. It will obviously be related to the alternative opportunity cost of capital, but will undoubtedly include some premium the firm considers appropriate given the environment—fraught with uncertainty as well as risks. Thus, the profit maximization criterion for the firm takes the form:

$$\underset{\{p(m, t), L(m, t), K(m, t): m = 1, \ldots, M\}; g_R(t); R}{\text{M a x i m i z e}} \qquad V(T) \qquad (3.17)$$

where

$$V(T) = \int_0^T \dot{V}(t)\, dt \qquad (3.18)$$

and

$$\dot{V}(t) = e^{-\rho t}\left\{ \sum_{m=1}^M \left[p(m, t)\dot{Y}(m, t) - w(t)L(m, t)\right.\right.$$

$$\left.\left. - r(t)\{K(m, t) + p(m, t)[Z(m, t) - Y(m, t)]\}\right] - R\right\}. \qquad (3.19)$$

The controls available for achieving the maximum profit are the budgeted R&D, the proportion of net cash flow $[g_R(t)]$ devoted to R&D, the factor allocations in production, and the price structure of the products. The other investment alternative, through $g_K(t)$, does not enter because of relation (3.10); this would not be the case, of course, if there were even more alternatives included in the model.[41] The discounted profits at time t, then, are simply the sum of sales less costs (or opportunity costs) of the machines in the firm's product line, less the budgeted R&D expenditure. On the assumption that the firm has access to competitive labor or capital markets, it views the wage rate, $w(t)$, and opportunity cost of capital, $r(t)$, as given.[42] Opportunity costs must be covered on both capital goods and inventories. The constraint of nonnegative inventories in this model,

$$Z(m, t) - Y_k(m, t) \geq 0, \qquad m = 1, \ldots, M \qquad (3.20)$$

takes the place of the usual market equilibrium of supply and demand. Within this framework, new firms will enter the industry as long as the expected profits, $V(T)$, are sufficiently large to attract their participation.

Optimal Firm Behavior

The model specification presented above is rather elaborate, precisely because my intention from the outset has been to consider a model that could lead to an empirically analyzable form; it has retained considerable detail even after a number of simplifying assumptions. At this point the analysis could proceed in either of two directions, theoretical or econometric. My primary objective is to pursue the latter course in the following chapters. But in this section I shall briefly comment on some of the theoretical implications.

41. See note 33 above.
42. Since these variables are exogenously given, allowing them to change over time requires that their movement during the time horizon be specified.

The necessary conditions for profit maximization are presented briefly in the appendix to this chapter. These have the usual interpretation of the equality at the margin of benefit and cost of each of the control variables available to the firm.[43] It may be useful, however, to consider specific examples of demand conditions and innovation possibilities and interpret the implications of the model.

First, let us collapse the system into one country and one firm and suppose that the levels of demand for the products of this firm vary with the level of innovative content up to a point [call it $\Xi^1(t)$], and inversely with increasing Ξ thereafter. Also, suppose that the value of Ξ at which demand is highest increases through time at a rate $\dot{\Xi}^1(t)$.[44] Even if these features of demand were known to the firm, its behavior is not yet determined. With sufficient resources and the absence of significantly diminishing returns to scale from research, the firm will attempt to center its product line around $\Xi^1(t)$ and maintain its innovation possibilities frontier at a growth rate of $\dot{\Xi}^1(t)$. To steer this course, given its precautionary characteristic in implementing research results (α), the firm will allocate relatively more of its net cash flow to research during those times when its product line begins slipping below " center " with respect to demand conditions—the periods when the relative return from research as opposed to capital goods investment increases. Conversely, it will allocate more to capital goods investment[45] if it finds the "center" of its product line above $\Xi^1(t)$. Although the model should convey some uncertainty about the outcome from current research expenditure, the optimal path for a firm characterized by differential equations for its operations will be instantaneously adjusted to such "under or over shooting."

So long as the marginal cost functions for the machines are similar,[46] the assumptions of continuously increasing and then decreasing levels of demand by levels of innovative content, and of completely atmospheric R&D impact [recall that $\Xi(m, t) = \sigma(m)\Xi(t)$]

43. The control variables—those aspects of the firm's operations over which it has control—include the fixed R&D budgetary level (R), the proportion of the yearly retained earnings devoted to innovational activity [$g_R(t)$], the allocation of factors of production [$L(m, t)$ and $K(m, t)$], and the pricing policy [$p(m, t)$].

44. This would be characterized by a shift through time in the demand function (3.15) based on Ξ. Although this "one hump" demand spectrum has been chosen for convenience, there is no reason why the distribution of demand should not be bimodal or even discontinuous. The bimodal description might be a convenient abstraction for the commercial and scientific uses of computers.

45. Or, the firm might allocate more resources to advertising under this circumstance to attempt to increase the level of demand across its entire product line.

46. Derived from equations (3.11) above.

imply that profit-maximizing pricing will determine production levels proportional to demand in this monopolistic context. That is, no machine in the product line will be produced at a lower rate than those in the product line of *both* higher and lower level of innovative content because of lower profitability.

When one considers more than one firm in the industry (still one country), the conclusion of production mirroring market levels of demand no longer follows; analysis of the behavior of a monopolist now becomes investigation of possible strategies of oligopolists.[47] The strategy for a firm at the time of its entry into the industry can be characterized within this model as choosing the levels of "innovative content" for its product line [the $\sigma(m)$] that will acquire the highest levels of demand (or make the biggest inroads on the "market shares" of its competitors). Even with the simplified one-dimensional representation of innovative content (Ξ), there are an infinite number of possible product variants. It is still reasonable to expect that each firm will face a continuous demand curve for each of its products.[48] Any one demand function will probably be quite price elastic in the vicinity of the price levels of its competitors in the relevant range of innovative content of that product, but the demand function should turn inelastic for significantly lower price levels, since product variation itself precludes the firm from capturing the entire market.

Expanding the discussion to more than one country, we again enter the context in which this chapter began. Firms *operate* within each country along the lines sketched above. They *enter* a new industry according to the considerations of the innovation/imitation approach: firms of one country introduce the new technological advances in another country, and after a period of time some firms in that second country may decide to become participants in the industry.

A question that has been quite popular is whether or not research and development has an effect on a country's exports. Several studies using correlation methods have found that there is a significant association between these variables, especially in the United States.[49]

---

47. See, for example, L. Shapley and M. Shubik, "Price Strategy Oligopoly with Product Variation," *Kyklos* 22, no. 1, 1969, pp. 30–44.

48. Ibid., pp. 34–38.

49. For example, W. Gruber, D. Mehta, and R. Vernon, "The R&D Factor in International Trade and International Investment of United States Industries," *Journal of Political Economy* 75, Feb. 1967, pp. 20–37; D. B. Keesing, "The Impact of Research and Development on United States Trade," *Journal of Political Economy* 75, Feb. 1967, pp. 38–48.

The model that has now been presented for new industries can indicate the type of relationship that has been explored by these authors, since it is clear that they do not hypothesize a direct structural relationship of research causing exports.

In the present model, net exports of a country consist of the value of machines produced by firms of that country but not used in the country, minus the value of machines used in the country but not produced by its firms. *Thus net exports will be affected within the present model by the relative innovative achievements of domestic versus foreign producers.* This will itself be a function of the amount of R&D undertaken by the firms in these countries, as portrayed by equations (3.6) and (3.7). It is clearly this type of structural relationship that is embedded in these aggregate correlation analyses.

Classification of Industries

A problem remaining after presentation of the features of the "new industry" theory is that of identifying which industries should be classified as "new" rather than "standard."[50] One procedure would be to poll a panel of experts to determine which industries are believed to operate with limited availability (between countries) of the newest technology and innovations. These industries could then be classified as "new."

Since the basis of the new industry hypothesis is the lack of general availability or commercial exploitation of technological formation in a particular field, one would expect that the exports of new industries would be concentrated in relatively few countries where the information is available.[51] Thus high concentration of total exports in relatively few countries could be a primary criterion for classification. One would also expect that new technologies currently being exploited would be participating to a rapidly growing extent in international trade. So the growth of trade in these categories could be another characteristic for which to look. Confounding both of these empirical measures in trade data is the option of direct investment in foreign countries. It is conceivable that this could hide characteristics of the industry below the surface of trade data,

50. No solution to this problem was given by I. B. Kravis, "'Availability' and Other Influences," or M. V. Posner, "International Trade and Technical Change." Several observers have noted the difficulty of distinguishing new and old goods or processes, or even new goods from new processes. See also D. Blondel, "Transmission Internationale des Innovations," *Revue Economique* 17, no. 3, May 1966, pp. 434–466.

51. This feature of trade patterns in past new industries was mentioned in Chapter 1, based on a survey in A. J. Harman, "Innovations, Technology, and the Pure Theory of International Trade," Chapter 2.

requiring more detailed knowledge of ownership and organization of individual foreign enterprises.

The concentration and growth of exports criteria can be applied to international activity in the computer industry. It should be classified as "new," since it is a highly technologically oriented industry, the technology has been implemented only since the early 1950s, and the technology is not nearly universally available.[52] As was described in Chapter 2, several U.S. companies have set up subsidiaries or arranged license agreements abroad. To see whether the concentration criterion would identify this industry as "new," even with the confounding of evidence from these direct foreign operations, refer to Table 3.2. The category for electronic computers within the Standard International Trade Classification[53] is 714.2 (1) —an optional subheading no country compiles. The full category 714.2—calculating machines, accounting machines, and similar machines incorporating a calculating device (including electronic computers)—is not presented in the *Yearbook of International Trade Statistics* volumes for 1963 and 1965 for all of the relevant countries. Thus category 714—office machinery—which includes typewriters, duplicating equipment, and so on, had to be used for the check of trade data. As can be seen from the last two columns, the United States has had a large and growing share of the export trade; its share was almost 37 percent in the 1963–1965 period. The three largest exporters accounted for 65 percent of the trade during this period and the next two countries bring the percentage to 85. Since Italy was very strong in marketing typewriters, and Sweden in desk calculators, the impression from these data is that the commodity concentration criterion is quite useful. The growth of this category of trade also appears to be high, with an annual rate of increase of about 17 percent. This measure, however, is biased in part by incomplete breakdowns of country trade data in the earlier years.

Despite the ability of trade data to distinguish the computer industry as "new," it is not the best information on which to base evaluation of the theoretical model. Broad features of the international aspects of the theory have already been verified by the description of the industry in Chapter 2. Production is, to a very large extent, undertaken by American firms and delivered to foreign users. However, important features of this "trade" are hidden by the SITC

52. C. Layton, in *Trans-Atlantic Investments*, classifies the computer and aircraft industries as "new industries."

53. See United Nations, *Standard International Trade Classification, Revised,* New York, Statistical Office, Department of Economic and Social Affairs, 1961, pp. 36, 135.

Table 3.2 Office Machinery (Category 714, SITC) Exports[a]

	1960	1961	1962	1963	1964	1965	Average share (percent)	
							1960–1962	1963–1965
Argentina				1.5 (0.2)	7.2 (0.6)	7.3 (0.6)	0.0	0.5
Canada		29.98 (3.5)	33.05 (3.5)	29.42 (2.9)	36.44 (3.2)	32.65 (2.5)	3.5	2.9
France	45.91 (7.5)	73.65 (8.6)	86.87 (9.1)	78.12 (7.8)	82.82 (7.4)	150.31 (11.4)	8.4	8.9
West Germany	104.7 (17.2)	144.8 (16.9)	165.4 (17.3)	164.0 (16.4)	197.3 (17.5)	243.0 (18.4)	17.1	17.4
Italy	81.35 (13.3)	102.40 (11.9)	116.51 (12.2)	119.10 (11.9)	114.04 (10.1)	135.73 (10.3)	12.5	10.8
Netherlands	30.18 (4.9)	33.67 (3.9)	42.57 (4.5)	43.59 (4.4)	44.89 (4.0)	50.07 (3.9)	4.4	4.1
Spain		2.41 (0.3)	2.00 (0.2)	2.44 (0.2)	3.18 (0.3)	3.05 (0.2)	0.2	0.2
Sweden	43.22 (7.1)	56.55 (6.6)	62.04 (6.5)	64.26 (6.4)	66.56 (5.9)	74.71 (5.6)	6.7	6.0
Switzerland	19.55 (3.2)	22.83 (2.7)	25.48 (2.7)	25.09 (2.5)	25.62 (2.3)	30.65 (2.3)	2.9	2.4
United Kingdom	77.90 (12.8)	82.24 (0.6)	93.49 (9.8)	110.66 (11.1)	112.25 (10.0)	124.49 (9.4)	10.7	10.2
United States	207.6 (34.0)	309.7 (36.1)	327.2 (34.3)	359.6 (36.0)	434.3 (38.6)	470.4 (35.5)	34.8	36.7
Total	610.41	858.23	954.61	997.78	1124.50	1323.26		

Source: United Nations, *Yearbook of International Trade Statistics, 1963–1965*, New York, Statistical Office, Department of Economic and Social Affairs, 1965 and 1967.
Note: [a] Values in millions of U.S. dollars. Numbers in parentheses show percent of total.

data, both by insufficient disaggregation and by production and delivery of U.S. machines to foreigners taking place in the same country (in which foreign subsidiaries are present).

The data also contain misleading export figures from some European countries. The primary example is IBM's facilities, specialized in different computer models in different countries. Thus export data for Italy would show an increase every time a British firm received delivery of an IBM 360/20, which is produced in Italy, *sold* to IBM (U.K.) and (usually) leased by the latter to the British user.[54] If sufficiently disaggregated corporate data could be obtained, it would be desirable to classify foreign subsidiaries of firms in new industries as foreign firms but with the same pattern of innovation implementation characteristics as the parent company for the machines in its product line.[55] This would take account of probably the most efficient channels of technological communication from the home country abroad. Also, it would provide a means of measuring the extent to which foreign countries' exports are actually dependent on the home country's firms, and the extent to which home country's exports in the industry are reduced because of foreign subsidiaries' production. Unfortunately, such detailed data are not available; thus, the tack to be followed will be direct consideration of computer models of designer firms, regardless of the country in which they are manufactured.

54. See, for example, T. Dakin, "Marketing: Computer Colossus Expands in Europe." *British Industry Week*, Oct. 13, 1967, pp. 15–16.

55. As another example, the entrance of Argentina into exports in the office machinery category may have resulted, in part, from the establishment of IBM production facilities in that country.

Appendix to Chapter 3
Conditions for Optimal Firm Behavior

Optimality conditions for the behavioral model of a firm in a new industry will be derived by means of optimal control theory.[56] Maximization of the present discounted value of profits (3.17) subject to the environmental constraints are derived from the Hamiltonian:[57]

$$\mathscr{H}(\Psi(i(m), t); \Xi(t), K(t), Z(m, t), Y(m, t),$$

$$p(m, t), L(m, t)K(m, t), g_R(t), R)$$

$$= e^{-\rho t}[\sum p(m, t)\dot{Y}(m, t) - w(t)L(m, t)$$

$$- r(t)\{K(m, t) + p(m, t)[Z(m, t) - Y(m, t)]\}]$$

$$+ \Psi(1, t)f^{12}(\cdot) + \Psi(2, t)\{[g - g_R(t)]C(t) - \delta K(t)\}$$

$$+ \sum_m \Psi(3(m), t)f^{2m}(\cdot) + \sum_m \Psi(4(m), t)f^{4m}(\cdot). \qquad (3.21)$$

Following Pontryagin's maximum principle, the partial derivatives of $\mathscr{H}$ with respect to the Ψs yield the differential equations for the phase variables: the environmental constraints. Within the allowable

---

56. L. S. Pontryagin *et al.*, *The Mathematical Theory of Optimal Processes*, New York, Interscience Publishers, 1962. This appendix does not really *explore* the model that has been hypothesized; it merely derives some of the conditions for optimality that would be necessary for such an exploration. The main purpose of this further elaboration is to verify the completeness of the model and indicate some of its features.

The firm's "control variables" are listed in the profit-maximizing condition (3.17), except that in the Pontryagin terminology R is a "parameter": it does not vary continuously with time but is set once and for all according to an optimality condition. These controls, then, are constrained by

$$\left.\begin{array}{l} p(m, t) \geq 0, \\ L(m, t) \geq 0, \\ K(m, t) \geq 0; \end{array}\right\} m = 1, \dots, M$$
$$g_R(t) \geq 0;$$
$$R \geq 0;$$

and

$$g - g_R(t) \geq 0.$$

57. The Ψ's will have the usual interpretation of imputed values of the phase variables. The imputed value, $\Psi(0)$, for present discounted profits through equation (3.19) has been set to unity. The entire Hamiltonian (with all relevant substitutions) is derived from equations (3.6) to (3.8), (3.10) to (3.13), and (3.15) and (3.16).

space of the phase variables, the selection of R is obtained by the following:[58]

$$-\frac{1}{\rho}(1 - e^{-\rho T}) + \Psi(1, T) \int_0^T f_1^{12}(\cdot)\frac{\partial f^{11}(\cdot)}{\partial R} - \Psi(2, T)$$

$$\times \int_0^T g_K(t)\, dt \le 0, \quad \text{and} \quad = 0 \text{ if } R > 0. \quad (3.22)$$

This expression indicates that the marginal cost of budgeted R&D, both in terms of the reduction in profits from the "last dollar" budgeted and through the reduction in funds available for capital goods investment, must be just equal to the marginal benefit of research through further innovative advances. The means of valuation are the shadow prices at the end of the time horizon, $\Psi(i, T)$. The further contribution to R&D is established by $\partial \mathcal{H}/\partial g_R(t)$, which reduces to

$$\Psi(1, t)f_1^{12}(\cdot)\frac{\partial f^{11}(\cdot)}{\partial g_R(t)} - \Psi(2, t) \le 0 \quad \text{and} \quad = 0 \text{ if } g_R(t) > 0. \quad (3.23)$$

So, the remaining allocation of investable resources between innovative activity and capital goods acquisition is established to yield the same marginal benefit from each.

The factors of production are employed according to the following conditions. For capital allocation,

$$\left[\frac{\partial \mathcal{H}}{\partial K(\hat{m}, t)}\right]_{K(t)} = e^{-\rho t}\Bigg\{(-r) \sum \left[\frac{\partial K(m, t)}{\partial K(\hat{m}, t)}\right]_{K(t)}\Bigg\}$$

$$+ \Psi(2, t)[g - g_R(t)]\Bigg\{(-\delta) \sum \left[\frac{\partial K(m, t)}{\partial K(\hat{m}, t)}\right]_{K(t)}\Bigg\}$$

$$+ \sum \Psi(3(m), t)f_2^{2m}(\cdot)\left(\frac{\partial K(m, t)}{\partial K(\hat{m}, t)}\right)_{K(t)} \le 0 \quad (3.24)$$

58. There are restrictions on the values of the phase variables:

$$\begin{aligned} Y(m, t) &\ge 0, \\ Z(m, t) &\ge 0, \end{aligned} \quad m = 1, \ldots, M$$
$$K(t) \ge 0;$$
$$(t) \ge 0;$$
$$Z(m, t) - Y_k(m, t) \ge 0, \quad m = 1, \ldots, M$$

and

$$\sum[p(m, t)f^{4m}Y_k^*(m, t), (1 - v)y_k(m, t); \gamma) - w(t)L(m, t)] - R \ge 0.$$

The last two constrain inventories and net cash flow to be nonnegative.

The optimality conditions on the boundaries of the phase space will not be explicitly derived. Ibid., Chapter 6. Thus the conditions presented here are pertinent when all phase variables are positive and inventories exist for each of the machines in the product line. Within this region, the pertinent mathematical conditions are as presented on pp. 58–61, 191–194, ibid.

which reduces, since the total amount of capital is held constant, to

$$\sum \Psi(3(m), t) f_2^{2m}(\cdot) \left[\frac{\partial K(m, t)}{\partial K(\hat{m}, t)} \right]_{K(t)} \leq 0 \quad \text{and}$$

$$= 0 \text{ if } K(\hat{m}, t) > 0, \quad \text{for each } \hat{m} = 1, \ldots, M. \quad (3.25)$$

For labor employed in the production of each machine:

$$\frac{\partial \mathcal{H}}{\partial L(m, t)} = -w(t)e^{-\rho t} + \Psi(1, t) \left[f_1^{12}(\cdot) \frac{\partial f^{11}(\cdot)}{\partial C(t)} \frac{\partial C(t)}{\partial L(m, t)} \right]$$

$$+ \Psi(2, t)\{-[g - g_R(t)]w(t)\}$$

$$+ \Psi(3(m), t) f_1^{2m}(\cdot) \leq 0 \quad \text{and}$$

$$= 0 \text{ if } L(m, t) > 0, \quad \text{for } m = 1, \ldots, M. \quad (3.26)$$

The first condition demands that capital be allocated to production of a particular model of machine until the imputed value from producing extra units of that machine just compensates for the imputed loss from lower production of all others. The other states that labor is hired for each machine until the costs in reduced profits and reduced investable resources just equals the benefits of the marginal product of the additional labor.

The last optimality conditions deal with pricing policy, from $\partial \mathcal{H} / \partial p(m, t)$. These conditions can be expressed in a simplified form [when (3.23) is satisfied] as:

$$[e^{-\rho t} + \Psi(2, t)g][f^{4m}(\cdot) + p(m, t) f_1^{3m}(\cdot) f_1^{4m}(\cdot)]$$

$$- r(t)e^{-\rho t}[Z(m, t) - Y(m, t)] + \Psi(4(m), t) f_1^{3m}(\cdot) f_1^{4m}(\cdot) \leq 0,$$

$$\text{and} = 0 \text{ if } p(m, t) > 0, \quad \text{for } m = 1, \ldots, M. \quad (3.27)$$

They can be interpreted as the conditions that adjustments in the price structure of the product line end when the marginal increase in revenue and benefit from additional investable resources from such adjustments are just equal to the marginal cost of reduction in the demand for each model [recall from equations (3.14) and (3.16) that $f_1^{3m}(\cdot) < 0$ and $f_1^{4m}(\cdot) > 0$].

4
Analysis of the Computer Industry

Model Specification for Empirical Estimation

The main feature of the environment of a firm in a " new industry " is the innovation implementation frontier and adjustment of actually implemented innovations to the frontier [see equations (3.6) and (3.7)].[1] The argument in the former function was simply the total resources committed to R & D over a relevant past period. This was derived from a fixed R & D budget plus an additional amount allocated from the remaining investable resources at the moment. Since none of the firms to be investigated actually distinguish permanent from temporary R & D allocations, actual measurement of these variables will have to be modified somewhat. The R & D component of reported operations by the firms will be the measure of $R(t)$; in addition, a retained earnings measure will enter independently in the equation. It should still indicate the value to the firm of being able to finance investment internally in innovative activities, as well as to imitate innovations of others through financing work that may not be included within the firm's reported R & D.

The model actually calls for $g_R(t)$, the proportion of retained earnings devoted to innovative activity. Since this information also is not available, $g(t)$ must be used. The inherent assumption in using $g(t)$ as a proxy for $g_R(t)$ is that, although the firm may shift the proportion of earnings retained between innovative and capital-goods investment, over the periods under consideration it has chosen to keep the proportion (μ) of $g(t)$ directed to $g_R(t)$ reasonably stable. This assumption seems plausible, since most firms are still in the stage of anticipating profits from their computer operations at some future date, which could entail devoting a (possibly large) stable fraction of $g(t)$ to establish places for themselves in the industry.

The form of the innovation implementation frontier will be specified as

$$\Xi^*(t) = a_0 \left[\sum_{i=t-\tau}^{t-1} R(i) \right]^{a_1} \left[\sum_{i=t-\tau}^{t-1} \frac{1}{\tau} g(i) \right]^{a_2} \tag{4.1}$$

and the adjustment to this frontier will be characterized by

$$\frac{\Xi(t)}{\Xi(t-1)} = \left[\frac{\Xi^*(t)}{\Xi(t-1)} \right]^{\alpha}. \tag{4.2}$$

---

1. Definitions of all variables are summarized in Table 3.1 above.

Equation (4.1) follows the form of equation (3.6)—research expenditure over a past period (back τ periods) is used as the relevant variable, since research is a form of investment and is expected to result in technological development over a period of time. The other term is the average retained earnings over τ periods.[2] This function attributes constant elasticities to each of the influences on maximum potential innovations; a_1 and a_2 are presumed to be positive. With the elasticity for the retained earnings variable assumed to be positive (and μ positive), the use of $g(t)$ rather than $g_R(t)$ in the equation will impart a downward bias on the constant term. The rate of increase in actually implemented innovations is represented by a multiplicative form of a lagged adjustment model.[3] Equation (4.2) states that there will be a lagged adjustment of $\Xi(t)$ to its potential value of $\Xi^*(t)$; α is assumed to be between 0 and 1. As was pointed out previously, the firm faces uncertainty, both in the demand for products close to its innovative frontier, and in the outcome of further research, which might make attainment of $\Xi^*(t)$ in the future much less costly. It was also noted that α could actually be considered as another control variable of the firm. Management could be more or less cautious in introducing further innovations in its product line from one period to another. It is thus conceivable that this parameter might be poorly estimated in an equation in which it is assumed to be constant over time. These equations can be estimated by the combined form as

$$\frac{\Xi(t)}{\Xi(t-1)} = \text{const} \left(\frac{[\sum R(i)]^{a_1} \left[\sum \frac{1}{\tau} g(i) \right]^{a_2}}{\Xi(t-1)} \right)^{\alpha}. \qquad (4.3)$$

The model emphasizes retained earnings as the primary source of financing of investment in innovative activity or in capital goods. A survey of several of the firms in the computer industry indicated that IBM achieved about 70 percent of its total cash flow from internal operations and the other 30 percent from floating new capital issues.[4]

2. Note that this form of equation (4.1) avoids the implication that for some t, $g(t) = 0$ implies $\Xi^*(t) = 0$; it does not exclude the possibility that average g may equal zero and imply $\Xi^*(t) = 0$. This is not unreasonable with g viewed as the source of financing of development work needed to realize an innovative (or imitating) idea as a product. In fact, it emphasizes the Department of Commerce study finding that expenditure other than for research plays an important role in innovating; see U.S. Department of Commerce, *Technological Innovation: Its Environment and Management*.

3. This equation, as with (4.7) below, can also be viewed as a discrete form of the differential equation of a Gompertz curve. This formulation is also used by G. C. Chow, "Technological Change and the Demand for Computers," *American Economic Review* 57, no. 5, December 1967, pp. 1117–1130.

4. "Cash and Computers," *Economist* 223, Apr. 22, 1967, pp. 368–369.

The computer specialists, especially the smaller firms, have even higher percentages. Therefore the retained earnings proportion (g) does seem to be a relevant variable for the computer industry. The proportion of earnings retained has been quite high, as expected, for all firms considered in this investigation—the lowest being over three-quarters for Burroughs.

The firm's production of its machines [see equation (3.11)] could be characterized by Cobb-Douglas production functions:

$$\Delta Z(m, t) = b_0(m)[Z(m, t - 1), t]L(m, t)^{b_1(m)}K(m, t)^{b_2(m)}. \quad (4.4)$$

These functions could allow for the possibilities of increasing returns to scale and "learning by doing" through previous production. With the assumption of homogeneous capital goods used in the production of all machines and exponential depreciation, changes in total capital stock can be represented in discrete form by

$$\Delta K(t) = g_K(t)C(t) - \delta K(t - 1). \quad (4.5)$$

The demand conditions faced by a firm in the industry are specified, at the country level of aggregation, to be [see equations (3.14) and (3.15)]:

$$Y_k^*(m, t) = c_0[T(m)]p(m)^{c_1}\Xi(m)^{c_2}I_k(t - 1)^{c_3} \quad (4.6)$$

and

$$\frac{Y_k(m, t)}{Y_k(m, t - 1)} = \left[\frac{Y_k^*(m, t)}{Y_k(m, t - 1)}\right]^{\gamma}. \quad (4.7)$$

The function for the equilibrium stock of machines demanded displays constant elasticities; following the specification for these functions in the theoretical section, the price elasticity should be negative ($c_1 < 0$) and the income elasticity positive ($c_3 > 0$). Since the $\Xi(m)$ characteristic of each machine will actually remain constant throughout the life of the machine in this empirical analysis, the appropriate time variable to represent competition to the firm's models is the time since each model was first introduced, represented by $T(m)$. The influence of $T(m)$ is expected to be negative. Two different views of this "time since introduction" competitive effect will be considered later in this chapter; this will be the only type of competition (constantly increasing with time) that I shall explore empirically. For the adjustment of the stock of computers to the equilibrium level, gamma ($0 < \gamma < 1$) is used to reflect the caution with which users commit themselves to a given state of technology as embodied in the machines. Since γ varies across firms, it should also indicate how successful selling efforts have been in establishing brand preference—a relatively high γ faced by a firm would indicate that that firm's machines are acquired relatively rapidly when need for them increases. It will estimate the combined form of the demand equations:

$$\frac{Y_k(m, t)}{Y_k(m, t-1)} = \mathrm{const}[T(m)]\left\{\frac{p(m)^{c_1}\Xi(m)^{c_2}I_k(t-1)^{c_3}}{Y_k(m, t-1)}\right\}^{\gamma}. \quad (4.8)$$

Characteristics of Corporate Activity

Innovative Activity

The innovative process will be explored for seven U.S. corporations as noted in Table 2.1. Probably the most important decision for the empirical analysis is the selection of an appropriate measure for $\Xi(m)$. Gruenberger listed what he considered to be "30 good, solid ideas" in the development of the computer up to 1962; some deal with hardware (magnetic cores, transistorization, thin films, two-headed tapes), some with design features (index registers, floating point, buffering, parity checking), and some with software (compilers, assemblers, self-written compilers, indirect addressing).[5] Knight is much more extensive in his identification of innovative activity embodied in computers and tried to attach a value to each of the disclosed innovations, as well as a value to "undisclosed engineering and production improvements."[6]

One of the purposes of the brief review of developments in computers presented in Chapter 2 was to emphasize that it is very difficult to enumerate the relevant advances in computer technology, let alone to assign a value for the embodiment of these advances in a computer. In fact, Knight makes an important point in emphasizing that there has been significant improvement in computer performance brought about by many small design or engineering modifications which often are not revealed explicitly in the professional literature. The problem,

5. F. Gruenberger, "Editors' Readout—.06 Idea per Kiloman Year, A Guest Editorial," *Datamation* 8, no. 9, Sept. 1962, p. 23.

6. K. E. Knight, "A Study of Technological Innovation—The Evolution of Digital Computers," Ph.D. dissertation, Carnegie Institute of Technology, 1963. His evaluation of innovations is based in part on comparing one computer with a previous one. His comparisons are invalid in many cases because he took as "previous" any computer with a lower number on his list of computers from 1 to 225 (see Table 4.9). Thus, some computers which should show an increase in value over the previous *year* do not, simply because one earlier on the list for the same year showed a greater improvement. This problem, as well as arbitrary and enormous estimates of value for early innovations, seriously undermine the legitimacy of Knight's listed evaluation of innovations; his method of evaluation using a "technology frontier" for a particular year has not been explored further in this analysis.

then, is how to devise a useful index of the cumulative value of innovations for a particular computer.

Knight developed a measure he calls "computing power" that seems to be quite appropriate for this purpose.[7] He first points out that previous work using one or two measures of a computer's performance—such as add time, memory access time, or number of index registers—have led to questionable implications.[8] Instead, he developed an algorithm (see Figure 4)[9] that "consists of three main components: (1) the internal calculating speed of the computer's central processor (t_c), (2) the time the central processor is idle and waiting for information input or output $(t_{I/O})$, and (3) the memory capacity of the computer" (T).[10] Each of the time variables is derived from a complex set of terms involving times for the various types of calculations for the former, and times for the various types of delays for primary as well as secondary (slower) sources of storage of information for the latter. Thus the measure Knight developed will take cognizance of most of the types of improvements in computers that were sketched in Chapter 2.[11] It will also limit the amount of double counting in the usefulness of innovations by considering only the *net* increase in computer performance resulting from the innovations.[12] Knight made a further embellishment on this index. He acknowledged that there are at least two basic uses for computers that have developed: for scientific and commercial work. Scientific problems require many more multiplications and processing operations in general, and fewer input-output operations between the central processor and data

7. Ibid., Chapter 4.

8. One study of measuring computer capabilities by a single attribute led to the unlikely conclusion that 1960 computers were only slightly better than those developed in the early 1950s. See C. P. Bourne and D. F. Ford, "The Historical Development and Predicted State-of-the-Art of the General Purpose Digital Computer," *Proceedings of the Western Joint Computer Conference*, May 3–5, 1960, pp. 1–21.

9. This algorithm has been reproduced from K. E. Knight, "Changes in Computer Performance: A Historical View," *Datamation* 12, no. 9, Sept. 1966, pp. 40–54.

10. K. E. Knight, *A Study of Technological Innovation*, p. IV–3.

11. There are, of course, shortcomings to the particular algorithm chosen by Knight. W. F. Sharpe (*The Economics of Computers*, New York, Columbia University Press, 1969, Chapter 11) discusses various other measures of "computer effectiveness," but notes that no other measure has been applied to so large a range of computers.

12. Knight's index has been called various things, including "operations per second" and "power." The broader characterization as an index of "performance" seemed more appropriate to the present application. The index has been used, independent of this investigation, within a different theoretical framework; see J. L. Barr and K. E. Knight, "Technological Change and Learning in the Computer Industry," *Management Science: Theory* 14, no. 11, July 1968, pp. 661–681.

storage facilities than do commercial uses. Even in the processing phase, commercial uses require relatively more additions than multiplications; additions take considerably less time. These differences were embodied in the values of the "semi-constant factors" that contribute to the values of t_c and $t_{I/O}$. Although the performance measure for the typical scientific problem and that for the typical commercial problem (as specified by these weighting factors) will be used in the analysis, I place primary reliance on the scientific measure of computer performance, since that has been the area of the main impetus for development through research. In fact, the two measures are quite highly correlated, so that the results should not vary substantially whichever measure is used.[13] With these two indexes as measures of $\Xi(m)$ for each computer model developed by a firm, the corresponding two measures of $\Xi(t)$ for that firm are simply the maximum of all $\Xi(m)$ of models that have been introduced by year t [see equation (3.4)].

Although this measure of the value of innovations does account for many of the characteristics of the product that are changed through innovation, several will be lost in this analysis. For example, the reliability of continuous operation of the system and the availability of quick servicing when there is a breakdown are important factors considered by a potential user of computer services. Broad consulting support (through both software provision and suggestions of applications) can add to the versatility of the machine, while modularity of design can allow less expensive future expansion of computer capacity.[14] The analysis must be viewed as an attempt to measure

13. The weights were chosen by Knight for one "typical" scientific or commercial problem; these performance variables used as Ξ still reflect only that one type of problem. Thus, machines not designed to handle that particular type of problem may appear to contain low innovative content. Although this is a shortcoming, it is my belief that with the analysis restricted to general purpose digital computers, the index is sufficiently general to convey most of the relevant information on implemented innovations.

The fact that these two measures are nearly identical also eliminates the concern that one might be using the wrong index in evaluating a particular firm's performance. For example, a company that is really trying to make a business of supplying machines for commercial applications might fare badly in an analysis using a scientific index that was really different from the commercial one.

14. I am indebted to Nelson Hanover and Dean George Brown for emphasizing these qualifications to the analysis. It should also be pointed out that, although computer development during the period of the present analysis was directed toward larger and larger systems, there is a serious debate in progress over the advantages of a large computer with many simultaneous users (time-sharing) versus small computers for individual use. See, for example, J. Main, "Computer Time-Sharing—Everyman at the Console," *Fortune* 73, Aug. 1967, pp. 88–91ff; and R. C. Stiefel, "Computers Large or Small? In Which Direction Will They Go?" *Computers and Automation* 15, Nov. 1966, pp. 18–19. See also "Approaching Multiple Access," *Economist* 222, Mar. 4, 1967, p. 850.

Figure 4. Measure of Computer Performance

$$\Xi(m) = \frac{10^{12} \dfrac{[(L-7)T \cdot WF]^i}{[32,000(36-7)]^i}}{t_c + t_{I/O}}$$

$$t_c = 10^4[C_1 A_{FI} + C_2 A_{FL} + C_3 M + C_4 D + C_5 L]$$

$$t_{I/O} = P \cdot OL_1 \left[10^6 \frac{W_{I1}B}{K_{I1}} + \frac{W_{O1}B}{K_{O1}} + N(S_1 + H_1) \right] R_1$$

$$+ (1-P)OL_2 \left[10^6 \frac{W_{I2}B}{K_{I2}} + \frac{W_{O2}B}{K_{O2}} + N(S_2 + H_2) \right]$$

VARIABLES—ATTRIBUTES OF EACH COMPUTING SYSTEM

$\Xi(m)$ = The performance of the mth computing system
L = The word lengths (in bits)
T = The total number of words in memory
t_c = The time for the Central Processing Unit to perform 1 million operations
$t_{I/O}$ = The time the Central Processing Unit stands idle waiting for I/O to take place
A_{FI} = The time for the Central Processing Unit to perform 1 fixed point addition
A_{FL} = The time for the Central Processing Unit to perform 1 floating point addition
M = The time for the Central Processing Unit to perform 1 multiply
D = The time for the Central Processing Unit to perform 1 divide
L = The time for the Central Processing Unit to perform 1 logic operation
B = The number of characters of I/O in each word
K_{I1} = The Input transfer rate (characters per second) of the primary I/O system
K_{O1} = The Output transfer rate (characters per second) of the primary I/O system
K_{I2} = The Input transfer rate (characters per second) of the secondary I/O system
K_{O2} = The Output transfer rate (characters per second) of the secondary I/O system
S_1 = The start time of the primary I/O system not overlapped with compute
H_1 = The stop time of the primary I/O system not overlapped with compute
S_2 = The start time of the secondary I/O system not overlapped with compute
H_2 = The stop time of the secondary I/O system not overlapped with compute
R_1 = 1 + the fraction of the useful primary I/O time that is required for nonoverlap rewind time

---

Figure 4 (continued)

Semi Constant Factor		Values	
Symbol	Description	Scientific Computation	Commercial Computation
WF	The word factor		
	a. fixed word length memory	1	1
	b. variable word length memory	2	2
C_1	Weighting factor representing the percentage of the fixed add operations		
	a. computers without index registers or indirect addressing	10	25
	b. computers with index registers or indirect addressing	25	45
C_2	Weighting factor that indicates the percentage of floating additions	10	0
C_3	Weighting factor that indicates the percentage of multiply operations	6	1
C_4	Weighting factor that indicates the percentage of divide operations	2	0
C_5	Weighting factor that indicates the percentage of logic operations	72	74
P	Percentage of the I/O that uses the primary I/O system		
	a. systems with only a primary I/O system	1.0	1.0
	b. systems with a primary and secondary I/O system	variable	variable
W_{I1}	Number of input words per million internal operations using the primary I/O system		
	a. magnetic tape I/O system	20,000	100,000
	b. other I/O systems	2,000	10,000
W_{o1}	Number of output words per million internal operations using the primary I/O system	the values are the same as those given above for W_{I1}	

Figure 4 (continued)

Semi Constant Factor		Values	
Symbol	Description	Scientific Computation	Commercial Computation
W_{12}, W_{02}	Number of input/output words per million internal operations using the secondary I/O system	the values are the same as those given above for W_{11}	
N	Number of times separate data is read into or out of the computer per million operations	4	20
OL_1	overlap factor 1—the fraction of the primary I/O system's time not overlapped with compute		
	a. no overlap—no buffer	1	1
	b. read or write with compute—single buffer	.85	.85
	c. read, write and compute—single buffer	.7	.7
	d. multiple read, write and compute—several buffers	.60	.60
	e. multiple read, write and compute with program interrupt—several buffers	.55	.55
OL_2	Overlap factor 2—the fraction of the secondary I/O system's time not overlapped with compute	values are the same as those give above for OL_1	
i	The exponential memory weighting factor	.5	.333

Reprinted (with notation slightly modified) from Knight, "Changes in Computer Performance; A Historical View," with permission from *Datamation*, published and copyrighted Sept. 1966 by L. D. Thompson Publications, Inc., 35 Mason St., Greenwich, Conn. 06830.

corporate innovative activity by some of the main results of this activity, keeping in mind that not all the results of the corporate efforts have been included in the measure.

The next decision that must be made, in order to estimate the parameters in equation (4.3), is the choice of τ, the length of the past period over which research expenditure and retained earnings were relevant to present level of potential computer performance. Clearly, research before the previous year is still relevant; but, in an effort to keep the sample size as large as possible, only two previous years are used for cumulative research (denoted R) and average retained earnings proportion (denoted g). There is some justification for this short lag in that computer models, particularly smaller ones, have come from the drawing board to the installation stage within two years.[15]

With the selection of τ equal to 2, the sample ranges for the corporations in the analysis are as given below.[16]

Corporation	Range
IBM	1944–1966 (M: 1949–1966)
Sperry Rand	1952–1966
Burroughs	1951–1966
NCR	1952–1966
CDC	1960–1966
DEC	1964–1966
SDS	1964–1966

15. Nelson Hanover, "An Analysis of the Electronic Computing Industry," unpublished. C. Freeman found the typical total development period to be somewhat longer in "Research and Development in Electronic Capital Goods," *National Institute Economic Review* 34, Nov. 1965, p. 67.

16. Some of the information needed to investigate this model is usually not made public. Firms were included if *some* R & D data were available. Please refer to the appendix to this chapter for a detailed description of the data, including a discussion of the procedures used for interpolation and extrapolation.

The IBM sample range was modified for some runs (referred to as *M*-runs) to start in 1949, since in 1944 it started with development of computers that were quite small and not internally programmed. These do not really fit under the current definition of "computer," and have been dropped from other researchers' analyses—see G. C. Chow, "Technological Change and the Demand for Computers," and N. Hanover, "Economic Aspects of Computer Use," Ph.D. thesis, Massachusetts Institute of Technology, forthcoming. The *M*-runs are included in Table 4.2 for comparison (and do display somewhat different results). However, I believe that the full period from 1944 is the relevant one to study IBM, since during that early period in the development of the computer those developing better designs did not *know* what the eventual configuration of a "modern" computer should be. Independent of the selection of the sample range, it may be that the coefficients shifted over time, or with experience in production—"learning by doing." These possibilities are investigated below.

Although the limited sample ranges for the more recent entries to the industry make separate estimation of the equation undesirable, there is good reason to believe that the coefficients should be nearly the same for all of these companies. First, these particular firms are among the main ones in the industry, having been successful in entering the industry. If the hypothesized model is correct, the effect of research or retained earnings on innovations should be applicable to each of these firms. The belief that the elasticities of these variables are the same for all the firms comes from the observation that scientific knowledge, which is one of the main influences on productivity of R & D expenditures and is left out of the equation, is rapidly available to all the firms in the industry. It is available through the tremendous number of professional journals and societies' meetings that have sprung up in the last several years in this field. Also, information has traveled between firms through one of the most mobile of professional labor forces. Finally, some of the fundamental research has been undertaken by universities under federal grants; the results of this work are available to industry.

The elasticities may be the same for the companies considered, but the initial scientific knowledge brought by the firm when it entered the industry may have varied across firms. Also, the proportion of retained earnings devoted to innovations (μ) may have varied from firm to firm. Therefore, the basic relationship that was investigated was a single equation fitted to the data for all companies but with the constant allowed to vary. The results of this form of the hypothesis are given in Table 4.1. The basic equation (4.3) is (from line 1 of the table):[17]

$$\frac{\Xi(t)}{\Xi(t-1)} = \text{const} \left(\frac{R^{(1.4)}_{3.53} g^{(1.3)}_{15.4}}{\Xi(t-1)} \right)^{.182}_{(2.5)} \qquad (4.9)$$

17. All equations were estimated in $\log_e$ form, and the Hildreth-Lu technique ("Demand Relations with Autocorrelated Disturbances," Technical Bulletin no. 276, E. Lansing, Mich., Michigan State University Agricultural Experimental Station, Nov. 1960, p. 276) was used to eliminate autocorrelation of the disturbance terms. Since it is an asymptotic maximum likelihood estimator, all standard errors of the coefficients are asymptotic. The estimated first order autocorrelation coefficient is denoted ρ and is presented with each equation in the tables. Except for Table 4.4 (where the equations were too large for the capacity of the machine with the regression package being used), many of the equations were actually estimated by the Cochrane-Orcutt method ("Application of Least Squares Regression to Relationships Containing Autocorrelated Error Times," *Journal of the American Statistical Association* 44, 1949, pp. 32–61), which produces identical results to the Hildreth-Lu method when it converges to the global minimum standard error of estimate. Checks were conducted to insure that this method was converging to the proper minimum.

The log form of the constants is: SDS, -2.01; CDC, -2.24; DEC, -2.78; B, -3.26; SR, -3.59; NCR, -3.79; and IBM, -4.06. This equation displays a reasonably good fit of the data.[18]

For comparison, a naïve model was hypothesized in which innovation, measured as $\Xi(t)/\Xi(t-1)$ or $\Xi(t)-\Xi(t-1)$, was "explained" simply by time and constants for each firm. The best result was with the linear difference form, producing an R^2 of .173. Most variations in firm constants were insignificant; with the ratio form the R^2 was .098 (comparisons of R^2 with different dependent variables are not actually very informative, since different "total variation to be explained" are involved). It should be emphasized that these compare to an R^2 of .192 for the basic equation (4.9) with the dependent variable actually used being a ratio. The model permits multiplication by Ξ_{t-1}, so that the dependent variable can then be expressed merely as the level of maximum computer performance, rather than the increase for a particular year. The predicted elasticities are the same, of course, whereas the R^2 suggests how well predicted levels fit actual levels. In a model fitting a step function (Ξ) by a log-linear function, it is not surprising that changes in Ξ (that is, the timing of innovations) are not very well predicted, whereas the level of Ξ is. The "R^2s" reported in the tables are all for equations fitted with the dependent variable as a level rather than a ratio.

The variables for Table 4.4 (and for the analysis of international activity) had to be modified by the Hildreth-Lu technique before it was possible to use the available canned computer programs. The estimation results were obtained using the "TSP" and "REGRII" programs available on the MIT Sloan School of Management Computer Facility's IBM 1620. The form of the equations that were estimated is

$$\log \Xi(t) = \log (\text{const}) + \alpha a_1 \log R + \alpha a_2 \log g + (1 - \alpha) \log \Xi(t-1).$$

I am indebted to Phillip Cooper for making available his derivations of tne necessary adjustment to the standard calculation of the asymptotic variance-covariance matrix to allow for the presence of a lagged endogenous variable.

M. Nerlove has conducted Monte Carlo experiments on various methods of estimation of models with similarly distributed disturbance terms in "Further Evidence on the Estimation of Dynamic Economic Relations from a Time Series of Cross- Sections," New Haven, Cowles Foundation for Research in Economics at Yale University, Discussion Paper no. 257, November 1968. These results were available after the analysis of this chapter had been completed, however.

18. According to formal t tests of the estimated coefficients, significance requires the t statistics (in parentheses below the estimated coefficients) to be about 2 for the full sample. However, strong "prior" beliefs have been expressed about the signs of the coefficients (i.e., $a_1 > 0$, $a_2 > 0$), so coefficients larger than one standard error will be discussed in interpreting the results. The case of $1 < t < 2$ occurs most frequently for estimates of the "a"s. Although the discussion is based on the best point estimate available for each of them, in such cases when their t statistics are only slightly above one their true values could deviate from these estimates.

Table 4.1 Innovative Activity—Basic Results

$$\frac{\Xi(t)}{\Xi(t-1)} = \text{const} \left\{ \frac{R^{(a_1+a_4D)}\, g^{(a_2+a_3S)}}{\Xi(t-1)} \right\}^{\alpha}$$

Line	α	a_1	a_4	a_2	a_3	Log Const (IBM)	SR	B	NCR	CDC	DEC	SDS	ρ	R^2
1	.182	3.53		15.4		−4.06	.47	.80	.27	1.82	1.28	2.05	−.203	.948
	(2.5)	(1.4)		(1.3)		(−1.7)	(1.0)	(1.7)	(.73)	(1.9)	(1.2)	(1.8)		
2C	.190	2.91		17.2		−3.03	.56	.91	.40	1.56	1.49	2.20	−.252	.948
	(2.8)	(1.5)		(1.6)		(−1.5)	(1.6)	(2.4)	(1.3)	(2.0)	(1.7)	(2.4)		
3	.060	2.54		26.1		.12							−.252	.943
	(1.6)	(.85)		(.94)		(.12)								
4	.242	2.24		22.1	−.000008	−2.66	.91	1.52	.66	2.03	1.34	2.12	−2.08	.950
	(2.8)	(1.4)		(1.5)	(−.99)	(−1.1)	(1.6)	(2.2)	(1.5)	(2.1)	(1.2)	(1.9)		
5	.325	1.47	1.71	10.8		−4.66	2.69	3.29	3.09	.82	.13	1.11	−.098	.950
	(3.1)	(1.3)	(1.4)	(1.5)		(−1.8)	(2.1)	(2.3)	(2.0)	(.72)	(.10)	(.83)		
6	.271		2.61	11.4		−1.07	2.95	3.67	3.72	−.65	−1.33	−.46	−.130	.948
	(2.7)		(1.5)	(1.4)		(−.94)	(2.3)	(2.6)	(2.5)	(−1.1)	(−1.5)	(−.54)		
7M	.179	3.31		12.5		−3.59	.33	.58	.10	1.73	1.19	1.93	−.215	.928
	(2.3)	(1.3)		(1.1)		(−1.5)	(.72)	(1.1)	(.27)	(1.8)	(1.1)	(1.8)		
8M	.232	2.28		19.2	−.000008	−2.57	.71	1.20	.44	1.93	1.26	2.03	−.220	.930
	(2.5)	(1.4)		(1.2)	(−.95)	(−1.0)	(1.2)	(1.6)	(.92)	(2.0)	(1.2)	(1.8)		
9M	.282	1.67	1.54	10.7		−4.21	2.13	2.64	2.42	.95	.30	1.21	−.136	.930
	(2.5)	(1.2)	(1.0)	(1.2)		(−1.7)	(1.5)	(1.6)	(1.3)	(.83)	(.23)	(.92)		
10M	.243		2.68	11.3		−1.01	2.71	3.40	3.46	−.58	−1.23	−.38	−.147	.928
	(2.2)		(1.2)	(1.1)		(−.76)	(1.8)	(2.0)	(1.9)	(−.95)	(−1.4)	(−.44)		

Notes: t statistics are presented in parentheses below each coefficient. Line notation C denotes commercial $\Xi_c(t)$ used; M denotes M-run.

When the level of Ξ is predicted by a similar naïve model, the R^2 is about the same as equation (4.9) for the log form, and somewhat lower for the linear difference form. Although by this criterion the fits are only slightly better for the model being explored here, estimates of the elasticities in the structural equations are crucial to the application of these equations in circumstances different from those accounted for by the sample. The evaluation of possible levels of computer performance of European firms' machines at some time in the future requires the use of these structural estimates. This evaluation is taken up in Chapter 5.

The estimates displayed in equation (4.9) indicate that a firm in the industry gets an elastic response to increase in research expenditures and a highly elastic response to increased proportions of earnings retained.[19] However, the magnitude of the adjustment factor α makes the effective elasticity of implemented innovations to increases in research expenditure (αa_1) inelastic. The constants for individual companies do reflect the type of ordering expected from the bias of μ imparted to them. That is, the firms that are specialized in the computer industry (except IBM) have higher constants than those widely diversified companies Sperry Rand and NCR.[20]

Line 2 of Table 4.1 presents the results of this equation for the index of "commercial" computer performance as opposed to the "scientific" index used in line 1. The fit is basically the same, but the elasticity of computer performance to research expenditure is slightly reduced. This is the direction of change that one would expect, since most of the research effort in improving computers has been directed toward internal calculating speeds for long scientific computations (needed, for example, in military applications where support for

19. There could be an identification problem in the influences on innovation from retained earnings—an increase in a firm's innovative activity might induce the firm to increase its retained earnings to finance development work or expanded capital equipment to produce the new machine. The possible importance of this interaction is reduced in the above formulation, however, by considering variation in retained earnings across firms as well as through time for a given firm.

20. See Chapter 2 for a description of each of these firms. The consistently low constant for IBM in this analysis can probably be best explained by its early entry into the development of computer technology. At the time of its entry, IBM had little scientific knowledge in this field; much of its innovative work was accomplished during the period of the investigation and is therefore accounted for by its research expenditure within the model. This also would explain the constant increasing and R elasticity decreasing when the M-run is performed (line 7). IBM is thereby considered to start its research activities in computer technology at a later date.

This low prior knowledge could also explain the low constants for the other early entrants, Sperry Rand and NCR, but does not explain why Burroughs' constant should be higher than these others.

research has originated). This variation in coefficients is interesting but hardly a well-established conclusion, since the coefficients do not differ significantly in any statistical sense.[21] Most of the following discussion will concentrate on the analysis using the "scientific" index of computer performance.

Since research expenditure is measured in dollars rather than relative to any size variable,[22] it is possible that some of the positive influence of R on computer performance comes because those firms that have large "Rs" are also large companies. In fact, the correlation between R and the total assets of the firm, S, both in $\log_e$ form, is .909—higher than between any other two of the independent variables entering the analysis. The influence of size could not be extracted independently from research expenditure because of the problem of multicollinearity. Thus the elasticity of R may include the influence of size as well as of research.

The retained earnings coefficient may be subject to a variation that has not so far been accounted for by the model. In equation (3.6) the retained earnings proportion devoted to innovative activity was assumed to be devoted to innovations in computer technology. In the actual corporations under consideration, some are widely diversified and undertaking research activities outside of the computer field. Two different approaches have been explored to account for diversification of innovative activity.

First, as a proxy for the amount of diversification of a particular firm, its size in assets (S) was used to modify the elasticity with respect to g. This proxy is reasonably good, being low for the smaller, undiversified firms and much larger for Sperry Rand and NCR. It is, of course, largest for IBM, which is mainly in the computer business; this is a shortcoming of the proxy. The equation to be fitted, then is

$$\frac{\Xi(t)}{\Xi(t-1)} = \text{const}\left\{\frac{R^{a_1}g^{(a_2+a_3S)}}{\Xi(t-1)}\right\}^{\alpha} \tag{4.10}$$

and it is assumed that a_3 will be negative. The main result of this form of the equation is

$$\frac{\Xi(t)}{\Xi(t-1)} = \text{const}\left(\frac{R^{(1.4)}_{2.24}g^{\left[22.1-.000008S_{(-.99)}\right]}_{(1.5)}}{\Xi(t-1)}\right)^{.242}_{(2.8)} \tag{4.11}$$

---

21. The actual variables for commercial and scientific Ξ also hardly differ, as noted earlier. Their correlation, with Ξ in $\log_e$ form is .988.

22. The assumption here is that all firms, regardless of size, face the same factor and equipment markets for the inputs to their research efforts, so actual expenditure is the relevant variable.

(from line 4 of Table 4.1). The modification of the retained earnings variable is negative but barely significant. With size entering now, the elasticity with respect to research is reduced, both through a decline in the estimated elasticity for implemented performance improvements (αa_1) and from a rise in the estimated adjustment coefficient (α). These shifts suggest that with size in the equation—even in this indirect form, shifting the retained earnings elasticity (g)—the effect of size appearing through the research variable has been substantially removed. The sizes of a_2 and a_3 do not give an adequate description of the elasticity with respect to g for different-size firms; for the sample ranges the g exponent in equation (4.11) would be as follows:

Corporation	Start	1966
IBM	20.82	−7.90
Sperry Rand	20.53	14.54
Burroughs	21.47	18.51
NCR	20.83	18.11
CDC	22.03	20.14
DEC	22.01	21.97
SDS	22.01	21.70

The negative value of the g elasticity since 1964 for IBM requires further interpretation. It is a result of the size variable's entering as a strictly linear influence on the elasticity. Note that, since g is always between 0 and 1, a negative exponent gives a value greater than one when g is raised to that exponent; also decreases in g are accompanied by increases in computer performance and at an increasing rate for $a_2 + a_3 S < -1$. The best interpretation for this phenomenon seems to be that after the firm reaches a certain size (assets of \$2.76 billion from this equation), it can afford to increase dividend payments to its stockholders without damaging its ability to finance innovations. Except for IBM, the g exponents reflect the diversification of the firms; the two most widely diversified companies have the lowest values.

The other method of allowing for diversification of innovative activity involved obtaining a direct measure of diversification based on sales, D. (See the appendix to this chapter for the method used to obtain this rather crude measure.) When this variable was entered in place of S (or even with S) in equation (4.10), it was estimated to have a negative coefficient also (even though higher values of D imply

greater specialization in revenue originating from computer operations). More plausible results were obtained using the formulation:

$$\frac{\Xi(t)}{\Xi(t-1)} = \text{const}\left\{\frac{R^{(a_1+a_4D)}g^{a_2}}{\Xi(t-1)}\right\}^{\alpha}. \tag{4.12}$$

The assumption in this formulation is that research effort in computers is stably proportional to the return (in revenue) from computer
sales. That is, some parts of a firm's operations may result in revenue
with little need for research devoted to this area (for example, Burroughs sells business forms as well as computers and desk calculators).
Of the remaining areas requiring research effort, the effort is proportional to the relative shares in sales of these areas. This formulation
was explored for the case (line 6) of zero elasticity for the completely
diversified company ($a_1 = 0$ by hypothesis) as well as for the case
(line 5) in which increased specialization increased the elasticity of
research. The former case resulted in the implication that Sperry
Rand's and Burroughs' R elasticities were about .9 and NCR's was
.26, while the other firms' were over 2.0. The latter hypothesis led to
the more plausible smaller variation in research elasticity:

$$\frac{\Xi(t)}{\Xi(t-1)} = \text{const}\left\{\frac{R^{\left[\begin{smallmatrix}1.47+1.71D\\(1.3)\ \ (1.4)\end{smallmatrix}\right]}g^{\begin{smallmatrix}10.8\\(1.5)\end{smallmatrix}}}{\Xi(t-1)}\right\}^{\begin{smallmatrix}.325\\(3.1)\end{smallmatrix}}. \tag{4.13}$$

These coefficients lead to estimated R elasticities in 1966 of 3.18 for
the specialized firms (CDC, DEC, and SDS), 2.81 for IBM, 2.10 for
Burroughs, 2.06 for Sperry Rand, and 1.64 for NCR. This form of the
diversification in research hypothesis was used in the explorations
reported below.

With the early years for IBM excluded (the M-runs), the results
show the same relative effects, but all coefficients are slightly smaller.
These results have been presented in Table 4.2; they will not be discussed further, since I believe that estimation from the beginning of
IBM's involvement in the computer industry is the relevant range of
time (see note 16).

The hypothesis throughout has been that the only estimated parameter that is explicitly allowed to vary across firms is the constant
term. The absence of dummies in line 3 of Table 4.1 shifts the other
coefficients substantially and makes the R and g coefficients less significant. The hypothesis that all firms have the same constant was
formally evaluated using the Chow test.[23] This hypothesis was not

---

23. With a lagged endogenous variable present, the Chow test is only asymptotic.

rejected at a 5 percent significance level for equation (4.9).[24] The better fit of the pertinent coefficients, rather than the overall fit, suggests the varying constant term model as the better hypothesis.

A further possible view of the model with constants alone varying among firms is that there is a distinct difference in the elasticities over different periods. This possibility is explored through the equations reported in Table 4.2. The two subperiods that were considered involve estimates during the first-generation technology (up to 1958), combining the second and third generations in a second period; and estimates over the first and second generations (up to 1963), and thereafter for the short period up to 1966. The latter trials were not very satisfactory because of the low sample size and the form of the $\Xi(t)$ data, which is a step function that does not necessarily vary for each firm each year or two. No consistent pattern is revealed in the relative sizes of the elasticities of the earlier period compared with the later one. Viewing the basic formulation (lines 1 and 2), the implication is that the research elasticity has increased slightly, whereas the importance of retained earnings has declined. Firms have also become slightly more cautious in implementing innovations in the second- and third-generation technologies. Still, when the analysis of variance F tests are performed, only the set of equations for the (4.12) formulation (lines 7 and 8) is significantly better than the corresponding equation in Table 4.1 at the 1 percent level, and no other set of equations is significantly better at even the 5 percent level. The evaluation of the coefficients over the period as a whole is therefore taken to be satisfactory.

Equations (4.9), (4.11), and (4.13) might be thought of as general descriptions of what a typical firm in the industry faces in its attempts to innovate. Part A of Table 4.3, on the other hand, displays the results of attempts to describe innovative effort of each separate firm by equation (4.3). The sample sizes are small; only IBM has estimated parameters that are significant. There is substantial variation of research elasticities among firms, with Sperry Rand's, Burroughs', and IBM's being quite high. CDC's is somewhat lower but is still greater than one; its implementation exponent (α) is high, as is IBM's. No meaningful results could be obtained for the two smallest firms, even when their data were pooled with CDC's to yield a "new firms" equation (Part B, line 1), in which α is outside the allowable range and a_2 is negative and insignificant.

24. Preliminary exploration of the model in the form of equation (4.10) did result in rejection of this hypothesis of equal constants at the one percent significance level.

Table 4.2 Test of Time Shift in Elasticities

$$\frac{\Xi(t)}{\Xi(t-1)} = \text{const} \left\{ \frac{R^{(a_1+a_4D)}\, g^{(a_2+a_3S)}}{\Xi(t-1)} \right\}^{\alpha}$$

Line	Years	α	a_1	a_4	a_2	a_3	Log Const (IBM)	SR	B	NCR	CDC	DEC	SDS	ρ	R^2
										Deviation from constant for					
1	To 58	.246 (1.5)	2.16 (.65)		24.2 (.95)		-2.14 (-.38)	1.10 (.95)	1.26 (1.2)	.34 (.48)				-.203	.905
2	59-66	.174 (.97)	2.55 (.65)		.67 (.05)		-2.37 (-.80)	.48 (.90)	.52 (.80)	-.07 (-.10)	1.70 (1.5)	1.14 (.96)	1.83 (1.5)	-.241	.836
3	To 63	.279 (2.9)	3.85 (1.7)		9.38 (1.0)		-7.99 (-2.3)	.80 (1.2)	.65 (1.0)	.23 (.50)	3.92 (2.4)			-.136	.937
4	64-66	1.16 (14.)	2.48 (5.8)		22.9 (5.0)		-11.8 (-2.4)	-2.54 (-2.4)	4.55 (5.6)	-1.25 (-1.9)	1.26 (1.0)	1.06 (.61)	2.69 (1.5)	.027	.993
5	To 58	.178 (1.0)	-2.44 (-.40)		50.9 (.87)	-.000050 (-.76)	6.84 (.64)	.51 (.39)	2.04 (1.6)	.45 (.64)				-.263	.908
6	59-66	.238 (1.2)	1.95 (.76)		10.6 (.52)	-.000004 (-.41)	-2.20 (-.75)	.96 (1.3)	1.32 (1.2)	.43 (.51)	2.20 (1.7)	1.51 (1.2)	2.24 (1.7)	-.237	.842
7	To 58	.782 (4.3)	.62 (.90)	3.28 (2.3)	-4.79 (-.83)		-14.6 (-2.6)	8.08 (3.8)	9.08 (3.8)	10.0 (3.6)				-.057	.936
8	59-66	.628 (3.1)	-1.48 (-1.0)	3.32 (1.6)	1.12 (.27)		2.25 (.48)	9.32 (2.6)	9.37 (2.6)	11.8 (2.3)	-3.38 (-1.2)	-4.56 (-1.5)	-3.38 (-1.1)	-.037	.860

Note: t statistics are presented in parentheses below each coefficient.

An attempt was made to analyze Sperry Rand and CDC together (Part B, lines 2 through 4), under the hypothesis that because CDC's research team broke away from Sperry Rand, they would have the same elasticity from research expenditure and differ only by amount of diversification (accounted for by S or D). Only with the account of diversification through formulation (4.12) were elasticities well estimated, suggesting that an important distinguishing feature between the two is a higher return from research for CDC.

Two other experiments were performed in the individual corporation analysis presented in Table 4.3. In Part B, line 5, the firms first to make a profit from their computer operations—IBM, CDC, and SDS—were analyzed. The results are somewhat different from those encountered for all firms, with the retained earnings elasticity and the implementation exponent α each nearly twice as high as in equation (4.9). Thus management willingness to risk early implementation of innovations may have been a factor in achieving early profits. The other experiment was to consider the older, established firms completely separately from the newer, smaller ones (see Part B, lines 6 through 8). The results of this are almost identical to those reported as equations (4.9), (4.11), and (4.13). Although this should not be too surprising—the two omitted firms accounted for only 4 of the 75 observations included in the full estimation—it might seem to detract from the characterization of those equations as "general descriptions of what a typical firm in the industry might face." In fact, when Chow tests are performed, the hypothesis that the coefficients do not vary between the first five firms and the last two is not rejected for any of the formulations of the model.[25]

A further elaboration of the analysis was investigated. Coefficients α and a_2 were held constant over all firms, but the research elasticity as well as the constant was allowed to vary across firms, as reported in Table 4.4. Without the constants varying across firms, most research elasticities are less significant than in the other formulations. With constant dummies in, all elasticities are fairly well estimated except DEC's, which is insignificant (line 1). As in the analysis reported in Table 4.3, further exploration of combinations of firms was undertaken, combination of DEC with SDS to obtain a "small firms"

25. The small sample for DEC and SDS with insufficient degrees of freedom to estimate their coefficients means that the residuals from this part of the "unrestricted fit" are simply zero. For the test in this form, see G. C. Chow, "Tests of Equality Between Sets of Coefficients in Two Linear Regressions," *Econometrica* 28, no. 3, July 1960, pp. 598–599; or F. M. Fisher, "Tests of Equality Between Sets of Coefficients in Two Linear Regressions: An Expository Note," *Econometrica* 38, no. 2, Mar. 1970, pp. 361–366.

Table 4.3 Test of Elasticities Varying by Firm

Part A, Individual firms

$$\frac{\Xi(t)}{\Xi(t-1)} = \text{const} \left(\frac{R^{a_1} g^{a_2}}{\Xi(t-1)} \right)^{\alpha}$$

Line	Corp.	Sample Size	α	a_1	a_2	Log Const	ρ	R^2
1	IBM	22	.864 (4.2)	4.45 (2.3)	11.0 (2.1)	−31.5 (−3.4)	.093	.975
2	SR	14	.137 (.41)	5.14 (.32)	2.77 (.13)	−5.29 (−1.2)	−.330	.888
3	B	15	.109 (.75)	4.77 (.38)	41.1 (.49)	−1.86 (−.17)	−.437	.946
4	NCR	14	.301 (.54)	.79 (.17)	33.0 (.26)	2.82 (.14)	−.203	.855
5	CDC	6	.928 (1.8)	1.72 (.96)	7.03 (.06)	−1.24 (−.23)	.241	.919

Part B, Groups of firms

$$\frac{\Xi(t)}{\Xi(t-1)} = \text{const} \left\{ \frac{R^{(a_1+a_4D)}\, g^{(a_2+a_3S)}}{\Xi(t-1)} \right\}^{\alpha}$$

Line	Corp.	α	a_1	a_4	a_2	a_3	Log Const (IBM)	Deviation from constant for						ρ	R^2
								SR	B	NCR	CDC	DEC	SDS		
1	CDC, DEC, SDS	1.09 (3.4)	1.85 (2.0)		-30.4 (-.57)		-3.13 (-.90)					-1.24 (-1.2)	-.19 (-.19)	.268	.936
2	SR, CDC	.067 (.28)	2.22 (.21)		18.5 (.18)		.12 (.05)							-.089	.879
3	SR, CDC	.226 (.91)	.425 (.32)		36.4 (.63)	-.000031 (-.64)	2.71 (.97)							-.112	.897
4	SR, CDC	.835 (3.7)	1.97 (2.0)	.707 (1.9)	6.42 (1.4)		-8.84 (-1.7)							.435	.912
5	IBM, CDC, SDS	.326 (2.7)	3.04 (1.4)		25.8 (1.5)		-5.64 (-1.4)				2.18 (1.5)		2.48 (1.4)	-.044	.969
6	Excluding DEC & SDS	.175 (2.4)	3.48 (1.3)		15.9 (1.2)		-3.76 (-1.5)	.45 (.97)	.79 (1.6)	.26 (.70)	1.72 (1.8)			-.208	.946
7	Excluding DEC & SDS	.237 (2.7)	2.13 (1.4)		22.7 (1.5)	-.000008 (-.98)	-2.30 (-.92)	.89 (1.6)	1.51 (2.2)	.65 (1.4)	1.93 (2.0)			-.212	.948
8	Excluding DEC & SDS	.309 (2.9)	1.45 (1.2)	1.71 (1.3)	11.1 (1.5)		-4.30 (-1.6)	2.54 (2.0)	3.13 (2.2)	2.92 (1.9)	.77 (.67)			-.111	.949

Note: t statistics are presented in parentheses below each coefficient.

Table 4.4 Test of Research and Development Elasticity Varying by Firm

$$\frac{\Xi(t)}{\Xi(t-1)} = const_f \left\{ R^{a_{1f}}\, g^{(a_2 + a_3 S + a'_4 D)}\, \frac{\Xi(t-1)}{\Xi(t-1)} \right\}^\alpha$$

Line	α	a_2	$a_{1\,\text{IBM}}$ Log Const (IBM)	$a_{1\,\text{SR}}$ SR	$a_{1\,\text{B}}$ B	$a_{1\,\text{NCR}}$ NCR	$a_{1\,\text{CDC}}$ CDC	$a_{1\,\text{DEC}}$ DEC	$a_{1\,\text{SDS}}$ SDS	ρ	R^2
	a_3					Deviation from constant for					
	a'_4										
1 **All firms separate**	.372 (3.0)	10.3 (1.5)	4.37 (1.7)	2.94 (1.6)	7.68 (1.7)	2.93 (1.5)	1.61 (1.4)	1.20 (.07)	5.99 (1.2)	−.100	
			−12.8 (−2.4)	6.59 (1.1)	−11.0 (−1.5)	5.82 (1.1)	13.3 (2.2)	13.6 (.27)	.08 (.01)		.961
2 **Same constant**	.148 (2.4)	18.5 (1.2)	3.10 (1.3)	3.34 (1.3)	3.60 (1.4)	3.25 (1.3)	4.06 (1.3)	3.73 (1.2)	4.36 (1.3)	−.213	
			−2.40 (−1.3)								.947
3 **Small firms—DEC and SDS**	.372 (3.1)	10.3 (1.5)	4.37 (1.7)	2.94 (1.7)	7.67 (1.8)	2.93 (1.5)	1.61 (1.4)	5.62 (1.2)	*	−.100	
			−12.8 (−2.5)	6.61 (1.1)	−11.0 (−1.5)	5.83 (1.2)	13.3 (2.2)	.05 (.00)	1.18 (.08)		.961
4 **UNIVAC based technology—SR and CDC**	.360 (2.9)	10.9 (1.5)	4.33 (1.6)	2.14 (1.6)	7.63 (1.7)	2.88 (1.4)	*	1.16 (.07)	6.18 (1.2)	−.100	
			−12.2 (−2.3)	9.22 (1.7)	−10.5 (−1.4)	5.69 (1.1)	11.0 (2.0)	13.1 (.26)	−.67 (−.04)		.960

#	Description	C1	C2	C3	C4	C5	C6	C7	C8	C9	C10	C11	C12	C13	C14	C15	C16	C17		
5	Small firms and UNIVAC based technology	.360 (3.0)	10.9 (1.5)		4.33 (1.6)	−12.2 (−2.4)	2.13 (1.7)	9.25 (1.8)	7.62 (1.7)	−10.5 (−1.4)	2.88 (1.4)	5.70 (1.1)	*	11.1 (2.0)	5.80 (1.2)	−.68 (−.04)	*	.45 (.03)	−.100	.960
6	Small firms—DEC and SDS	.373 (3.0)	12.0 (1.3)	−.000001 (−.31)	4.01 (1.5)	−11.5 (−1.8)	2.72 (1.5)	6.18 (1.0)	7.25 (1.6)	−10.6 (−1.4)	2.74 (1.4)	5.32 (1.0)	1.61 (1.4)	12.0 (1.7)	5.63 (1.2)	−1.33 (−.08)	−.19 (−.01)		−.100	.961
7	Small firms—DEC and SDS	.406 (3.3)	19.7 (1.6)	−39.3 (−1.2)	3.76 (1.7)	−12.4 (−2.4)	2.94 (1.8)	5.47 (.95)	4.20 (1.2)	1.00 (.09)	1.94 (1.2)	9.47 (1.6)	1.67 (1.5)	12.5 (2.1)	4.90 (1.1)	.84 (.05)	1.92 (.13)		−.100	.962
8	Small firms and UNIVAC based technology	.397 (3.2)	20.7 (1.6)	.000001 (.22)	3.96 (1.6)	−13.1 (−1.9)	2.28 (1.7)	9.00 (1.5)	3.77 (1.0)	3.68 (.26)	1.86 (1.1)	10.7 (1.4)	*	11.1 (1.8)	4.91 (1.1)	1.74 (.11)	*	2.80 (.18)	−.100	.962

Notes: t statistics are presented in parentheses below each coefficient. Firms mentioned in line descriptions are those for which research elasticities are assumed to be the same. "*" denotes that the appropriate elasticity is presented in the column for the other firm with the same value.

elasticity (reported in line 3) and of CDC with Sperry Rand to obtain a "UNIVAC-based-technology" elasticity (line 4). The only difference from previous formulations is that the use of the proportion of sales diversification index (D) is entered to modify the retained earnings elasticity (with coefficient a'_4). The negative estimated coefficient mentioned above also appears in this formulation. All estimated elasticities are greater than one, and only NCR, CDC, and DEC have estimated elasticities less than two in some formulations. The most interesting equation of this investigation seems to be the one with the "small firms" combined research elasticity (line 3 of Table 4.4):

$$\frac{\Xi(t)}{\Xi(t-1)} = a_{0f}\left(\frac{R_f\, g^{(1.5)}{}^{10.3}}{\Xi(t-1)}\right)^{.372}_{(3.1)}. \tag{4.14}$$

Corporation	log const	R_f
IBM	-12.8 (-2.5)	4.37 $R^{(1.7)}$
Sperry Rand	-6.21 (-1.1)	2.94 $R^{(1.7)}$
Burroughs	-23.8 (-2.5)	7.67 $R^{(1.8)}$
NCR	-6.98 (-1.2)	2.93 $R^{(1.5)}$
CDC	$.49$ $(.10)$	1.61 $R^{(1.4)}$
DEC	-12.8 $(-.89)$	5.62 $R^{(1.2)}$
SDS	-11.6 $(-.81)$	

In this formulation, the research elasticity is increased slightly by not accounting for diversification through size a_3 (compare line 6 with line 3), except for the "small firms" elasticity, which is unaffected by the inclusion of S. Accounting for diversification through D has a similar effect (see line 7). All firms achieve elastic responses in potential innovations from increases in their research expenditures. Among the larger, established firms, the extent of diversification is reflected in lower research elasticities but overcome in part by higher constant terms. The lowest elasticity and highest constant for CDC may be the result of important but not exclusively financial inputs to the research process, and outstanding development team led by Seymour Cray. This formulation, then, seems to be a very adequate and reasonable description of individual corporate innovative behavior; the actual and fitted values of the computer performance index are presented graphically in Figure 5.

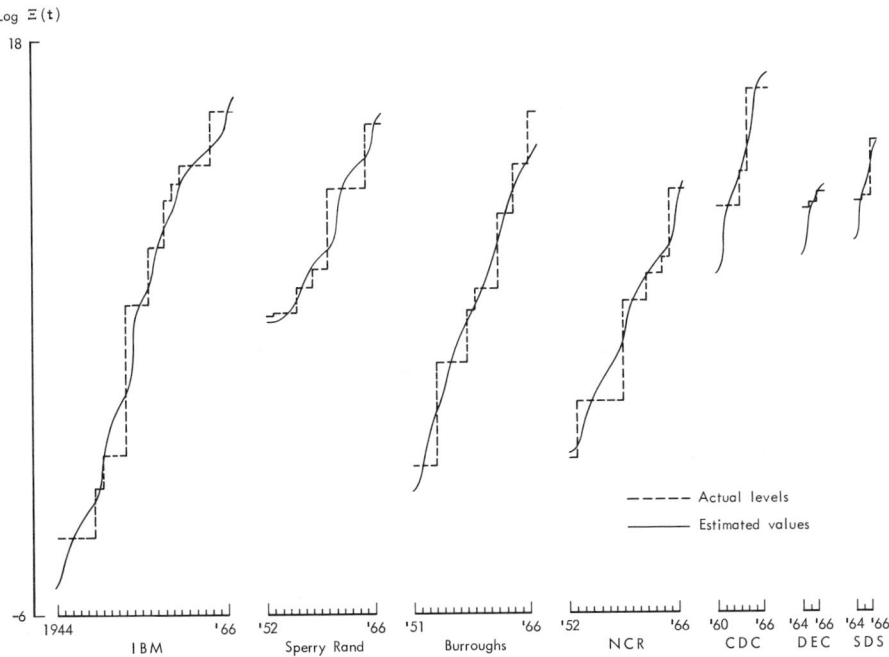

Fig. 5. Actual and estimated values of computer performance.

Attempts were made to incorporate aspects of the different firms' experience in the industry explicitly in the analysis. First, the proportion of disclosed innovations actually performed by a firm was entered, in lagged form, as a modification to the research elasticity.[26] The hypothesis was that a firm that had innovated in the past would know how to use its research expenditures more effectively for future innovation. The resulting coefficients, although usually positive, were quite insignificantly different from zero and are not reported. The problem in attempting this formulation appears to have been that too few innovations have actually been disclosed, and the number of disclosures depends very much on which company performed the innovation.

The attempt was then made, as reported in Table 4.5, to use the proportion of new models produced by the firm to all new models for the year (again, in lagged form, denoted C) as a proxy for experience in innovating—a "learning by doing" hypothesis. When this variable is entered as a modification to the research elasticity ($R^{a_1 + a_6 C}$, see

26. Disclosed innovations were obtained from Knight's thesis, "A Study of Technological Innovation—The Evolution of Digital Computers," Appendix B.

Table 4.5. Innovation through Learning by Doing

$$\frac{\Xi(t)}{\Xi(t-1)} = \text{const} \left\{ \frac{R^{(a_1+a_4D+a_6C)}C^{a_5}g^{(a_2+a_3S)}}{\Xi(t-1)} \right\}^{\alpha}$$

Line	α	a_1	a_4	a_6	a_5	a_2	a_3	Log Const (IBM)	\ Deviation from constant for SR	B	NCR	CDC	DEC	SDS	ρ	R^2
1	.161 (2.0)	3.65 (1.2)			.617 (.62)	16.6 (1.1)		-3.60 (-1.4)	.50 (1.1)	.88 (1.8)	.37 (.92)	1.78 (1.8)	1.26 (1.2)	1.99 (1.7)	-.214	.948
2	.224 (2.3)	2.25 (1.2)			.396 (.55)	23.2 (1.3)	-.000008 (-.94)	-2.30 (-.91)	.92 (1.6)	1.57 (2.2)	.74 (1.6)	2.00 (2.1)	1.32 (1.2)	2.08 (1.8)	-.216	.950
3	.301 (2.5)	1.45 (1.1)	1.76 (1.2)		.221 (.40)	11.2 (1.4)		-4.21 (-1.5)	2.58 (2.0)	3.20 (2.2)	3.01 (1.9)	.81 (.72)	.14 (.11)	1.08 (.82)	-.115	.950
4C	.156 (2.2)	3.08 (1.3)			1.02 (1.1)	19.8 (1.4)		-2.44 (-1.2)	.64 (1.8)	1.05 (2.6)	.57 (1.7)	1.55 (2.1)	1.48 (1.7)	2.17 (2.4)	-.281	.949
5C	.192 (2.2)	2.36 (1.3)			.815 (1.1)	22.3 (1.3)	-.000005 (-.62)	-1.89 (-.92)	.82 (1.9)	1.37 (2.4)	.74 (1.9)	1.66 (2.2)	1.52 (1.7)	2.22 (2.4)	-.269	.950
6C	.227 (2.6)	1.41 (1.0)	1.39 (1.2)		.712 (1.2)	14.5 (1.6)		-2.14 (-1.1)	1.78 (2.2)	2.36 (2.5)	2.13 (2.0)	.76 (.84)	.64 (.63)	1.38 (1.3)	-.246	.951
7	.136 (2.0)	4.21 (1.3)		-1.82 (-1.7)		12.8 (.89)		-3.07 (-1.4)	-.01 (-.02)	.08 (.15)	-.37 (-.90)	1.12 (1.2)	.62 (.60)	1.32 (1.2)	-.241	.953
8	.181 (2.1)	2.82 (1.3)		-1.24 (-1.7)		19.7 (1.1)	-.000005 (-.55)	-2.19 (-.96)	.33 (.57)	.63 (.83)	-.05 (-.10)	1.32 (1.4)	.71 (.69)	1.43 (1.3)	-.243	.954
9	.224 (2.2)	2.08 (1.2)	1.50 (.91)	-.982 (-1.7)		10.0 (1.0)		-3.41 (-1.4)	1.37 (1.1)	1.64 (1.1)	1.39 (.90)	.56 (.54)	-.04 (-.04)	.79 (.65)	-.177	.954
10C	.150 (2.2)	3.27 (1.3)		-1.05 (-1.6)		16.7 (1.3)		-2.34 (-1.2)	.26 (.68)	.44 (.99)	-.01 (-.04)	1.09 (1.4)	1.02 (1.2)	1.72 (1.8)	-.278	.951

Notes: t statistics are presented in parentheses below each coefficient. Line notation C denotes $\Xi_c(t)$ (commercial) used.

lines 7 through 10) the coefficient is significant but negative (contrary to expectation). The variable was also tested as an independent influence on innovative achievement on the hypothesis that the "learning" that results from producing many different models may be not so much in the technical aspects of research as in the design features of putting the various modules together, or increasing consistency of performance through feedback from the service personnel. Thus the model was converted from the basic ones to

$$\frac{\Xi(t)}{\Xi(t-1)} = \text{const} \left\{ \frac{R^{(a_1+a_4D)}g^{(a_2+a_3S)}C^{a_5}}{\Xi(t-1)} \right\}^\alpha . \tag{4.15}$$

In this form the results are quite similar to equations (4.9), (4.11), and (4.13) with the elasticity of the experience variable (C) less than one and not significantly different from zero. The more significant application of this formulation is to the index of commercial computer performance (lines 4 through 6). It was stated earlier that much of the research that has been undertaken in the industry has been directed toward the technology needed for scientific (and military) applications.[27] However, these results suggest that experience in producing computer models has had a more significant influence on the innovations implemented for commercial applications.[28]

Productive Activity

The model identifies as characteristics of corporate activity both the innovative nature of the firm and its productive capacity. It would be very interesting to explore the production functions applicable to the various computer models of each firm.[29] Unfortunately, the data just are not available for such an analysis. There is no information in public documents on the allocation of capital and labor by particular firms to the production of individual machines in their product line. On the other hand, it is fundamental to the model to distinguish the innovative content of a firm's activity. Therefore it seems quite inappropriate to aggregate the output of computers for an individual

27. See Chapter 2.
28. However, this distinction between "learning" in scientific versus commercial applications cannot really be distinguished very well from the two indexes used here. The indexes are nearly identical—their correlation (with the indexes in log form) is .9878, higher than the correlation between any other two variables included in the analysis (including their own lagged values and a time dummy).
29. The discussion in Chapter 2, particularly IBM's behavior, strongly suggests that there are significant economies of scale in production of individual models.

firm to determine an aggregate production function for each firm.[30] This book is directed toward the explanation of comparative advantage by industries; to this end the production functions called for in the model are probably of minor importance when compared with the explanation of innovative activity.[31] Therefore the investigation of corporate activity will not be pursued further here. Instead, the shape of the demand functions faced by the firms will be investigated.

International Activity

Of the major world markets for computers, data were lacking for Japan. The cross-country demand analysis will therefore include only the United States and Western Europe.[32] The theoretical model assumes that each firm faces a demand curve of finite price elasticity [see equations (3.14) and (4.8)]. Although the firms have similar products, their service and software provisions are different, and these contribute to the differentiation among firms of the total product. Consideration must also be given to the degree of price competition between alternative manufacturers' machines. The consistent downward trend in the price of computer services over the past two decades allows the use of a "time since introduction" variable as a proxy for this competitive effect. That is, a downward price trend through time combined with a policy of fixing the price[33] (usually rental, since about 75 percent of computers in business are rented)[34] for a particular model throughout its entire life implies that as time goes on from the introduction of a model it will become less and less

30. The lack of a suitable aggregate of firm output makes the existence of an output aggregate for the industry dependent on which firms are in the industry; see F. M. Fisher, "Embodied Technology and the Existence of Labor and Output Aggregates," *Review of Economic Studies*, Oct. 1968, assumption 2.1. This is indeed a strange kind of aggregate. Therefore, the emphasis in Chapter 3 that a production function for the entire industry (requiring an output aggregate) is *not* a useful way of approaching the analysis of "new" industries is based in part on this presumed lack of a firm output aggregate.

31. This belief in the relative importance of innovative activities in some industries led to the "new" industries exceptions to the Heckscher-Ohlin theory in the first place.

32. See the appendix to this chapter for a discussion of these data.

33. The established price for a system is the result of a long-standing policy of the market leader, IBM. The validity of applying the same price to U.S. and European rentals is confirmed by W. de Bruijn, "Automation in Europe," *Datamation* 12, no. 9, Sept. 1966, pp. 25–27, "computer prices are generally based on dollars and are equal all over the world."

34. W. W. Finke, "Computers: Yesterday, Today and Tomorrow," *Credit and Financial Management* 68, Jan. 1966, pp. 18–20.

competitive. The hypothesis will be made that there is a constant elasticity for the competitive influence accounted for by T_m, so that equation (4.6) takes the form

$$Y_k^*(m, t) = c_0\, T(m)^{c_4} p(m)^{c_1} \Xi(m)^{c_2} I_k(t-1)^{c_3} \qquad (4.16)$$

and the *a priori* expectation is that the elasticity of the time variable will be negative.

It was mentioned earlier that other aspects of the product beside those accounted for by the "computer performance" variable may be important in a prospective customer's decision to do business with a particular firm. Some of these, including the constant improvement in reliability and provisions for servicing by the manufacturer and increases in the personnel available to operate the computers, will have a definite influence on demand. Although no explicit account is taken of these factors, reliability and servicing availability are a part of the product differentiation characteristic of each company and may be among the factors contributing to differences in the adjustment coefficients or constant terms across companies. The increasing number of qualified personnel should contribute to the size of what should be a positive income elasticity of demand for computers, since the steady increase in industrial production exhibits the same growth through time as has this professional labor category. Since the data are a combination of cross-section and time series, the cross-country variation must also be considered. Although it is quite likely that the larger industrial production variable for the United States as compared with Europe as a whole corresponds roughly to the latter's relative dearth of qualified personnel, there is no information on the extent to which differences in industrial production among European countries also reflect the relative availabilities.

The nature of the pricing mechanism in the rental of computers is rather different from that usually assumed to exist in a market situation. As has been emphasized in several places, IBM has established as a characteristic of the industry its own long-standing policy of fixing the price (rental) of a particular model of computer at the time of its introduction. This policy clearly does not imply that prices are established independently of market conditions—the reaction at the market place to systems recently introduced undoubtedly influences the pricing of future systems with similar operating characteristics. But, for purposes of estimating the demand function a firm faces, the system of price-quantity relations is recursive rather than simultaneous.[35] Thus price is a predetermined variable in the equation determining quantity demanded of a particular model, and ordinary least squares is an appropriate technique for estimating the coefficients of the function.

An econometric problem is likely to arise from the cross-sectional aspect of this demand analysis. It is reasonable to expect that the variance of the disturbance term varies (that is, that the assumption of homoscedasticity is violated). The obvious alternative assumption is that the variance of the disturbance term varies with the "income" variable, industrial production. This problem should therefore be resolved as a result of the regression analysis being applied to equation (4.8) in $\log_e$ form; this transformation should remove the heteroscedasticity.[36]

There is a possible distortion in viewing the results of estimating equation (4.8) as a demand equation. This involves the interpretation of γ, the lagged adjustment coefficient. In the model γ is the rate at which a country approaches the optimal level of installations of a particular system (given its price and quality characteristics) from the previous year's level of such installations. If, however, the computer manufacturers are not prepared to meet increased demand in the year in which it materializes, then installations may approach their optimal level at a rate slower than pure demand considerations would imply. There is some evidence that this limiting supply factor may have influenced the availability of systems; thus the adjustment coefficient γ may be viewed as probably having a downward bias and therefore being a lower bound to the true demand adjustment coefficient. Since the coefficients for the optimal level of installations are derived by division by γ, they must therefore be viewed as upper bounds to the true values for these elasticities to the equilibrium stock of computer systems.

The estimates of the model coefficients for equation (4.8) are presented in Table 4.6. Since IBM is the dominant firm in the marketing

35. Actually there are two other ways in which simultaneity could still be a problem. First, another relation involving price and quantity exists from the first order conditions for profit maximization—the marginal revenue equals marginal cost relationship presented in the appendix to Chapter 3 as equation (3.27). Thus if prices are set with perfect foresight, simultaneity could still exist. The other possibility is that the disturbance term of the equation under investigation is correlated with the disturbances of the other equations in the system. Both of these possibilities are being ruled out; it seems reasonable to assume that prices are set rather arbitrarily and with quite imperfect foresight.

36. The actual estimation technique used was the Hildreth-Lu method (see "Demand Relations with Autocorrelated Disturbances") to eliminate autocorrelation of the disturbance terms; this method was also used for the innovations analysis (see note 17 above). The first order autocorrelation coefficient estimated for each equation is ρ in the tables below.

of systems in all countries under investigation, the relevance of the hypothesized form of the model must rest in large part on the fit and coefficients obtained for this firm. Its fit is also most relevant from a statistical point of view because the sample size is largest and made up of the largest number of different machines.

The coefficients in each form of the equation for IBM are all statistically significant, and all signs are as expected. The first form of the equation neglects the competitive position of a particular system through time, since no "time since introduction" variable $[T(m)]$ is included. In this form the relative adjustment of actual systems to the optimal level (γ) is estimated to be about 30 percent. The price elasticity of demand for particular models (c_1) is negative and greater than two and one-half, whereas the countries' income elasticity of demand (c_3) is over one and one-half. The shift of the demand equation for models with higher performance characteristics (c_2) is downward at an increasing rate, which reflects the widely observed fact that there is greater demand for systems at the smaller capacity and speed end of the product line than at the upper end.

The competitive effect is explored in two ways in this international setting. First, as shown in (4.16) above, the variable $T(m)$ is entered and its elasticity (c_4) is estimated—negative as anticipated:[37]

$$\frac{Y_k(m, t)}{Y_k(m, t-1)} = .44T(m)^{(-1.24)}_{(-20)} \left[\frac{p(m)^{(-2.25)}_{(-3.7)} \Xi(m)^{(-2.67)}_{(-4.9)} I_k(t-1)^{(2.10)}_{(4.3)}}{Y_k(m, t-1)} \right]^{.116}_{(6.4)}.$$

(4.17)

The major shifts in the other coefficients from introduction of the competitive effect are a decline in the adjustment coefficient, an increase in the (negative) elasticity for computer performance, and an increase in the income elasticity.

The other approach to determine the competitive effect is through the equation:

$$Y_k^*(m, t) = c_0 T_{US}^{c_5} T_E^{c_6} p(m)^{c_1} \Xi(m)^{c_2} I_k(t-1)^{c_3}. \qquad (4.18)$$

In place of one variable $T(m)$ the same variable is entered but with separate elasticities to be estimated for the United States and for Europe (including the United Kingdom). The hypothesis underlying this formulation is that the amount of competition encountered by a firm is different—and greater—in the United States than abroad. This

37. The coefficient for the time variable and the constant are not divided by γ in the results reported in the tables; the form of the equations actually estimated is:

$$\log Y_k(m, t) = \log c_0 + c_4 \log T(m) + \gamma c_1 \log p(m)$$
$$+ \gamma c_2 \log \Xi(m) + \gamma c_3 \log I_k(t) + (1-\gamma) \log Y_k(m, t-1).$$

A similar equation is used for separating the competitive effect as in (4.18).

Table 4.6 Corporate Demand Equations Using Country Data

$$\frac{Y_k(m,t)}{Y_k(m,t-1)} = [c_o\,T(m)^{c_4}]\left\{\frac{p(m)^{c_1}\,\Xi(m)^{c_2}\,I_k(t-1)^{c_3}}{Y_k(m,t-1)}\right\}^{\gamma}$$

$$= [c_o\,T_{US}^{c_5}\,T_E^{c_6}]\left\{\frac{p(m)^{c_1}\,\Xi(m)^{c_2}\,I_k(t-1)^{c_3}}{Y_k(m,t-1)}\right\}^{\gamma}$$

γ	c_1	c_2	c_3	Log Const	c_4	c_5	c_6	ρ	R^2
IBM (Sample size = 298, machines = 16)									
.298	−2.54	−1.78	1.67	−8.82				−.45	.889
(16.)	(−10.)	(−9.8)	(9.3)	(−17.)					
.116	−2.25	−2.67	2.10	−.818	−1.24			−.35	.938
(6.4)	(−3.7)	(−4.9)	(4.3)	(−1.4)	(−20.)				
.086	−2.58	−3.30	3.98	−1.61		−1.51	−1.22	−.40	.939
(4.7)	(−3.0)	(−3.9)	(4.0)	(−2.8)		(−17.)	(−21.)		
Sperry Rand (Sample size = 156, machines = 8)									
.099	−3.90	−3.29	3.19	−4.84				−.80	.908
(4.6)	(−3.9)	(−3.9)	(3.8)	(−10.)					
.070	−3.49	−3.47	4.23	−3.13	−.410			−.75	.916
(3.2)	(−2.5)	(−2.7)	(2.8)	(−5.9)	(−6.3)				
.080	−3.15	−3.13	3.47	−2.96		−.337	−.415	−.75	.916
(3.0)	(−2.4)	(−2.6)	(2.8)	(−5.0)		(−2.6)	(−6.4)		
CDC (Sample size = 114, machines = 8)									
.128	−1.51	−1.10	2.97	−4.88				−.50	.948
(4.8)	(−3.2)	(−3.2)	(3.8)	(−11.)					
.106	−.691	−.758	3.36	−3.29	−.266			−.50	.951
(4.0)	(−1.3)	(−2.0)	(3.3)	(−5.6)	(−4.0)				
−.006	7.83	9.42	−60.2	−3.55		−.664	−.247	−.60	.952
(−.14)	(.14)	(.14)	(−.14)	(−6.5)		(−4.5)	(−4.1)		

Honeywell (Sample size = 104, machines = 6)

.077 (2.3)	-1.43 (-1.6)	-1.91 (-2.0)	4.80 (2.1)	-3.53 (-6.2)				-.55	.911
.016 (.48)	2.38 (.40)	-2.30 (-.41)	19.4 (.47)	-1.55 (-2.4)	-.482 (-6.2)			-.50	.925
-.125 (-3.1)	-.580 (-1.3)	-.031 (-.11)	-3.52 (-3.0)	-2.82 (-4.5)		-1.17 (-7.6)	-.454 (-6.4)	-.55	.931

GE (Sample size = 61, machines = 5)

.044 (.73)	-133. (.71)	-67.3 (-.71)	2.83 (.54)	-52.5 (-3.0)				.25	.950
.041 (.67)	-122. (-.64)	-62.1 (-.64)	3.03 (.51)	-44.1 (-2.1)	-.157 (-.73)			.25	.951
.169 (1.9)	-34.9 (-1.4)	-17.8 (-1.5)	.319 (.49)	-51.4 (-2.5)		.442 (1.2)	-.166 (.79)	.25	.954

NCR (Sample size = 58, machines = 3)

.189 (3.8)	-2.58 (-1.3)	-1.96 (-1.2)	3.28 (3.0)	-4.84 (-3.9)				-.80	.938
.049 (1.5)	-5.08 (-.96)	-4.37 (-1.0)	5.72 (1.3)	-3.29 (-2.5)	-.417 (-3.8)			-.70	.944
-.003 (-.06)	90.7 (.06)	80.2 (.06)	-119. (-.06)	-3.85 (-2.9)		-.736 (-3.3)	-.442 (-4.2)	-.80	.944

DEC (Sample size = 50, machines = 4)

.396 (2.5)	5.77 (2.0)	5.01 (2.0)	1.59 (1.5)	9.63 (1.8)				.30	.795
.230 (1.6)	6.60 (1.4)	5.64 (1.4)	2.11 (1.2)	6.75 (1.6)	-.727 (-1.9)			.10	.860
.381 (1.6)	4.38 (1.3)	3.75 (1.3)	1.08 (1.2)	8.58 (1.9)		-.06 (-.07)	-.772 (-2.0)	.10	.863

Miscellaneous Corps. (Sample size = 199, machines = 7)

.120 (6.7)	5.76 (4.8)	3.25 (4.6)	2.60 (4.6)	2.44 (3.7)				-.40	.958
.069 (3.9)	2.60 (1.5)	.88 (.88)	3.05 (2.8)	.428 (.65)	-.445 (-8.0)			-.40	.964
-.022 (-1.2)	1.68 (.35)	3.25 (.76)	-15.9 (-1.2)	-2.63 (-3.9)		-.971 (-12.)	-.436 (-9.1)	-.50	.968

Notes: t statistics are presented in parentheses below each coefficient. " Miscellaneous corporations" includes machines marketed by Burroughs, RCA, Bendix, Monroe, and General Precision.

hypothesis seems especially applicable to IBM, which is a very important participant of the computer industry of all the countries under investigation; if the competitive pressures are lower abroad, then the demand for IBM machines should reflect this difference; indeed, it does. The estimates indicate that the downward shift in the demand for a system is about 30 percent faster when marketed in the United States than in Europe. The same types of shifts in other coefficients occur when this form of competitive influence is introduced. The adjustment coefficient is reduced and the performance and income elasticities increase, each even more than when $T(m)$ alone was used. The estimates of c_1 remain essentially the same under all forms of the equation.

Six other firms, and one combination of five firms, were also analyzed using these same formulations of the demand equation. Estimation was attempted for an individual firm when the necessary data were available for three or more machines. However, the resulting estimates were often insignificant for some coefficients when five or fewer machines were included as the sample for a firm. Although the sample sizes were still reasonably large, the variation in $p(m)$ and $\Xi(m)$ is strictly between machines; thus there was not much information available for the determination of the price elasticity and demand shift by performance characteristics for these firms.

There are several uniformities in the significant coefficient estimates for the individual firm equations.[38] Nearly all the significantly positive adjustment coefficients are less than those for IBM.[39] With the competitive factor taken into account, IBM's constant term is also greater than that of most of the other firms. Thus these firms face a lower level and slower rate of acceptance of their machines than does the market leader. The income elasticities are usually well estimated when the competitive effect is not separated, and they generally have a value of three or higher—usually higher than that observed for IBM. The competitive influence shows up significantly and negatively in almost every case; the competitive comparison between the United States and Europe shows the United States to be the more competitive market for all companies except Sperry Rand and DEC. For Honeywell

38. Coefficients greater than twice their standard errors are considered here and are thereby deemed "significant." These coefficients are often statistically significant at the 5 percent significance level.

39. The downward bias mentioned earlier makes actual value of c_1, c_2, and c_3 vary substantially when γ is close to zero, and often destroys the usefulness of this formulation for the form of the equation in which competitive effects between the United States and Europe are separated. In these cases, the point estimates of γ are often negative.

the competition is much more severe in the home market than in Europe. Sperry Rand displays the highest price elasticities and largest downward shifts in the demand for high performance models. By contrast, CDC faces a price inelastic demand for its products under formulation (4.16) and has among the lowest price elasticities. This company appears to have been rather successful in differentiating its product to obtain a circle of "regular" customers. CDC is particularly noteworthy in having the lowest shift factor to increased performance of its machines. This seems to confirm its reputation as a leader in the field of large capacity, high speed systems.

The equation for the five other firms' machines, denoted "miscellaneous corporations" was estimated under the hypothesis that the remaining international computer firms (for which very little data were available) face the same demand function. The results apparently indicate that this is not the case. They seem rather to indicate that, aside from income elasticities and competitive factors influencing their demand similar to the firms noted above, the more successful among these firms (in terms of the number of installations of the machines considered) are those with the higher performance, high price product line of machines.

One further approach to the demand analysis is reported in Table 4.7. Only firms with eight or more different machines in their sample are included The European installations are now viewed as being present either in the European Economic Community or in the United Kingdom. This formulation was explored since, for some firms, the sample sizes were enlarged simply by specifying that a firm had no installations of some models in a particular country for all years. The inherent assumption in using those data is that each firm surveyed all countries and made deliberate decisions concerning which countries *not* to enter. Although I believe that this assumption is approximately correct, it can be checked by observing to what extent the estimated elasticities change when the firms are thought to discriminate only between the broad economic areas, undertaking operations inside or outside the European Economic Community as well as in the United States.

Comparing these results with those in Table 4.6, one can see that the broad conclusions are still valid. There are changes that occur using the EEC perspective. The adjustment coefficients increase (but with IBM's still usually the largest). The negative price and performance elasticities are reduced; CDC still faces inelastic price elasticity of demand in the $T(m)$ case, and the least demand shift for higher computer performance in the two significant cases. The income

Table 4.7. Demand Equations Using US, EEC, and UK Data

$$\frac{Y_k(m,t)}{Y_k(m,t-1)} = [c_0 T(m)^{c_4}] \left\{ \frac{p(m)^{c_1}\, \Xi(m)^{c_2}\, I_k(t-1)^{c_3}}{Y_k(m,t-1)} \right\}^{\gamma}$$

$$= [c_0\, T_{US}^{c_5}\, T_{EEC}^{c_6}\, T_{UK}^{c_7}] \left\{ \frac{p(m)^{c_1}\, \Xi(m)^{c_2}\, I_k(t-1)^{c_3}}{Y_k(m,t-1)} \right\}^{\gamma}$$

γ	c_1	c_2	c_3	Log Const	c_4	c_5	c_6	c_7	ρ	R^2
IBM (Sample size = 164, machines = 16)										
.401 (15.)	-1.94 (-8.1)	-1.41 (-8.1)	2.19 (8.6)	-12.9 (-14.)					-.35	.891
.198 (8.5)	-1.46 (-3.6)	-1.68 (-5.2)	2.42 (5.2)	-3.37 (-3.7)	-1.26 (-16.)				-.35	.941
.152 (6.7)	-1.51 (-3.0)	-1.92 (-4.5)	6.40 (5.5)	-8.69 (-7.6)		-1.76 (-17.)	-1.34 (-17.)	-.918 (-9.9)	-.35	.949
Sperry Rand (Sample size = 83, machines = 8)										
.274 (8.9)	-1.84 (-5.2)	-1.75 (-5.9)	2.13 (5.7)	-7.74 (-9.0)					-.70	.904
.212 (6.2)	-1.70 (-3.3)	-1.79 (-4.1)	2.42 (4.3)	-5.60 (-5.6)	-.422 (-3.8)				-.70	.910
.211 (5.6)	-1.69 (-3.2)	-1.79 (-3.8)	3.24 (4.0)	-7.52 (-4.9)		-.524 (-2.8)	-.553 (-4.7)	-.209 (-1.5)	-.70	.913
CDC (Sample size = 62, machines = 8)										
.221 (6.6)	-1.31 (-3.7)	-1.05 (-3.8)	3.24 (4.9)	-9.10 (-11.)					-.40	.962
.165 (5.5)	-.499 (-1.2)	-.742 (-2.3)	3.80 (4.2)	-5.81 (-6.4)	-.495 (-5.8)				-.45	.970
.018 (.50)	-1.38 (-.33)	-3.96 (-.46)	59.3 (.50)	-10.4 (-13.)		-1.22 (-10.)	-.632 (-10.)	.008 (.11)	-.60	.981

Note: t statistics are presented in parentheses below each coefficient.

elasticities are also changed, increasing for IBM and CDC and declining somewhat for Sperry Rand. Sperry Rand is again shown to find slightly greater competitive pressure within the EEC, while both IBM and CDC find competition stiffest in the U.S. market. Finally, it is interesting to note that IBM has found continental European competition tougher (although more fragmented) than competition with the other major producer in the British market, ICT.

One other observation can be made that is not readily apparent from the results reported in Tables 4.6 and 4.7. In estimating the parameters of the equations, fluctuations of observed demand for a company's computers about the values predicted from the estimated equations have been assumed to be generated by a random process. If, however, a particular machine's installations had been systematically influenced by a phenomenon not included in the equation, one would expect to find deviations from the predicted level to be compatible with the influence of this phenomenon.[40] In particular, in the discussion of IBM and CDC in Chapter 2, it was observed that IBM was accused of deliberately announcing the development of its very large 360/91 prematurely in an attempt to discourage customers from ordering CDC's 6600s. If this occurred, one would expect the actual installation of the 6600 to be below predicted levels when it was first introduced, and recover or exceed predicted levels only after it became apparent that the IBM machine would not actually be available. This pattern of deviations does appear when viewing CDC's 6600, using either country or US, EEC, and UK data. The actual and predicted values for United States installations are:

| Year | Actual values | Predicted using estimates from | |
		country data	US, EEC, UK data
1965	6	6.10	8.09
1966	21	13.97	15.16

These deviations of predicted from actual installation levels for the United States do not actually verify the achievement of a result IBM is alleged to have sought, but they are compatible with that interpretation.

40. Of course, if all the data are affected by the phenomenon, then the equation is misspecified and the estimated parameters will be biased. It is assumed here that this influence affects relatively little of the data, so any bias from including the affected observations is minimal.

Synthesis

Let us pause for a moment and reflect back on the model presented in Chapter 3 and the empirical results that have now been discussed. The model determined comparative advantage within a "new" industry by the innovative achievements of various countries' firms. Based on the overview of the computer industry presented in Chapter 2, I have proceeded with the empirical analysis on the presumption that that is a reasonable characterization of the American advantage in this industry.

The next interesting question is "what is there about American firms in the industry that has enabled them to predominate?" This question has generated a great deal of print copy in the last decade. My approach has been to formulate an empirically analyzable model of a firm in a technologically advancing industry and to analyze this model with data on some of the main American firms.

Although the limitations of the data are discussed in the appendix to this chapter, a couple of features should be reviewed here before I summarize the results. Since the R&D information required for the analysis is often not revealed by firms, the criterion for the selection of firms for the innovation analysis was the availability of *some* R&D expenditure data. For those companies with incomplete reports— IBM, Sperry Rand, Burroughs, and SDS—approximations had to be made. For the demand analysis, installations data were not complete for some countries and the coverage of machines in a firm's product line may not have been adequate to reflect its commercial acceptance. Faced with shortcomings in the data, I still consider the empirical analysis to be both of methodological interest and indicative of the conclusions that would result from more accurate and detailed information.

The analysis of innovative achievements of firms started from a model that distinguished between conceptually separate long-term budgeted R&D and short-term additional commitments. The data were not sufficient to maintain this distinction. Thus the innovation "production function"—the innovation implementation frontier in which total expenditure on R&D is the "input" and improved performance of the product is the "output"—had to be modified into a hybrid function. This new function incorporated the two financial characteristics of the firm (R&D expenditure and proportion of earnings retained), but the two are not completely separate. The results for the two main formulations, the basic equation (4.9) and the varying firm-research elasticities (4.14), indicate that there are *elastic* responses of the "innovative frontier" of a company from its financial commitments to that end. However, this is distinguished within the model from the response in actually implemented increased performance, which is presumed to proceed at a somewhat slower pace because of precautionary motives. After accounting for this precautionary influence (through the parameter α), the effective elasticities of R for some firms are close to, or less than, unity; therefore these firms are required to devote resources to research in equal proportions or more than in proportion to the results they wish to achieve. This methodology is quite useful in that it incorporates quantitative proxies for some of the main innovative characteristics of the firms: the ability to participate in the advancement of the technology (a_1 and a_2), some aspects of " management " of the effort (as measured by α), and the cost of such participation (the expenditure to achieve increased performance, R).

Better measures of a firm's management of its overall participation in the computer industry are obtained through the demand analysis, in which we need not postulate that successful participation requires the most technologically sophisticated products. Demand is analyzed for each firm's range of computer performance. However, the particular formulation of the equation—constant elasticities for price, performance, and industrial production—precluded the investigation of the one- or two-hump demand profile with respect to performance described in Chapter 3 (see pp. 56–58). That is, demand is monotonically related to performance by assumption; the results indicate that demand (measured by the number of installations) is negatively related. This result is compatible with the one-hump demand description, given that the peak level of demand has centered over increasingly higher levels of computer performance through time, perhaps because of continuously improving abilities to handle the more powerful equipment. Thus one would expect firms to center their product line above this maximum-demand performance level in anticipation of the danger of technological obsolescence.

IBM's historical command over the market is reflected quite clearly in this analysis; it faces one of the most rapid rates of acceptance of its machines (as measured by the adjustment coefficient γ). CDC's established position in the very high performance market is indicated by the least decline in demand for a given increase in performance, and Sperry Rand is faced with one of the highest (negative) price elasticities. Among the general conclusions from these equation estimates are the general applicability of the model's demand representation to the firms in the computer industry and the elastic response of demand to higher levels of industrial production.

Appendix to Chapter 4
Description of Data

Corporate Data

Table 4.8 gives the measurements actually used in the analysis of the innovation implementation function. The uniformity of this final table does not reveal the full extent of the necessary adjustment in the data; this section will deal with those adjustments.

First of all, the corporations included in the analysis were selected on the basis of availability of *some* R&D data for them.[41] However, not all firms included revealed R&D expenditures for all years. In particular, actual data on R&D were obtained for IBM for 1942–1955 ("development and engineering expenditure"), Sperry Rand for 1950–1955 ("research and experimental costs" for Remington Rand for 1950–1955 and the combined corporation Sperry Rand for 1954–1955), Burroughs for 1963–1966, NCR for all years, CDC for all years, DEC for all years, and SDS for 1962 to June 1965 ("engineering, research and development"). The method used to obtain approximate figures for the missing data for IBM, Sperry Rand, Burroughs, and SDS was to determine the average proportions of R&D to total "cost of sales" in which the research expenditure figure was included. The proportion was then used in the other years to fill in blanks.[42] Although clearly there is good reason to believe that R&D expenditure is not held at a constant proportion of cost of sales, this method

41. Corporate financial data were obtained from Moody's *Industrial Manual; American and Foreign* (New York, Moody's Investor's Service, annual) except for IBM for early years and CDC for R&D, where annual reports were used. Digital Equipment data were obtained from a prospectus for stock sale, *Digital Equipment Corporation, Prospectus*, Preliminary, July 18, 1966, for sale of 375,000 shares of common stock (Lehman Brothers, New York, 1966) as well as from Moody's. Along with the R&D data, some 1966 Moody's figures were corrected in the 1967 annual report of CDC. The figures for SDS were obtained from Moody's except for the R&D figures and some depreciation data, which were obtained from the company and incorporated in a report by Hayden, Stone, Inc., "A Report on Scientific Data Systems, Inc.," Boston, Investment Research Dept., 1965.

42. The proportion used for IBM was .04716 (based on the average of 1946–1955 ratios); Sperry Rand's was .02946; Burroughs' was .06906 as proportion of "other costs" (not total); and SDS was .151 as a proportion of "costs and expenses" including R&D (based on average of 1963–1964 ratios). For SDS, the 1965 figure was calculated using the figures for the full year 1964 and first six months of 1964 and 1965 assuming that the expenditure during 1965 followed the same pattern as in 1964. Thus, the estimate by proportion of costs was only made for 1966 which didn't enter the estimation analysis since R enters in lagged form.

should provide figures of the right order of magnitude and indicate some characteristic of each corporation's individual research budgeting (since the proportions are different for each corporation). Along with the order of magnitude, the variability of R&D was kept low by relating it to this cost figure. This seems desirable in that the $R(t)$ variable in the model is budgeted R&D and is intended not to be very sensitive to temporary influences on corporate profits. Furthermore, random deviations from actual expenditures should tend to cancel when the data were used, since the accumulation of R over *two* previous years or more is required by the model.

One check on this method has arisen. During initial experimentation with this equation, the figures for CDC were based on actual values only for 1965 to 1966, the others being estimated as described above (the proportion used was .13457 based on the 1965–1966 figures with weights of 2 and 1, respectively, since CDC had a sizable but temporary profit squeeze with higher costs in 1966). Then, in its 1967 annual report, CDC listed its actual R&D expenditure series for 1958 to 1964.[43] My estimates produced an average absolute deviation that was about 20 percent of the average of actual values, whereas the average of net deviations was only 3 percent of the average of actual values (that is, deviations tended to cancel).

Also, partial checks of the method could be made from data presented for IBM and Sperry Rand in C. Freeman's survey of R&D in electronic capital goods.[44] His Table 10 presents total figures for 1951–1959 for both "private venture R&D" and "government R&D contracts." Although each of his private venture totals are within about 3 percent of the totals of figures for IBM and Sperry Rand in the figures presented here, the government awards do not appear in the present figures. If these funds have been growing over the periods under investigation, the elasticities derived from these data will be overestimates.

The other corporate data in Table 4.8 were available, except for total assets for DEC for from 1962 to 1965. These figures were estimated as .611106 times the total sales for those years, the ratio being the average of the ratios of those variables for 1966 and 1967.

The other major problem with these data was that Sperry Rand

43. Control Data Corp., Annual Report, 1967," Minneapolis, 1967, pp. 20–21.
44. C. Freeman, "Research and Development in Electronic Capital Goods," *National Institute Economic Review* 34, Nov. 1965; see especially footnote (1), p. 65, and Table 10, p. 73.

Table 4.8 Data for Innovative Activity Analysis

INTERNATIONAL BUSINESS MACHINES CORPORATION

YEAR	R	NI	D	DIV	S	$\Xi_s(t)$	$\Xi_c(t)$	C	DVS
1942	1127.	8680.	10240.	7447.	120590.	0.0	0.0	0.0	0.0
1943	1354.	9205.	11340.	7817.	154510.	0.0025	0.135	0.0	0.220
1944	2333.	9711.	12000.	8207.	136490.	0.0379	0.406	1.000	0.250
1945	2756.	10894.	15294.	8616.	134370.	0.0379	0.406	0.0	0.286
1946	2747.	18766.	11873.	8587.	148400.	0.0379	0.406	0.0	0.329
1947	3636.	23554.	14172.	9107.	184270.	0.0379	0.406	0.0	0.371
1948	3358.	28101.	17955.	10023.	241970.	0.0379	0.406	0.0	0.414
1949	4809.	33277.	23630.	10519.	267340.	2.1260	14.370	0.333	0.457
1950	5338.	33301.	30787.	11044.	299950.	5.6660	34.060	0.200	0.500
1951	8117.	27892.	39161.	11577.	394110.	5.6660	34.060	0.0	0.517
1952	10454.	29875.	49945.	12173.	428220.	5.6660	34.060	0.0	0.535
1953	12205.	34119.	61231.	12779.	520430.	992.7000	615.700	0.105	0.552
1954	14586.	46537.	72032.	15558.	565470.	992.7000	615.700	0.105	0.570
1955	16537.	55873.	83071.	16386.	629510.	992.7000	1063.000	0.059	0.587
1956	22624.	68785.	106560.	19937.	769040.	10670.0000	3785.000	0.273	0.605
1957	31426.	89292.	146340.	25407.	1086900.	10670.0000	7473.000	0.235	0.622
1958	34864.	126190.	177590.	30765.	1261100.	18690.0000	10230.000	0.100	0.640
1959	38375.	145630.	204590.	37074.	1390600.	97350.0000	45470.000	0.125	0.657
1960	41937.	168180.	218040.	54852.	1535300.	172200.0000	48360.000	0.143	0.675
1961	49115.	207220.	249180.	63266.	1768600.	371700.0000	631000.000	0.200	0.692
1962	55895.	241380.	273050.	82814.	1984500.	371700.0000	631000.000	0.150	0.710
1963	77784.	364250.	282950.	118040.	3083300.	371700.0000	631000.000	0.211	0.727
1964	88662.	431160.	478310.	165960.	3309100.	371700.0000	631000.000	0.095	0.745
1965	99228.	476900.	526310.	210760.	3744900.	3560800.0000	1437800.000	0.200	0.762
1966	120790.	526130.	640620.	230670.	4660700.	3560800.0000	1437800.000	0.111	0.780

1950	2858.7	12544.0	4906.7	5002.4	151770.0	682.5000	301.800	0.200	0.200
1951	3556.2	14864.0	5613.5	5184.8	190940.0	682.5000	301.800	0.167	0.225
1952	3941.5	14392.0	6615.0	5435.0	204630.0	682.5000	301.800	0.0	0.250
1953	3945.3	23616.0	7422.0	10199.0	207210.0	749.2998	666.200	0.105	0.275
1954	5879.8	40439.0	9003.6	12711.0	252680.0	749.2998	666.200	0.053	0.300
1955	12384.0	45900.0	15660.0	16957.0	485550.0	749.2998	666.200	0.0	0.225
1956	19644.0	48796.0	20766.0	21487.0	670770.0	2295.0000	1460.000	0.091	0.236
1957	25949.0	31854.0	24680.0	22953.0	734340.0	2295.0000	2363.000	0.118	0.246
1958	28248.0	27603.0	29412.0	23083.0	769480.0	4433.0000	5527.000	0.200	0.257
1959	25133.0	34838.0	33778.0	23084.0	831530.0	4433.0000	5527.000	0.0	0.268
1960	22146.0	29920.0	38918.0	18847.0	883710.0	142600.0000	40450.000	0.114	0.279
1961	24207.0	25234.0	44677.0	1141.3	878500.0	142600.0000	40450.000	0.160	0.289
1962	23641.0	15939.0	50027.0	460.0	894040.0	142600.0000	76050.000	0.200	0.300
1963	23364.0	23453.0	57435.0	460.0	891800.0	142600.0000	76050.000	0.105	0.315
1964	26009.0	23095.0	78680.0	460.0	908670.0	142600.0000	544200.000	0.095	0.330
1965	26358.0	29047.0	79401.0	460.0	940260.0	2075100.0000	2088100.000	0.080	0.345
1966	29089.0	47261.0	82408.0	460.0	1011100.0	2075100.0000	2088100.000	0.185	0.346

Table 4.8 (continued)

BURROUGHS CORPORATION

YEAR	R	NI	D	DIV	S	$\Xi_s(t)$	$\Xi_c(t)$	C	DVS
1949	3510.	7480.	1515.	4496.	65546.	0.0	0.0	0.0	0.0
1950	3601.	8020.	2049.	4497.	73138.	1.0000	1.000	0.0	0.050
1951	4911.	10615.	2418.	4498.	103150.	5.6050	7.718	0.167	0.060
1952	7313.	9002.	3292.	4498.	129200.	5.6050	7.718	0.0	0.070
1953	8051.	7826.	3111.	4498.	134680.	5.6050	7.718	0.0	0.080
1954	8305.	9147.	2451.	4997.	138080.	80.8400	187.300	0.053	0.090
1955	9675.	12150.	4872.	5392.	181800.	80.8400	187.300	0.059	0.100
1956	11312.	14197.	5908.	5792.	233370.	80.8400	187.300	0.0	0.120
1957	12202.	10075.	8266.	6039.	271530.	80.8400	187.300	0.059	0.140
1958	12859.	6408.	10667.	6327.	299640.	810.2000	1616.000	0.160	0.160
1959	15098.	10745.	12427.	6616.	325770.	2354.0000	1616.000	0.125	0.180
1960	16426.	9236.	14032.	6637.	334210.	2354.0000	1616.000	0.029	0.200
1961	16638.	10489.	14668.	6643.	355120.	2354.0000	1616.000	0.0	0.228
1962	17487.	9493.	14347.	6677.	379010.	43000.0000	15910.000	0.150	0.257
1963	16189.	9224.	17457.	7050.	390280.	43000.0000	15910.000	0.0	0.285
1964	15185.	10712.	21758.	7408.	404090.	376270.0000	544200.000	0.143	0.313
1965	15768.	19778.	29838.	7393.	443510.	376270.0000	544200.000	0.0	0.342
1966	18776.	32485.	33969.	8166.	509160.	3127200.0000	2755700.000	0.111	0.370

NATIONAL CASH REGISTER COMPANY

1950	2121.	12143.	5453.	4857.	134710.	0.0	0.0	0.0	0.0
1951	2104.	12013.	5841.	6102.	153390.	1.0000	1.000	0.0	0.030
1952	2570.	10133.	7779.	5907.	167990.	1.2600	2.998	0.110	0.035
1953	3803.	11088.	8268.	6055.	174940.	16.9900	34.440	0.105	0.039
1954	5328.	12729.	9352.	6532.	183420.	16.9900	34.440	0.053	0.044
1955	7741.	15388.	11572.	7256.	210720.	16.9900	34.440	0.059	0.049
1956	8383.	18420.	13892.	7627.	257660.	16.9900	34.440	0.0	0.053
1957	13650.	18190.	14699.	8473.	267530.	16.9900	34.440	0.0	0.058
1958	15242.	15512.	17284.	8479.	271120.	16.9900	34.440	0.0	0.063
1959	14175.	19076.	19946.	9093.	289070.	1136.0000	2445.000	0.062	0.067
1960	15515.	20024.	21418.	9548.	340280.	1136.0000	2445.000	0.0	0.072
1961	17100.	21709.	27422.	9554.	356320.	1136.0000	2445.000	0.040	0.077
1962	19455.	20645.	32066.	9861.	452640.	3408.0000	11460.000	0.100	0.081
1963	20027.	20082.	38710.	9959.	462500.	3408.0000	11460.000	0.0	0.086
1964	22039.	22503.	46164.	9981.	481050.	6164.0000	17251.000	0.048	0.091
1965	25289.	24725.	51438.	10168.	494110.	132060.0000	153770.000	0.080	0.095
1966	29655.	27219.	63462.	10551.	566440.	132060.0000	153770.000	0.0	0.100

Table 4.8 (continued)

CONTROL DATA CORPORATION

YEAR	R	NI	D	DIV	S	$\Xi_s(t)$	$\Xi_c(t)$	C	DVS
1958	51.0	-192.0	0.0	0.0	0.0	0.0	0.0	0.0	1.000
1959	75.3	395.2	458.2	20.3	4324.6	2295.0000	2363.000	0.0	1.000
1960	501.3	682.1	981.7	21.0	12218.0	58290.0000	20390.000	0.057	1.000
1961	1360.6	1140.5	3279.0	20.9	27659.0	58290.0000	20390.000	0.040	1.000
1962	3662.2	2174.6	6777.1	20.4	53667.0	58290.0000	20390.000	0.0	1.000
1963	8626.5	4569.0	11189.0	20.9	97426.0	459060.0000	156370.000	0.053	1.000
1964	13020.0	6993.0	15445.0	37.2	170740.0	7021600.0000	4091200.000	0.190	1.000
1965	13461.0	3117.5	22380.0	570.0	239960.0	7021600.0000	4091200.000	0.080	1.000
1966	14119.0	3364.0	34585.0	1023.5	311260.0	7021600.0000	4091200.000	0.074	1.000

DIGITAL EQUIPMENT CORPORATION

YEAR	R	NI	D	DIV	S	$\Xi_s(t)$	$\Xi_c(t)$	C	DVS
1962	854.7	993.5	0.0	0.0	5024.0	4455.0000	2173.000	0.050	1.000
1963	1500.5	1032.2	0.0	0.0	6353.1	6338.0000	12519.000	0.053	1.000
1964	2040.5	817.9	0.0	0.0	7813.0	46359.0000	32803.000	0.048	1.000
1965	2427.0	1202.3	589.0	0.0	11762.0	68497.0000	32803.000	0.080	1.000
1966	3221.8	2976.4	625.5	0.0	18122.0	107670.0000	352530.000	0.074	1.000

SCIENTIFIC DATA SYSTEMS, INC.

YEAR	R	NI	D	DIV	S	$\Xi_s(t)$	$\Xi_c(t)$	C	DVS
1962	507.	1.	15.	0.	0.	9244.0000	4964.000	0.100	1.000
1963	569.	1311.	88.	0.	5672.	43876.0000	10646.000	0.053	1.000
1964	1787.	2179.	549.	0.	18820.	73181.0000	21035.000	0.048	1.000
1965	3942.	3759.	1479.	113.	44784.	92692.0000	150100.000	0.080	1.000
1966	4978.	4332.	3147.	225.	65775.	894560.0000	554280.000	0.111	1.000

Note: The variables listed for each corporation for each year include: (in thousands of dollars) research and development expenditure (R), net income after taxes and depreciation (NI), depreciation and amortization deduction (D), dividend paid (DIV), and total assets (S). The ratio of retained to gross earnings is thus

$$g = \frac{NI + D - DIV}{NI + D}.$$

Other variables are scientific computer performance [$\Xi_s(t)$] maximum achieved to that year, commercial computer performance [$\Xi_c(t)$] maximum, proportion of all new models listed for the year that were introduced by this corporation (C), and extent of diversification of the corporation through proportion of total revenue from computer operations (DVS).

113

had March 31 as its year end, and CDC and DEC had June 30. For these companies, 1967 figures were obtained and interpolation was performed on all financial variables to yield December 31 estimated figures (see below, pp. 130–131, for the method of interpolation).

The final variable based on corporate data is the diversification index reported in the last column of Table 4.8. This is a very crude index, based on linear interpolation of quite fragmentary information on the proportion of total corporate revenue from computer operations. IBM's 1966 figure of .78 was reported by Merrill Lynch;[45] the series is derived by interpolation between this figure and estimates of the company's involvement in the industry of .5 for 1950 and .25 for 1944. Sperry Rand reported the proportions of its sales in computers for 1962 (.30), 1965 (.345), and 1966 (.346). Based on an estimate of .225 for 1955, the combined company's index for intermediate years was calculated by interpolation. For 1950 to 1954 the involvement was put somewhat higher for Remington Rand than for the combined Sperry Rand (see Chapter 2) by setting values by interpolation between .20 for 1950 and .30 for 1954. Burroughs' 1967 figure (.3985) was gleaned from a sketch of its operations reported throughout its annual report.[46] Interpolation was used to get yearly figures between this one and estimates for 1960, 1955, and 1950 of .20, .10, and .05, respectively. The NCR figure for 1966 (.10) was also obtained from the Merrill Lynch report.[47] Annual figures were obtained by interpolation between this and an estimate for 1951 of .03. Finally CDC, DEC, and SDS were considered essentially computer specialists, so that all years' entries were set at 1.0 for these companies.

The computer performance measures are calculated for each system based on the algorithm presented in Figure 4. The ones employed here, $\Xi_s(t)$ and $\Xi_c(t)$, are simply the maximum scientific and commercial performance measures to the current year of all computer models designed by the corporation in question (see Table 4.9).[48]

45. Merrill Lynch, Pierce, Fenner & Smith, Inc., "Investing in the Computer Industry," Boston, Securities Research Division, 1967.

46. "Burroughs Corporation, 1967 Annual Report," Detroit, Mich., 1968.

47. Merrill Lynch, "Investing in the Computer Industry," p. 38.

48. Several errors in Knight's calculations (presented in his "Changes in Computer Performance: A Historical View,") of these indexes have been corrected by Nelson Hanover. The corrected versions are used here. Four lagged values of these figures were filled in so that entire ranges of the other available variables could be used. These were selected to be lower than the first actual Knight value and are listed for IBM, Burroughs, NCR, and CDC as the first nonzero entry. The CDC figures for 1957 are actual corresponding figures for Sperry Rand (see p. 14).

Table 4.9. Reference List of Computer Models Surveyed

No.	Computer name	Date introduced	CM	No.	Computer name	Date introduced	CM
1	Harvard Mark I	1944	1	37	Jaincomp C	Aug. 1953	
2	Bell Lab Computer Model IV	Mar. 1945		38	Flac	Sept. 1953	6
3	Eniac	1946		39	Oracle	Sept. 1953	
4	Bell Lab Computer Model V	Late 1947		40	Univac 1103	Sept. 1953	2
5	Harvard Mark II	Sept. 1948		41	Univac 1102	Dec. 1953	2
6	Binac	Aug. 1949	2	42	Udec I	Dec. 1953	3
7	IBM CPC	1949	1	43	NCR 107	1953	4
8	Bell Lab Computer Model III	1949		44	Miniac	Dec. 1953	
9	SEAC	May 1950		45	IBM 701	1953	1
10	Whirlwind I	Dec. 1950		46	IBM 604	1953	1
11	Univac 1101 Era 1101	Dec. 1950	2	47	AN/UJQ-2(YA-1)	1953	
12	IBM 607	1950	1	48	Johnniac	Mar. 1954	
13	Avdiac	1950		49	Dyseac	Apr. 1954	
14	Adec	Jan. 1951		50	Elcom 120	May 1954	13
15	Burroughs Calculator	Jan. 1951	3	51	Circle	June 1954	
16	SWAC	Mar. 1951		52	Burroughs 204 & 205	July 1954	3
17	Univac I	Mar. 1951	2	53	Modac 5014	July 1954	
18	ONR Relay Computer	May 1951		54	Ordfiac	July 1954	13
19	Fairchild Computer	June 1951		55	Datatron	Aug. 1954	3
20	National 102	Jan. 1952	4	56	Modac 404	Sept. 1954	
21	IAS	Mar. 1952		57	Lincoln Memory Test	Dec. 1954	
22	Maniac I	Mar. 1952		58	TIM II	Dec. 1954	
23	Ordvac	Mar. 1952		59	Caldic	1954	
24	Edvac	Apr. 1952		60	Univac 60 & 120	Nov. 1954	2
25	Teleregister Special Purpose Digital Data Handling	June 1952		61	IBM 650	Nov. 1954	1
26	Illiac	Sept. 1952		62	WISC	1954	
27	Elcom 100	Dec. 1952	13	63	NCR 303	1954	4
28	Harvard Mark IV	1952		64	Mellon Inst Digital Computer	1954	
29	Alwac II	Feb. 1953	14	65	IBM 610	1954	1
30	Logistics Era	Mar. 1953		66	Alwac III	1954	14
31	Oarac	Apr. 1953	10	67	IBM 702	Feb. 1955	1
32	ABC	May 1953		68	Monrobot III	Feb. 1955	15
33	Raydac	July 1953		69	Norc	Feb. 1955	
34	Whirlwind II	July 1953		70	Miniac II	Mar. 1955	
35	National 102A	Summer 1953	4	71	Monrobot V	Mar. 1955	15
36	Consolidated Eng. Corp. Model 36-101	Summer 1953		72	Udec II	Oct. 1955	3
				73	RCA BIZMAC I & II	Nov. 1955	6
				74	Pennstac	Nov. 1955	
				75	Technitral 180	1955	
				76	National 102D	1955	4
				77	Monrobot VI	1955	15
				78	Modac 410	1955	
				79	Midac	1955	
				80	Elcom 125	1955	13

Table 4.9 (continued)

No.	Computer name	Date introduced	CM	No.	Computer name	Date introduced	CM
81	Burroughs E101	1955	3	130	RPC 9000	1959	16
82	Bendix G15	Aug. 1955	12	131	Librascope		
83	Alwac IIIE	Nov. 1955	14		Air Traffic	1959	16
84	Readix	Feb. 1956		132	Jukebox	1959	
85	IBM 705, I, II	Mar. 1956	1	133	Datamatic 1000	1959	8
86	Univac 1103A	Mar. 1956	2	134	CCC Real Time	1959	
87	AF CRC	Apr. 1956	4	135	Burroughs E102	1959	3
88	Guidance			136	Burroughs D204	1959	3
	Function	Apr. 1956		137	AN/TYK 6V		
89	IBM 704	Apr. 1956	1		BASICPAC	1959	
90	IBM 701 (CORE)	1956	1	138	CDC 1604	Jan. 1960	7
91	Narac	July 1956		139	Librascope 3000	Jan. 1960	16
92	LGP 30	Sept. 1956	16	140	Univac Solid		
93	Modac 414	Oct. 1956			State 80/91 1	Jan. 1960	2
94	Elecom 50	1956	13	141	Philco 2000-211	Mar. 1960	5
95	Udec III	Mar. 1957		142	Univac Larc	May 1960	2
96	George I	Sept. 1957		143	Libratrol 500	May 1960	16
97	Univac File 0	Sept. 1957	2	144	Monrobot XI	May 1960	15
98	Lincoln TXO	Fall 1957		145	IBM 7070	June 1960	1
99	Univac II	Nov. 1957	2	146	CDC 160	July 1960	7
100	IBM 705 III	Late 1957	1	147	IBM 1401		
101	Teleregister				(Mag. Tape)	Sept. 1960	1
	Telefile	Late 1957		148	AN/FSQ 31 & 32	Sept. 1960	1
102	Recomp I	Late 1957		149	Merlin	Sept. 1960	
103	IBM 608	1957	1	150	IBM 1401 (Card)	Sept. 1960	1
104	Mistic	1957		151	Mobidic B	Fall 1960	
105	Maniac	1957		152	RPC-4000	Nov. 1960	16
106	IBM 609	1957	1	153	PDP-1 (MT)	Nov. 1960	9
107	IBM 305	Dec. 1957	1	154	PDP-1 (PT)	Nov. 1960	9
108	Corbin	1957		155	Packard Bell		
109	Burroughs E103	1957	3		250 (PT)	Dec. 1960	
110	AN/FSQ 7 & 8	1957		156	Honeywell 800	Dec. 1960	8
111	Alwac 880	1957	14	157	General Mills		
112	Univac File I	Jan. 1958	2		AD/ECW-57	Dec. 1960	
113	Lincoln CG24	May 1958		158	Philco 3000	Late 1960	5
114	IBM 709	Aug. 1958	1	159	Maniac III	Late 1960	
115	Univac 1105	Sept. 1958	2	160	Sylvania S9400	Late 1960	
116	Lincoln TX2	Fall 1958		161	Target Intercept	Late 1960	2
117	Philco 2000-210	Nov. 1958	5	162	Westinghouse		
118	Recomp II	Dec. 1958			Airborne	1960	
119	Burroughs 220	Dec. 1958	3	163	RCA 300	1960	6
120	Mobidic	1958–1960		164	Mobidic CD &		
121	Philco CXPO	1958	5		7A AN/MYK	1960	
122	Monrobot IX	1958	15	165	Litton C7000	1960	
123	GE 210	June 1959	10	166	Libratrol 1000	1960	16
124	Cyclone	July 1959		167	GE 312	1960	10
125	IBM 1620	Oct. 1959	1	168	Diana	1960	
126	NCR 304	Nov. 1959	4	169	DE 60	Feb. 1960	
127	IBM 7090	Nov. 1959	1	170	Burroughs D107	1960	3
128	RCA 501	Nov. 1959	6	171	AN/USQ 20	1960	2
129	RW 300	Nov. 1959		172	AN/TYK 4V Compac	1960	1

Table 4.9 (continued)

No.	Computer name	Date introduced	CM	No.	Computer name	Date introduced	CM
173	General Mills Apsac	Jan. 1961		215	ASI 420	Dec. 1962	
174	Univac Solid State 80/90 II	Jan. 1961	2	216	Burroughs B200 Series-Card System	Dec. 1962	3
175	Bendix G20 & 21	Feb. 1961	12	217	RW 400 (AN/FSQ 27)	1962	
176	RCA 301	Feb. 1961	6	218	CDC 3600	June 1963	
177	BRLESC	Mar. 1961		219	IBM 7040	Apr. 1963	1
178	GE 225	Mar. 1961	10	220	IBM 7044	July 1963	1
179	CCC-DDP-19 (Card)	May 1961		221	RCA 601	Jan. 1963	6
180	CCC-DDP-19 (MT)	May 1961		222	Honeywell 1800	Nov. 1963	8
181	IBM Stretch (7030)	May 1961	1	223	Philco 1000 Transac S1000	June 1963	5
182	NCR 390	May 1961	4	224	Philco 2000-212	Feb. 1963	5
183	Honeywell 290	June 1961	8	225	Librascope L3055	Dec. 1963	16
184	Recomp III	June 1961		226	HW Electronics 15K	Feb. 1963	
185	CDC 160A	July 1961	7	227	GE 215	June 1963	10
186	IBM 7080	Aug. 1961	1	228	DDP-24	June 1963	8
187	RW 530	Aug. 1961		229	CDC 3600	June 1963	7
188	IBM 7074	Nov. 1961	1	230	UNIVAC 1050	Sept. 1963	2
189	IBM 1410	Nov. 1961	1	231	UNIVAC 1004	Sept. 1963	2
190	Honeywell 400	Dec. 1961	8	232	PDP-5	Oct. 1963	9
191	Rice Univ.	Dec. 1961		233	IBM 1460	Oct. 1963	1
192	Univac 490	Dec. 1961	2	234	IBM 1440	Nov. 1963	1
193	AN/TYK 7V	1961	1	235	Honewell 1400	Dec. 1963	8
194	Univac 1206	1961	2	236	ASI 2100	Dec. 1963	
195	Univac 1000 & 1020	1961	2	237	SDS 9300	Dec. 1963	11
196	ITT Bank Loan Process	1961		238	Burroughs 273	Jan. 1964	3
197	George II	1961		239	GE-235	Jan. 1964	10
198	Oklahoma Univ.	Early 1962		240	IBM 7010	Jan. 1964	1
199	NCR 315	Jan. 1962	4	241	Burroughs B160-180	Apr. 1964	3
200	NCR 315 CRAM	Jan. 1962	4	242	CDC 160G	Apr. 1964	7
201	Univac File II	Jan. 1962	2	243	IBM 7094 II	Apr. 1964	1
202	HRB-Singer Sema	Jan. 1962		244	CDC 3200	May 1964	7
203	Univac 1004	Feb. 1962	2	245	GE 415	May 1964	10
204	ASI 210	Apr. 1962		246	UNIVAC 1004 II, III	June 1964	2
205	Univac III	June 1962	2	247	SDS-930	June 1964	11
206	Burroughs B200 Series B270 & 280	July 1962	3	248	GE 425	June 1964	10
207	SDS 910	Aug. 1962	11	249	GE 205	July 1964	10
208	SDS 920	Sept. 1962	11	250	Honeywell 200	July 1964	8
209	PDP-4	Sept. 1962	9	251	RCA 3301	July 1964	6
210	Univac 1107	Oct. 1962	2	252	PDP-6	July 1964	9
211	IBM 7094	Nov. 1962	1	253	CDC 6600	Sept. 1964	7
212	IBM 7072	Nov. 1963	1	254	UNIVAC 418	Sept. 1964	2
213	IBM 1620 MOD III	Dec. 1962	1	255	NCR 315-100	Nov. 1964	4
214	Burroughs B5000	Dec. 1962	3	256	GE 635	Nov. 1964	10
				257	CDC 3400	Nov. 1964	7
				258	Burroughs B5500	Nov. 1964	3

Table 4.9 (continued)

No.	Computer name	Date introduced	CM	No.	Computer name	Date introduced	CM
259	SDS 925	Feb. 1965	11	286	DDP-124	Jan. 1966	8
260	SDS 92	Feb. 1965	11	287	Honeywell 1200	Jan. 1966	8
261	CDC 3100	Feb. 1965	7	288	IBM 360/20	Jan. 1966	1
262	ASI 6020	Mar. 1965		289	UNIVAC 1005		
263	DDP-224	Mar. 1965	8		II, III	Feb. 1966	2
264	DDP-116	Apr. 1965	8	290	UNIVAC 1005 I	Feb. 1966	2
265	GE 625	Apr. 1965	10	291	Honeywell 120	Feb. 1966	8
266	PDP-8	Apr. 1965	9	292	IBM 360/65	Mar. 1966	1
267	PDP-7	Apr. 1965	9	293	UNIVAC 494	Mar. 1966	2
268	IBM 360/40	May 1965	1	294	SDS 940	Apr. 1966	11
269	IBM 360/30	May 1965	1	295	RCA Spectra		
270	NCR 315 RMC	July 1965	4		70/55	July 1966	6
271	UNIVAC 1108 II	Aug. 1965	2	296	RCA Spectra		
272	GE 435	Aug. 1965	10		70/45	July 1966	6
273	IBM 360/50	Sept. 1965	1	297	RCA Spectra		
274	IBM 1130	Sept. 1965	1		70/35	July 1966	6
275	NCR 590	Sept. 1965	4	298	Philco 200-213	Oct. 1966	5
276	ASI 6240	Oct. 1965		299	IBM 360/44	Oct. 1966	1
277	UNIVAC 491			300	Honeywell 4200	May 1967	8
	& 492	Oct. 1965	2	301	SDS Sigma 7	Dec. 1966	11
278	RCA Spectra			302	PDP-8/S	Sept. 1966	9
	70/15	Oct. 1965	6	303	PDP-9	Dec. 1966	9
279	Raytheon 520	Oct. 1965		304	SDS Sigma 2	Jan. 1967	11
280	IBM 360/75	Nov. 1965	1	305	Burroughs B2500	Feb. 1967	3
281	Honeywell 2200	Dec. 1965	8	306	Burroughs B3500	May 1967	3
282	CDC 3800	Dec. 1965	7	307	UNIVAC 9300	June 1967	2
283	RCA Spectra			308	UNIVAC 9200	June 1967	2
	70/25	Dec. 1965	6	309	Burroughs B6500	Feb. 1967	3
284	Friden 6010	Jan. 1966		310	CDC 3500	Sept. 1967	7
285	CDC 6400	Jan. 1966	7				

Sources: Reprinted with permission from articles by K. E. Knight in *Datamation*, Sept. 1966 and Jan. 1968, published and copyrighted by L. D. Thompson Publications, Inc., 35 Mason St., Greenwich, Conn. 06830 (except for the CM column, which was compiled mainly from appendixes in Knight, *A Study of Technological Innovation—The Evolution of Digital Computers*; and N. Hanover, *Economic Aspects of Computer Use*.

Note: Column CM lists the corporate manufacturer by number as follows:

Corporation Number	Name
1.	International Business Machine Corp.
2.	Sperry Rand Corp.
3.	Burroughs Corp.
4.	National Cash Register Co.
5.	Philco Corp.
6.	Radio Corporation of America
7.	Control Data Corp.
8.	Honeywell
9.	Digital Equipment Corp.
10.	General Electric Co.
11.	Scientific Data Systems
12.	Bendix Corp.
13.	Underwood Corp.
14.	El-Tronics
15.	Monroe-Calculating Machine Co.
16.	General Precision Equipment Corp.

Computer No. 218 is also listed as No. 229; it was not counted as two separate machines.

Finally, the proportion of new systems installed by the firm to "all new models introduced in that year is given as *C* in Table 4.8. "All" is intended to indicate that the Knight list of computer models was used as the basis for this proportion. The inherent assumption in doing so is that Knight has overlooked other models by each corporation to the same degree, so that the numbers of models may be incorrect but the proportions are not biased across firms or years. For some models it was known that the actual first installation was in November or December; therefore, as an index of experience it might more properly be included in the following years' proportion. But this information was available only for the better-known models, and the possible bias between corporations in this measure seemed best avoided by including the model, despite the month, in the listed year of its introduction.

Table 4.10 presents the values of industrial production for the eight countries for the relevant years. Benelux was obtained from figures for each country converted to U.S. dollars separately and then added. The actual figures were derived from indexes of industrial production (1958 = 100) for each country, found in the United Nations *Statistical Yearbook* for 1966, combined with the value of industrial production for 1958 derived from its component parts: mining, manufacturing, and electricity and gas. For some countries not all components were available for 1958. In this case the component for the closest year available was reduced to a 1958 figure by assuming that its rate of growth was the same as for the entire industrial production in the

Demand Analysis Data

Table 4.10 Industrial Production Data (millions of dollars)

Year	United States	West Germany	United Kingdom	France	Benelux	Italy
1955	167333.0					
1956	173062.8					
1957	174442.5					
1958	162317.4					
1959	182931.7					
1960	188304.4	30252.3	28901.9	22683.8	7926.7	10590.8
1961	190041.2	32286.1	28901.9	23714.8	8360.5	11583.7
1962	204925.7	33557.2	29157.7	24952.1	8785.3	12659.4
1963	215330.3	34828.3	30436.5	26189.4	9316.8	13735.0
1964	229192.2	37878.9	32482.7	28045.4	10096.8	13900.5
1965	248410.5	39912.7	33250.0	28457.8	10499.5	14562.4
1966	270761.7	41107.5	33915.0	30458.1	11076.8	16167.6

intervening period. This adjustment was needed only for Germany's electricity and gas and Belgium's mining, for which 1961 data were available.

For 1966 the industrial production index was not yet available, but the growth of January to June production for 1966 over 1965 was indicated. The 1966 index was derived by assuming that this rate of growth prevailed throughout the year. For the United States, the actual index was available for 1966 (only the December part preliminary) in the 1967 *Economic Report of the President* (Table B43). The figure did not differ from the one calculated for the United States by the above method. The U.S. index was taken from the *Economic Report* for all years from 1955 to 1966, so that more "significant" figures could be used for the calculation. Foreign values were converted to U.S. dollars at 1958 exchange rates. The figures listed and used in the analysis are in millions of U.S. dollars.

Table 4.11 contains computer characteristics and installations data for corporations that had European installations data; only machines that had such data are included in the sample for each corporation. The name of each machine used is given in Table 4.9. The information on each machine in Table 4.11 includes two sets of two characteristics, and an accounting for each year since production began of the number of installations in each country, listed in the same order as in Table 4.10. The characteristics are Knight's operations per second and dollars per operation ("scientific" on the first line and "commercial" on the second).[49] The U.S. installations data were made available for this analysis by Nelson Hanover. He developed the figures from various reports, including the Diebold *Automatic Data Processing Newsletter* computer censuses and *Computers and Automation*—monthly computer censuses.[50] The Hanover U.S. data gave year-end installations figures for 1957 and 1959 through 1966 plus a census as of September 1956. Year-end figures for 1956 and 1958 were obtained by interpolation (using the method described below); no rounding to integers was performed before the analysis. Thus interpolated figures can often be identified in the table by nonzero fractions of "installations."

---

49. Knight calculated "operations per second," P, and "seconds per dollar," C. The first characteristic here is his P; the second is

$$\frac{1}{(P \times C)}$$

The corrected values of P and C, as determined by Hanover, "Economic Aspects of Computer Use," were used.

50. Ibid., Appendix.

Table 4.11 Demand Analysis Data

Year	United States	West Germany	United Kingdom	France	Benelux	Italy

INTERNATIONAL BUSINESS MACHINE CORPORATION

18 MACHINES INCLUDED IN SAMPLE (404 MACHINE-YEARS OF DATA)

MACHINE 61 CHARACTERISTICS

		110.80	0.57891E-04			
		291.10	0.22035E-04			
1955	0.0					
1956	443.43					
1957	650.00					
1958	925.00					
1959	1200.00					
1960	1090.00					
1961	725.00	70.00	16.00	60.00	20.00	25.00
1962	735.00	30.36	15.45	44.25	8.96	4.64
1963	460.00	17.32	6.71	32.62	6.00	2.00
1964	280.00	13.00	3.00	28.00	7.00	2.00
1965	192.00	7.00	2.00	21.00	7.00	2.00
1966	130.00	4.00	0.0	3.00	3.00	

MACHINE 107 CHARACTERISTICS

		94.47	0.64941E-04			
		96.47	0.63595E-04			
1957	20.00					
1958	575.00					
1959	575.00					
1960	900.00					
1961	1050.00	50.00	4.00	20.00	5.00	25.00
1962	925.00	48.90	12.59	14.23	4.31	14.46
1963	600.00	24.49	11.40	17.31	4.62	11.00
1964	400.00	12.00	9.00	18.00	5.00	9.00
1965	168.00	8.00	7.00	14.00	5.00	9.00
1966	138.00	2.00	5.00	5.00	0.0	

MACHINE 125 CHARACTERISTICS

		94.79	0.31805E-04			
		47.20	0.63872E-04			
1959	0.0					
1960	100.00					
1961	410.00	40.00	0.0	3.00	2.00	4.00
1962	1345.00	59.59	20.00	7.13	20.59	19.59
1963	1180.00	65.00	30.00	54.31	21.98	23.66
1964	1258.00	75.00	30.00	62.00	25.00	34.00
1965	1448.00	80.00	30.00	74.00	28.00	36.62
1966	1470.00	65.00	24.00	61.00	28.00	

MACHINE 145 CHARACTERISTICS

		2813.00	0.14825E-04			
		5139.00	0.81147E-05			
1960	30.00					
1961	160.00	12.00	0.0	3.00	1.00	5.00
1962	160.00	27.59	3.33	9.59	2.66	6.84
1963	214.00	24.25	5.00	11.43	3.00	10.35
1964	256.00	21.00	4.47	12.00	2.00	11.00
1965	176.00	21.00	4.00	13.00	2.00	9.67
1966	175.00	10.00	3.00	15.00	1.00	

MACHINE 150 CHARACTERISTICS

		340.90	0.13644E-04			
		967.80	0.48059E-05			
1960	20.00					
1961	438.00	130.00	8.00	60.00	10.00	18.00
1962	1100.00	376.68	166.01	120.14	119.59	219.59
1963	1587.00	559.02	265.00	250.50	167.31	250.40
1964	1894.00	730.00	266.93	375.00	176.00	330.00
1965	1688.00	905.00	270.00	525.00	185.00	370.00
1966	1913.00	790.00	261.00	458.00	196.00	

Table 4.11 (continued)

Year	United States	West Germany	United Kingdom	France	Benelux	Italy
MACHINE 189 CHARACTERISTICS						
		1673.00	0.95867E-05			
		4638.00	0.34581E-05			
1961	3.00	5.00	0.0	2.00	0.0	1.00
1962	140.00	24.59	15.33	27.59	7.33	19.59
1963	260.00	29.58	29.31	29.93	12.41	22.80
1964	550.00	55.00	23.24	36.00	17.00	35.00
1965	735.00	60.00	19.00	38.00	19.00	35.00
1966	805.00	35.00	24.00	20.00	18.00	
MACHINE 211 CHARACTERISTICS						
		175900.00	0.64735E-06			
		95900.00	0.11874E-05			
1962	1.00	2.67	0.67	1.33	0.0	0.0
1963	220.00	4.47	1.50	4.35	0.0	1.00
1964	235.00	6.00	2.62	5.00	0.0	3.00
1965	125.00	6.00	3.00	6.00	1.00	1.67
1966	115.00	5.00	5.00	4.00	2.00	
MACHINE 219 CHARACTERISTICS						
		21420.00	0.10482E-05			
		9079.00	0.24729E-05			
1963	22.00	1.50	0.0	1.50	0.0	1.00
1964	70.00	5.00	0.0	8.00	2.00	4.00
1965	115.00	6.00	0.0	10.00	3.00	5.49
1966	120.00	5.00	0.0	16.00	4.00	
MACHINE 233 CHARACTERISTICS						
		1611.00	0.89598E-05			
		7200.00	0.20047E-05			
1963	120.00	2.50	3.00	0.50	0.0	0.50
1964	925.00	18.00	6.00	6.00	2.00	6.00
1965	2200.00	23.00	8.00	12.00	4.00	8.62
1966	1760.00	15.00	18.00	10.00	4.00	
MACHINE 234 CHARACTERISTICS						
		1412.00	0.38616E-05			
		5559.00	0.98085E-06			
1963	420.00	10.00	12.50	4.00	4.50	6.00
1964	1350.00	105.00	39.69	16.00	13.00	30.00
1965	2600.00	210.00	100.00	20.00	45.00	163.33
1966	3400.00	205.00	120.00	20.00	53.00	
MACHINE 240 CHARACTERISTICS						
		5729.00	0.55982E-05			
		11537.00	0.27799E-05			
1963	7.00	0.50	0.0	1.00	0.0	0.0
1964	57.00	3.00	0.0	5.00	0.0	0.0
1965	180.00	6.00	0.0	6.00	0.0	0.0
1966	215.00	4.00	4.00	6.00	0.0	
MACHINE 268 CHARACTERISTICS						
		33438.00	0.55300E-06			
		50073.00	0.36928E-06			
1965	450.00	5.00	15.00	2.00	2.00	0.0
1966	1450.00	45.00	41.00	27.00	20.00	
MACHINE 269 CHARACTERISTICS						
		7942.00	0.17277E-05			
		17104.00	0.80222E-06			
1965	600.00	14.00	30.00	4.00	5.00	0.0
1966	2750.00	160.00	86.00	68.00	47.00	
MACHINE 273 CHARACTERISTICS						
		187488.00	0.19416E-06			
		148967.00	0.24437E-06			
1965	20.00	1.00	0.0	0.0	0.0	0.0
1966	150.00	8.00	8.00	6.00	1.00	

Table 4.11 (continued)

Year	United States	West Germany	United Kingdom	France	Benelux	Italy

SPERRY RAND CORPORATION

8 MACHINES INCLUDED IN SAMPLE (204 MACHINE-YEARS OF DATA)

MACHINE 140 CHARACTERISTICS

Year	United States	West Germany	United Kingdom	France	Benelux	Italy
		329.10	0.24367E-04			
		489.60	0.16379E-04			
1960	0.0					
1961	0.0	0.0	0.0	0.0	0.0	0.0
1962	529.00	0.0	3.33	0.0	8.00	0.0
1963	370.00	0.0	5.00	0.0	11.49	0.0
1964	282.00	0.0	5.00	0.0	12.00	0.0
1965	215.00	0.0	5.00	0.0	13.00	0.0
1966	178.00	0.0	5.00	0.0	12.00	

MACHINE 192 CHARACTERISTICS

Year	United States	West Germany	United Kingdom	France	Benelux	Italy
		17770.00	0.22564E-05			
		15050.00	0.26642E-05			
1961	2.00	0.0	0.0	0.0	0.0	1.00
1962	4.00	0.0	0.0	0.0	0.0	1.00
1963	23.00	0.0	1.00	0.50	0.0	1.00
1964	36.00	1.00	2.00	1.00	0.0	1.00
1965	79.00	1.00	2.00	1.00	0.0	1.00
1966	60.00	1.00	5.00	1.00	0.0	

MACHINE 205 CHARACTERISTICS

Year	United States	West Germany	United Kingdom	France	Benelux	Italy
		22720.00	0.16235E-05			
		22790.00	0.16186E-05			
1962	4.00	5.33	0.0	0.0	0.67	0.67
1963	41.00	8.00	0.0	0.0	1.00	3.35
1964	78.00	8.00	0.0	0.0	1.00	4.00
1965	86.00	8.00	0.0	0.0	2.00	4.00
1966	75.00	10.00	0.0	0.0	2.00	

MACHINE 210 CHARACTERISTICS

Year	United States	West Germany	United Kingdom	France	Benelux	Italy
		138700.00	0.57817E-06			
		76050.00	0.10545E-05			
1962	1.00	1.33	0.0	0.67	0.0	0.0
1963	13.00	2.00	0.50	1.00	0.0	0.0
1964	21.00	2.00	1.62	1.00	0.0	0.0
1965	29.00	3.00	2.00	1.00	0.0	0.0
1966	15.00	3.00	3.00	1.00	0.0	

MACHINE 274 CHARACTERISTICS

Year	United States	West Germany	United Kingdom	France	Benelux	Italy
		16.38	0.88121E-04			
		56.76	0.25430E-04			
1965	25.00	0.0	3.00	0.0	0.0	0.0
1966	1000.00	30.00	9.00	18.00	11.00	

MACHINE 280 CHARACTERISTICS

Year	United States	West Germany	United Kingdom	France	Benelux	Italy
		3560854.00	0.23779E-07			
		1437806.00	0.58891E-07			
1966	17.00	0.0	1.00	0.0	0.0	

MACHINE 288 CHARACTERISTICS

Year	United States	West Germany	United Kingdom	France	Benelux	Italy
		1932.00	0.21585E-05			
		4497.00	0.92732E-06			
1966	1300.00	250.00	37.00	98.00	43.00	

MACHINE 292 CHARACTERISTICS

Year	United States	West Germany	United Kingdom	France	Benelux	Italy
		1385573.00	0.52072E-07			
		809738.00	0.89103E-07			
1965	2.00	0.0	0.0	0.0	0.0	0.0
1966	32.00	0.0	0.0	1.00	0.0	

Table 4.11 (continued)

Year	United States	West Germany	United Kingdom	France	Benelux	Italy
MACHINE 230 CHARACTERISTICS						
		12028.00	0.73315E-06			
		19675.00	0.44820E-06			
1963	15.00	0.0	0.0	0.0	0.0	0.50
1964	125.00	1.00	3.00	0.0	2.00	4.00
1965	270.00	16.00	6.00	2.00	4.00	20.25
1966	295.00	43.00	12.00	2.00	6.00	
MACHINE 231 CHARACTERISTICS						
		97.12	0.24769E-04			
		1473.00	0.16331E-05			
1963	100.00	33.24	27.50	4.50	22.36	39.31
1964	700.00	130.00	182.31	12.00	36.00	57.00
1965	1350.00	175.00	211.00	45.00	48.00	71.69
1966	1500.00	196.00	210.00	67.00	67.00	
MACHINE 254 CHARACTERISTICS						
		58767.00	0.27292E-06			
		166564.00	0.96290E-07			
1963	1.00	0.0	0.0	0.0	0.0	0.0
1964	9.00	0.0	0.0	0.0	0.0	0.0
1965	56.00	0.0	0.0	0.0	0.0	0.0
1966	100.00	2.00	8.00	1.00	3.00	
MACHINE 271 CHARACTERISTICS						
		2075181.00	0.46380E-07			
		2088142.00	0.46092E-07			
1965	0.0	0.0	0.0	0.0	0.0	0.0
1966	0.0	0.0	2.00	5.00	0.0	

NATIONAL CASH REGISTER COMPANY

3 MACHINES INCLUDED IN SAMPLE (76 MACHINE-YEARS OF DATA)

Year	United States	West Germany	United Kingdom	France	Benelux	Italy
MACHINE 182 CHARACTERISTICS						
		2.03	0.14980E-02			
		10.43	0.29213E-03			
1960	3.00					
1961	60.00	0.0	1.00	0.0	0.0	0.0
1962	295.00	0.0	0.33	0.0	2.67	0.0
1963	505.00	0.0	2.50	0.0	5.00	0.0
1964	780.00	0.0	5.62	8.00	7.00	0.0
1965	1060.00	0.0	6.00	8.00	9.00	0.0
1966	725.00	0.0	6.00	8.00	13.00	
MACHINE 199 CHARACTERISTICS						
		3408.00	0.44709E-05			
		11460.00	0.13296E-05			
1962	20.00	6.00	15.59	0.67	0.0	0.0
1963	71.00	8.48	17.43	1.62	1.50	0.0
1964	132.00	10.00	22.23	2.00	3.00	0.0
1965	192.00	13.00	33.00	2.00	8.00	1.00
1966	195.00	14.00	34.00	3.00	9.00	
MACHINE 270 CHARACTERISTICS						
		132060.00	0.12145E-06			
		153770.00	0.10430E-06			
1965	12.00	0.0	0.0	0.0	0.0	0.0
1966	36.00	7.00	3.00	3.00	2.00	

Table 4.11 (continued)

Year	United States	West Germany	United Kingdom	France	Benelux	Italy

CONTROL DATA CORPORATION

9 MACHINES INCLUDED IN SAMPLE (167 MACHINE-YEARS OF DATA)

MACHINE   138 CHARACTERISTICS

Year	United States	West Germany	United Kingdom	France	Benelux	Italy
		58290.00	0.93542E-06			
		20390.00	0.26741E-05			
1960	10.00					
1961	27.00	0.0	0.0	0.0	0.0	0.0
1962	40.00	0.67	0.0	0.0	0.0	0.0
1963	54.00	1.00	0.0	0.0	0.0	0.0
1964	61.00	1.00	0.0	0.0	0.0	0.0
1965	58.00	1.00	0.0	0.0	0.0	0.0
1966	59.00	1.00	0.0	0.0	0.0	

MACHINE   185 CHARACTERISTICS

Year	United States	West Germany	United Kingdom	France	Benelux	Italy
		1015.00	0.71084E-05			
		1780.00	0.40534E-05			
1961	30.00	0.0	0.0	0.0	0.0	0.0
1962	93.00	1.33	0.0	0.0	0.0	0.0
1963	193.00	2.00	0.0	0.50	0.50	0.0
1964	278.00	3.00	0.0	1.00	1.00	0.0
1965	308.00	4.00	0.0	5.00	1.00	0.0
1966	417.00	3.00	2.00	5.00	1.00	

MACHINE   229 CHARACTERISTICS

Year	United States	West Germany	United Kingdom	France	Benelux	Italy
		459065.00	0.17469E-06			
		156375.00	0.51282E-06			
1963	11.00	1.00	0.0	1.00	0.0	0.0
1964	32.00	2.00	0.0	3.00	1.00	0.0
1965	49.00	2.00	0.0	4.00	2.00	0.0
1966	45.00	2.00	0.0	5.00	2.00	

MACHINE   244 CHARACTERISTICS

Year	United States	West Germany	United Kingdom	France	Benelux	Italy
		195256.00	0.98566E-07			
		87510.00	0.21992E-06			
1964	31.00	1.00	0.0	0.0	1.00	0.0
1965	89.00	3.00	0.0	3.00	2.00	0.0
1966	66.00	2.00	2.00	4.00	4.00	

MACHINE   253 CHARACTERISTICS

Year	United States	West Germany	United Kingdom	France	Benelux	Italy
		7021619.00	0.17138E-07			
		4091293.00	0.29413E-07			
1964	2.00	0.0	0.0	0.0	0.0	0.0
1965	6.00	0.0	0.0	0.0	0.0	0.0
1966	21.00	0.0	0.0	2.00	0.0	

MACHINE   257 CHARACTERISTICS

Year	United States	West Germany	United Kingdom	France	Benelux	Italy
		269859.00	0.12481E-06			
		157202.00	0.21426E-06			
1964	3.00	0.0	0.0	0.0	0.0	0.0
1965	16.00	3.00	0.0	0.0	0.0	0.0
1966	19.00	3.00	0.0	0.0	0.0	

MACHINE   261 CHARACTERISTICS

Year	United States	West Germany	United Kingdom	France	Benelux	Italy
		118462.00	0.10831E-06			
		74391.00	0.17247E-06			
1965	58.00	0.0	0.0	0.0	0.0	0.0
1966	85.00	2.00	0.0	0.0	0.0	

MACHINE   282 CHARACTERISTICS

Year	United States	West Germany	United Kingdom	France	Benelux	Italy
		690510.00	0.11614E-06			
		150726.00	0.53204E-06			
1965	0.0	1.00	0.0	0.0	0.0	0.0
1966	15.00	1.00	0.0	0.0	0.0	

MACHINE   285 CHARACTERISTICS

Year	United States	West Germany	United Kingdom	France	Benelux	Italy
		696086.00	0.11520E-06			
		193785.00	0.41382E-06			
1966	12.00	1.00	0.0	0.0	0.0	

Table 4.11 (continued)

Year	United States	West Germany	United Kingdom	France	Benelux	Italy

HONEYWELL, INC.

10 MACHINES INCLUDED IN SAMPLE (160 MACHINE-YEARS OF DATA)

MACHINE 156 CHARACTERISTICS

Year	United States	West Germany	United Kingdom	France	Benelux	Italy
		28790.00	0.23390E-05			
		23760.00	0.28342E-05			
1960	3.00					
1961	33.00	0.0	0.0	0.0	0.0	0.0
1962	49.00	0.0	0.67	0.0	0.0	0.0
1963	57.00	0.0	1.00	0.0	0.0	0.0
1964	64.00	0.0	1.62	0.0	0.0	0.0
1965	86.00	0.0	2.00	0.0	0.0	0.0
1966	89.00	0.0	4.00	0.0	0.0	

MACHINE 190 CHARACTERISTICS

Year	United States	West Germany	United Kingdom	France	Benelux	Italy
		1354.00	0.10305E-04			
		2752.00	0.50701E-05			
1961	1.00	0.0	0.0	0.0	0.0	0.0
1962	34.00	0.0	1.33	0.0	0.0	0.0
1963	85.00	0.0	3.46	0.0	0.0	0.0
1964	105.00	0.0	8.48	0.0	0.0	0.0
1965	122.00	0.0	22.00	0.0	0.0	0.0
1966	115.00	0.0	13.00	0.0	0.0	

MACHINE 222 CHARACTERISTICS

Year	United States	West Germany	United Kingdom	France	Benelux	Italy
		110600.00	0.50767E-06			
		57750.00	0.97226E-06			
1963	1.00	0.0	0.50	0.0	0.0	0.0
1964	5.00	0.0	1.00	0.0	0.0	0.0
1965	16.00	0.0	1.00	0.0	0.0	0.0
1966	22.00	0.0	1.00	0.0	0.0	

MACHINE 235 CHARACTERISTICS

Year	United States	West Germany	United Kingdom	France	Benelux	Italy
		1770.00	0.13591E-04			
		6821.00	0.35267E-05			
1963	1.00	0.0	0.50	0.0	0.0	0.0
1964	9.00	0.0	1.62	0.0	0.0	0.0
1965	12.00	0.0	2.00	0.0	0.0	0.0
1966	12.00	0.0	2.00	0.0	0.0	

MACHINE 250 CHARACTERISTICS

Year	United States	West Germany	United Kingdom	France	Benelux	Italy
		1148.00	0.83838E-05			
		7027.00	0.13697E-05			
1964	230.00	2.00	3.46	0.0	1.00	0.0
1965	710.00	14.00	50.00	2.00	6.00	0.0
1966	1020.00	41.00	51.00	4.00	6.00	

MACHINE 264 CHARACTERISTICS

Year	United States	West Germany	United Kingdom	France	Benelux	Italy
		2175.00	0.67843E-06			
		4023.00	0.36679E-06			
1965	37.00	0.0	0.0	0.0	0.0	0.0
1966	148.00	0.0	1.00	0.0	0.0	

MACHINE 281 CHARACTERISTICS

Year	United States	West Germany	United Kingdom	France	Benelux	Italy
		12222.00	0.10498E-05			
		14332.00	0.89523E-06			
1966	22.00	0.0	2.00	0.0	0.0	

MACHINE 286 CHARACTERISTICS

Year	United States	West Germany	United Kingdom	France	Benelux	Italy
		5812.00	0.68989E-06			
		7618.00	0.52634E-06			
1966	27.00	0.0	1.00	0.0	0.0	

MACHINE 287 CHARACTERISTICS

Year	United States	West Germany	United Kingdom	France	Benelux	Italy
		2130.00	0.40648E-05			
		10907.00	0.79380E-06			
1966	60.00	2.00	4.00	3.00	2.00	

MACHINE 291 CHARACTERISTICS

Year	United States	West Germany	United Kingdom	France	Benelux	Italy
		2100.00	0.25063E-05			
		9526.00	0.55250E-06			
1966	360.00	3.00	8.00	1.00	3.00	

Table 4.11 (continued)

Year	United States	West Germany	United Kingdom	France	Benelux	Italy
DIGITAL EQUIPMENT CORPORATION						
4 MACHINES INCLUDED IN SAMPLE (74 MACHINE-YEARS OF DATA)						
MACHINE 209 CHARACTERISTICS						
		220.20	0.94690E-05			
		75.97	0.27446E-04			
1962	6.00	0.0	0.0	0.0	0.0	0.0
1963	22.00	0.0	0.0	0.0	0.0	0.0
1964	54.00	0.0	0.0	0.0	0.0	0.0
1965	55.00	0.0	0.0	0.0	0.0	0.0
1966	57.00	1.00	1.00	0.0	0.0	
MACHINE 232 CHARACTERISTICS						
		6338.00	0.50602E-06			
		12519.00	0.25619E-06			
1963	5.00	0.50	0.0	0.0	0.0	0.0
1964	85.00	2.00	0.0	0.0	0.0	0.0
1965	112.00	1.00	0.0	0.0	1.00	0.0
1966	116.00	1.00	2.00	0.0	1.00	
MACHINE 266 CHARACTERISTICS						
		1768.00	0.24496E-05			
		991.00	0.43702E-05			
1965	103.00	3.00	0.0	0.0	3.00	0.0
1966	580.00	14.00	42.00	0.0	9.00	
MACHINE 267 CHARACTERISTICS						
		68497.00	0.14051E-06			
		29571.00	0.32548E-06			
1965	36.00	1.00	0.0	0.0	1.00	0.0
1966	110.00	5.00	10.00	0.0	3.00	
GENERAL ELECTRIC COMPANY						
5 MACHINES INCLUDED IN SAMPLE (91 MACHINE-YEARS OF DATA)						
MACHINE 178 CHARACTERISTICS						
		6566.00	0.19541E-05			
		7131.00	0.17992E-05			
1961	38.00	0.0	0.0	0.0	0.0	0.0
1962	104.00	0.0	0.0	2.00	0.0	0.0
1963	172.00	0.0	0.0	3.00	0.0	0.0
1964	120.00	0.0	0.0	4.00	0.0	0.0
1965	138.00	0.0	0.0	5.00	0.0	0.0
1966	203.00	0.0	0.0	5.00	0.0	
MACHINE 245 CHARACTERISTICS						
		7472.00	0.17171E-05			
		15688.00	0.81785E-06			
1964	23.00	0.0	0.0	3.00	0.0	0.0
1965	90.00	2.00	1.00	5.00	3.00	1.00
1966	205.00	2.00	1.00	7.00	5.00	
MACHINE 248 CHARACTERISTICS						
		11485.00	0.13965E-05			
		22160.00	0.72376E-06			
1964	12.00	0.0	0.0	1.00	0.0	0.0
1965	50.00	2.00	0.0	2.00	1.00	1.00
1966	85.00	2.00	1.00	4.00	2.00	
MACHINE 256 CHARACTERISTICS						
		338958.00	0.26016E-06			
		253898.00	0.34732E-06			
1965	4.00	2.00	0.0	0.0	0.0	0.0
1966	18.00	2.00	1.00	0.0	0.0	
MACHINE 272 CHARACTERISTICS						
		24803.00	0.96988E-06			
		56623.00	0.42484E-06			
1965	20.00	0.0	0.0	0.0	0.0	0.0
1966	32.00	0.0	1.00	2.00	1.00	

Table 4.11 (continued)

Year	United States	West Germany	United Kingdom	France	Benelux	Italy

BURROUGHS CORPORATION

    1 MACHINES INCLUDED IN SAMPLE (29 MACHINE-YEARS OF DATA)

MACHINE 216 CHARACTERISTICS

	United States	West Germany	United Kingdom	France	Benelux	Italy
		114.30	0.54647E-04			
		437.20	0.14287E-04			
1962	55.00	0.67	1.33	0.0	0.0	0.0
1963	103.00	1.00	1.41	0.0	0.50	0.0
1964	203.00	5.00	3.00	0.0	2.00	0.0
1965	310.00	13.00	29.00	2.00	7.00	0.0
1966	315.00	17.00	23.00	11.00	11.00	

RADIO CORPORATION OF AMERICA

    1 MACHINES INCLUDED IN SAMPLE (35 MACHINE-YEARS OF DATA)

MACHINE 176 CHARACTERISTICS

	United States	West Germany	United Kingdom	France	Benelux	Italy
		323.00	0.27301E-04			
		1055.00	0.83586E-05			
1961	47.00	1.00	33.00	2.00	0.0	0.0
1962	180.00	5.81	32.33	59.59	9.33	0.0
1963	390.00	23.31	37.09	93.31	16.00	0.0
1964	540.00	28.00	62.31	103.00	20.00	0.0
1965	622.00	38.00	68.00	115.00	22.00	0.0
1966	645.00	40.00	68.00	132.00	20.00	

BENDIX CORPORATION

    2 MACHINES INCLUDED IN SAMPLE (76 MACHINE-YEARS OF DATA)

MACHINE 82 CHARACTERISTICS

	United States	West Germany	United Kingdom	France	Benelux	Italy
		57.34	0.41533E-04			
		30.25	0.78728E-04			
1955	0.0					
1956	22.42					
1957	54.00					
1958	160.31					
1959	161.00					
1960	197.00					
1961	194.00	0.0	0.0	0.0	0.0	1.00
1962	190.00	0.0	0.0	0.0	0.0	1.76
1963	164.00	0.0	0.0	0.0	0.0	2.00
1964	175.00	0.0	0.0	0.0	0.0	2.00
1965	166.00	0.0	0.0	0.0	0.0	2.00
1966	158.00	0.0	0.0	0.0	0.0	

MACHINE 175 CHARACTERISTICS

	United States	West Germany	United Kingdom	France	Benelux	Italy
		37260.00	0.80912E-06			
		17060.00	0.17672E-05			
1961	10.00	0.0	0.0	0.0	0.0	0.0
1962	18.00	0.0	0.0	0.0	0.0	0.67
1963	26.00	0.0	0.0	0.0	0.0	1.00
1964	28.00	0.0	0.0	0.0	0.0	1.00
1965	23.00	0.0	0.0	0.0	0.0	1.00
1966	25.00	0.0	0.0	0.0	0.0	

Table 4.11 (continued)

Year	United States	West Germany	United Kingdom	France	Benelux	Italy

MONROE-CALCULATING MACHINE COMPANY

    1 MACHINES INCLUDED IN SAMPLE (36 MACHINE-YEARS OF DATA)

MACHINE   144 CHARACTERISTICS

		4.84	0.23201E-03			
		10.30	0.10900E-03			
1960	5.00					
1961	70.00	0.0	0.0	0.0	0.0	0.0
1962	210.00	0.0	3.33	0.0	1.33	0.0
1963	336.00	0.0	6.32	1.50	2.00	0.0
1964	450.00	0.0	14.31	4.00	4.00	0.0
1965	580.00	3.00	18.00	11.00	4.00	0.0
1966	460.00	4.00	19.00	11.00	3.00	

GENERAL PRECISION EQUIPMENT CORPORATION

    2 MACHINES INCLUDED IN SAMPLE (76 MACHINE-YEARS OF DATA)

MACHINE   92 CHARACTERISTICS

		41.94	0.49716E-04			
		32.75	0.63666E-04			
1956	20.40					
1957	102.00					
1958	226.00					
1959	350.00					
1960	430.00					
1961	445.00	0.0	0.0	0.0	0.0	0.0
1962	400.00	12.67	0.0	0.0	0.0	0.0
1963	450.00	29.31	0.0	0.0	0.0	0.0
1964	430.00	28.00	0.0	0.0	0.0	0.0
1965	300.00	31.00	0.0	0.0	0.0	0.0
1966	136.00	33.00	0.0	0.0	0.0	

MACHINE   152 CHARACTERISTICS

		89.91	0.44596E-04			
		54.11	0.74101E-04			
1960	0.0					
1961	39.00	0.0	0.0	0.0	0.0	0.0
1962	67.00	2.67	0.0	0.0	0.0	0.0
1963	100.00	4.47	0.0	0.0	0.0	0.0
1964	98.00	6.00	0.0	0.0	0.0	0.0
1965	70.00	9.00	0.0	0.0	0.0	0.0
1966	65.00	10.00	0.0	0.0	0.0	

Sources: Permission to reproduce the data in this table has been granted by the various sources from which it was derived:

1. *Datamation*, for the machine characteristics (see sources in Table 4.9).

2. Nelson Hanover, for compilation of installations data for the United States, based in large part on: (a) Computer censuses in *Computers and Automation*: vol. 16, Feb. 1967; vol. 15, Feb. 1966; vol. 14, Feb. 1965; vol. 13, Feb. 1964; vol. 12, Feb. 1963; vol. 9, July 1960; vol. 7, May 1958; and vol. 5, Dec. 1956; copyrighted and published by Berkeley Enterprises, Newtonville, Mass. (b) Censuses of United States computers in *Automatic Data Processing Newsletter*: vol. 11, no. 17; Jan. 23, 1967; vol. 10, no. 16, Jan. 3, 1966; vol. 9, no. 18, Feb. 1, 1965; vol. 8, no. 18, Feb. 3, 1964; vol. 7, no. 17, Jan. 21, 1963; vol. 6, no. 17, Jan. 22, 1962; vol. 5, no. 17, Jan. 23, 1961; vol. 4, no. 17, Jan. 11, 1960; and vol. 2, no. 21, Mar. 3, 1958; copyrighted and published by Management Science Publishing, the Diebold Group, New York, N. Y.

3. *Automatic Data Processing Newsletter*, censuses of European computer installations: vol. 11, no. 23, Apr. 17, 1967; vol. 11, no. 12, Nov. 14, 1966; vol. 11, no. 1, June 6, 1966; vol. 10, no. 10, Oct. 11, 1965; vol. 9, no. 24, Apr. 26, 1965; vol. 9, no. 14, Dec. 7, 1964; vol. 8, no. 14, Dec. 9, 1963; and vol. 6, no. 24, Apr. 30, 1962; for installations data in the other countries.

For the European installations data, exclusive reliance has been placed on the Diebold *Newsletter* eight computer censuses since 1961 —as of December 31 for 1961, 1964 (except for the United Kingdom), 1965, and 1966 (except for Italy); and as of June 30 for 1963, 1964, 1965, and 1966 (except for Italy).[51] From these fairly detailed figures, year-end installations figures were derived directly or by interpolation from available data for from 1961 to 1966 for Germany, the United Kingdom, France, and Benelux, and for from 1961 to 1965 for Italy.[52] The assumption was made that all unmentioned models of early computer censuses indicated zero installations, so that the sample points for the analysis (listed as "machine years of data") included zeros for the earlier years, and sometimes zeros for all years for some machines and countries other than the United States. Only one machine, number 194, was excluded from the sample because no U.S. installations figures were available, although European figures were. In the analysis, which required that $\log_e$ of each variable be taken, 0 was in effect read as 1 by setting the corresponding value of zero items equal to zero.

For the analysis including the United States, the European Economic Community, and the United Kingdom, data for the European Economic Community were generated by adding over columns 2, 4, 5, and 6 of industrial production and installations data in Tables 4.10 and 4.11.[53] The last five firms are grouped together and are referred to as the miscellaneous corporations in the discussion.

Method of Interpolation

At various stages of data collection, interpolation was necessary to make the sample points of the analysis conformable. The two major cases calling for interpolation were for corporate financial data for which the year end was not December 31, and for machine installations data from non-December censuses.

Rather than simply specify linear (or log) interpolation throughout, I have used the data that are available to suggest the smoothing

51. By 1960, Europe was "at the state [of experience in application of electronic data processing] in which America was in 1954; the beginning," P. Reveillon "A Comparison of the Approaches to E.D.P. Systems in America and in Europe," in OEEC, *Integrated Data Processing and Computers*, Paris, EPA Project 6/02B, 1961, p. 295

52. Some estimates had to be made for early breakdowns of some corporations' lines of computers. These were relatively few, including for IBM: system 360 breakdown for 1965; NCR: between 315 and 315 RMC for 1966; and GE: breakdowns throughout were somewhat incompletely given.

53. Installations for Italy for 1966 were estimated simply as "no change" from 1965.

function between available values of the variable. Specifically, to determine an interpolated value for a variable x between time t_1 and t_2, the method used was to look at an observation at t_3 after t_2 (but not necessarily an equal interval of time) and check to see which of the following conditions held:[54]

$$\text{(a)} \qquad \frac{x_{t_3} - x_{t_2} > x_{t_2} - x_{t_1}}{t_3 - t_2 < t_2 - t_1}\text{.} \qquad \text{(b)} \qquad \text{(c)}$$

Condition (a) was taken to indicate that the data looked like an exponential function, so that interpolation was performed on $\log_e x_{t_1}$ and $\log_e x_{t_2}$. Conversely, condition (c) indicated the data approximated a log function, so that interpolation was between $e^{x_{t_1}}$ and $e^{x_{t_2}}$. On condition (b), or if x_t made e^{x_t} too large for the capacity of the IBM 1620 on which these calculations were performed (that is, $x_t > 220$), linear interpolation was used. Also, if either x_{t_1} or x_{t_2} was equal to zero, linear interpolation was used.

54. When "t_2" was the last observation of the sample period, the notation should be read as interpolation between t_2 and t_3 with t_1 being the additional observation time for determining the type of interpolation.

5

Implications for the Future

Two main issues were left unresolved in the discussion of foreign activity in Chapter 2. These involved the possible efforts of Britain's International Computers and France's Compagnie Internationale de l'Informatique in the development of a large scientific computer and an evaluation of the benefit to firms in the industry from a more fully integrated Europe. The empirical results presented in Chapter 4 can be applied to these issues.

Assumptions for Evaluation of Future Developments

The innovation implementation analysis has produced structural estimates of just the elasticities that are relevant to ICL's and CII's possible development efforts. In trying to produce a large-scale scientific computer, they will be endeavoring to approach the industry's current innovation possibilities frontier.

Investigation of this question, however, has little to do with the commercial success, or even viability, of these companies, or of the American firms with which they will be compared. For example, NCR has fared rather poorly in the innovation implementation analysis—it has nearly the lowest research elasticity combined with a low constant term in equation (4.14). Figure 5 (or Table 4.8) reveals that NCR has the lowest value for cumulative computer performance of any of the corporations considered. Yet it has intentionally concentrated its efforts in the business applications of computers, especially in financial and retailing areas. Thus NCR may achieve commercial success without pressing its research efforts to extend the technological frontier of the industry.

For CII, on the other hand, commercial success is not the objective in attempting to produce a really large computer—independent French technology is.[1] Therefore, a comparison of projected levels of achievement of computer performance for CII or ICL with the highest American achievement up to a particular year is a valid method of evaluating these development efforts.

For these comparative projections into the future, equations (4.9) and (4.14) will be used. The former provides for variations only in

1. Exploration of the historical background and economic-political ramifications of this type of independence is the objective of R. Gilpin's book, *France in the Age of the Scientific State*, Princeton, Princeton University Press, 1968.

the constant term; the latter allows the research elasticity to vary across firms as well. The prediction of maximum future levels of the computer performance index for each company involves the generation of future retained earnings proportions and research expenditure data for all companies, and the selection of $\Xi(t-1)$, as well as constants and elasticities for equations (4.9) and (4.14) for the European companies.

Primary attention will be focused on the results of research expenditure; retained earnings proportions will therefore be held constant throughout the prediction period. For the U.S. firms, averages were taken of g (in log form) over the entire period of the estimation analysis and over the previous three years (1964–1966). These were also compared with the g observed for 1966. In all cases the recently observed proportions were considered the most appropriate estimate to the future levels. The average over the previous three years results in gs of: IBM, .8167; Sperry Rand, .9947; Burroughs, .7636; and NCR, .8415. The policy of retaining all earnings is assumed to continue at DEC (1.0). For the remaining two, the 1966 value showed a decisive increase in distribution of earnings from the recent average; this is assumed to be a new policy decision, and thus the 1966 values of g will be used for CDC, .9880; and SDS, .9892. For Britain's ICL, recent data for the major parent company, ICT, was obtained from *Moody's Industrial Manual.*[2] The proportion of earnings retained was reasonably stable for 1964 to 1966, so that the average (.8587) will be used. Data for the other major contributor to the ICL venture, English Electric, were also checked to insure that its dividend policy was not drastically different from ICT's. *Moody's Investment Handbook* indicated retained earnings proportions for 1965–1966 in the neighborhood of .89; therefore the ICT average was accepted as the joint company's g.[3] No corporate data could be found for France's CAE or SEA, which were combined to form CII; its proportion will be set at 1.0 to yield the most optimistic computer performance results from CII's research efforts.

Research expenditure projections were obtained by different methods for the United States and foreign firms. Data for U.S. companies were extrapolated from a regression of the previous two years research expenditure (R), in log form, on time $(T = \text{yearly date})$ and a constant. Each regression covered the entire period over

---

2. *Moody's Industrial Manual: American and Foreign*, New York, Moody's Investors Service, June 1967, p. 1446; June 1966, p. 2471.

3. *Moody's Investment Handbook: Part One, Industrial Trustee Companies*, London, Moody's Services, Apr. 1968.

which the firm had been analyzed in Chapter 4. The extrapolation equation is

$$R = d_0\, e^{d_1 T}.$$

The resulting estimates of these coefficients are presented in Table 5.1.

Table 5.1 Coefficients of the R Extrapolation Equations for U.S. Firms

Corporation	$\log d_0$	d_1	R^2
IBM	−369.2	.194	.99
	(−54.)	(55.)	
Sperry Rand	−304.6	.161	.75
	(−6.0)	(6.2)	
Burroughs	−180.1	.097	.86
	(−8.7)	(9.2)	
NCR	−333.0	.175	.91
	(−11.1)	(11.5)	
CDC	−1756.8	.899	.95
	(−9.8)	(9.9)	
DEC	−620.9	.320	.98
	(−6.2)	(6.3)	
SDS	−1635.1	.836	.99+
	(−27.5)	(27.7)	

Note: In parentheses below each estimated coefficient is its t statistic.

The extrapolated figures for R display an annual rate of increase (of $\log R$) that declines slowly over the period from 1967 to 1979. These growth rates, as percentages for 1967 and 1979, are approximately: 1.56 to 1.31 for IBM, 1.39 to 1.20 for Sperry Rand, .90 to .81 for Burroughs, 1.56 to 1.31 for NCR, 7.68 to 4.00 for CDC, 3.66 to 2.54 for DEC, and 8.83 to 4.29 for SDS. The three newer firms displayed projected growth rates of R much greater than for the other firms; it seemed plausible that these rates might be characteristic of their early phase of entry into the industry rather than sustainable growth rates.[4] Therefore, one-half the predicted growth rates of R were also

4. A write-up on SDS by Standard and Poor in June 1968, for example, noted that 1966 expenditure on R & D represented a peak in proportion to revenue: 11.9 percent for 1966 vs. 8.5 percent for 1967. This fact lends support to the impression that recent experience up until 1966 may not represent the longer-term planned rates of growth of R & D expenditure. On the other hand, Max Palevsky, president of SDS, emphasized at the company's 1969 annual meeting that this expenditure was being maintained at about 8 percent of the firm's rapidly growing revenue. The merger into Xerox Corp. may contribute to SDS's ability to maintain sizable R & D commitments.

used for these companies to generate projected R values for the prediction period—this is the $\frac{1}{2}$ case for CDC, DEC, and SDS noted in the projections (Tables 5.3 and 5.4 below).

For the European firms, 2 percent and 3 percent constant rates of growth of research and development expenditure (in *log form*) were assumed to prevail (these are the 2 percent and 3 percent cases referred to below). These rates seemed appropriate in light of the estimated growth rates of the American firms' research budgets. Given the total research expenditure over a specified number of years, an iterative routine was used to determine the annual expenditure series, growing at the specified rate, that would yield such a total over the number of years involved. Then it was merely necessary to determine the total expenditure for each company.

For CII, the published figures in 1967 indicated that the French government intended to provide $80 million over a five-year period in research contracts and to loan another $8 million in development aid.[5] It was also expected that CII would put up about $98 million in addition, "to develop a range of four middle-sized computers."[6] But since these additional funds were referred to as "private capital . . . being put into the CII venture,"[7] and since the total gross revenue from sales in 1966 was only $34 million, the $88 million figure (implying total dependence on government appropriations for research) was chosen as the most likely amount that CII could make use of between 1967 and 1971.

It was widely publicized in 1968 that ICL would receive $32.4 million in research and development grants from the British government for a four-year period, and another $8.4 million for its 10.5 percent stock participation.[8] Since this company is quite large and has characteristically financed at least a portion of its research activities,[9] the assumption made here was that the government's research grants represent 50 percent of the total funds that would be devoted to R&D over the period from 1968 to 1971.

These basic total research amounts for each country have been

5. R. Mooney, "France Entering Computer Battle," *New York Times*, Apr. 15, 1967, p. 55.

6. "Computers: Green Light for Plan Calcul," *Economist* 223, Apr. 22, 1967, p. 379.

7. R. Mooney, "France Entering Computer Battle," pp. 55–56.

8. A. Shuster, "British Will Create a Computer Giant to Assist Exports," *New York Times*, Mar. 22, 1968, pp. 69, 79; J. M. Lee, "Britain to Finance Computer Merger," *New York Times*, June 12, 1968, pp. 61, 72.

9. See Chapter 2 for more complete descriptions of ICL and CII which help justify the shares of corporate and government support of R & D that have been assumed for this analysis.

converted to dollars at the 1967 exchange rates. On the assumption that expenditure on research in Europe goes further than does expenditure in American research laboratories, an additional increment of 30 percent was chosen to account for this possible difference in purchasing power for research (this is the $1.3 \times R$ case).[10]

With these total expenditure assumptions, the corresponding 1968 estimated expenditures for each company are presented in Table 5.2. All other years' figures can, of course, be derived using the specified growth rates. Most of these figures are above the $5.6 to $11.2 million minimum level of "defensive" research and development that Freeman terms the "threshold" level of R&D expenditure for the computer industry.[11]

Table 5.2. 1968 Research and Development Expenditure Estimates for CII and ICL (millions of dollars)

Corporation	2% Case		3% Case	
	R	$1.3 \times R$	R	$1.3 \times R$
CII	13.96	18.01	12.13	15.58
ICL	11.90	15.33	10.08	12.92

The R used for the European companies' predictions is, of course, the sum of the two previous years' research expenditures, as the model specifies. Thus estimates for two years prior to the periods mentioned above were required. Because the French efforts involve a relatively bigger increase in computer industry involvement under the *Plan Calcul* than does the ICL merger, it was assumed that the 1965 expenditure for research was one-half that predicted for 1967, and the

10. This extra value from a research dollar in Europe might result from lower salaries for research personnel (of course, *after* salaries are standardized to account for any lower quality caused by a "brain drain" to the United States). C. Freeman has commented in his "Research and Development in Electronic Capital Goods," *National Institute Economic Review* 34, Nov. 1965, pp. 40–91, that "research and development costs in America are probably $1\frac{1}{2}$ to 2 times as high as in Europe" for electronic capital goods. However, this category includes several products in which technology and trained personnel are much more prevalent in Europe than they are for computers. Therefore, a somewhat more modest adjustment seemed appropriate. See also C. Freeman et al., *The Research and Development Effort in Western Europe, North America, and the Soviet Union*, Paris, OECD, 1965; and E. D. Brunner, *The Cost of Basic Scientific Research in Europe; Department of Defense Experience*, 1956–1966, RM-5275-PR, The Rand Corporation, Apr. 1967.

11. C. Freeman, "Research and Development in Electronic Capital Goods," p. 69. Even for the figures that are very close to the suggested "threshold" range, subsequent years are well above it because the R&D expenditure figures are assumed to be growing.

1966 expenditure prediction for ICL was placed at two-thirds of the predicted 1968 figure. The 1966 and 1967 figures were calculated by the same rate of increase over the previous year that was specified for the case being explored.

As final input data for these foreign firms, lagged values of $\Xi(t - 1)$ had to be chosen to start the analysis. Two starting values were tried for each firm. As a lower bound, each was set at one [the $\Xi(t - 1) = 1$ case] to start the projections in 1966 for CII and 1967 for ICL. The other starting value was chosen in relation to the $\Xi(t)$ achieved by SDS and RCA, with which the foreign firms have been associated. Since the former Compagnie Européene d'Automatisme Electronique (now part of CII) had license agreements with SDS, CII's $\Xi(t)$ for 1966 was set at one-half of SDS's 1966 figure (that is, 447280). Similarly, ICL's was based on RCA's 1966 Ξ, since ICT has had agreements with RCA in the past and English Electric still did at the time of the merger. By setting ICL's 1967 Ξ at two-thirds of RCA's 1966 figure (that is, 894088), it was expected that the advantage of ICL (which had experience with major lines of computers both from ICT's developments and English Electric's) over CII in computer design experience would be represented.[12]

Equation coefficients for the foreign firms also needed to be selected. For equation (4.14), CII was assumed to have benefited from its association with SDS to the extent of having the same innovations implementation function; ICL was placed in the "small firm research" category and assumed to have the same research elasticity as SDS and DEC and a constant that was an average of those of these companies. Similarly, in using equation (4.9)—in which all companies have the same research elasticity—CII was given SDS's constant term and ICL received the average constant of the two small firms.

Resulting Projections

Projections have been calculated to 1980; I do not mean to suggest that conditions prevailing up to 1966 can be realistically extrapolated so far to determine the level of future computer performance. Rather, the method to be used probably will give reasonable comparisons between firms and will also indicate the magnitude of the research expenditures needed by the foreign firms after the period

12. The choice of lagged values of R&D expenditure was also made with this relative level of experience in mind. In fact, however, it turned out that the predictions are quite insensitive to the early research budgets or the choice of $\Xi(t - 1)$.

for which plans have already been stated. This latter result is an important aspect of the projection for ICL and CII, since annual research budgets have been assumed to increase at a constant exponential rate.[13] In other words, each of these companies' total of annual expenditures is derived by assuming that R&D expenditure, in log form, will increase at a constant rate of 2 or 3 percent per year.

It is now time to examine the projections of $\Xi(t)$, "cumulative computer performance" or "computing power," for the various firms and cases. These are presented in Tables 5.3 and 5.4 for

Table 5.3 Projections of Maximum Computer Performance $[\Xi(t)]$ Using Equation (4.9)

Corporations	1966	1967	1969	1971	1973	1975	1977	1979	1980
American								
IBM	15.1	15.7	17.0	18.3	19.6	20.9	22.3	23.6	24.3
Sperry Rand	14.5	15.7	17.6	19.3	20.9	22.2	23.5	24.8	25.3
Burroughs	15.0	15.1	15.6	16.1	16.6	17.3	17.9	18.5	18.9
NCR	11.8	12.6	14.1	15.5	16.8	18.1	19.4	20.7	21.3
CDC	15.8	18.1	23.3	28.8	34.6	40.6	46.7	52.9	56.0
DEC	11.6	12.3	14.0	15.8	17.8	19.9	22.1	24.2	25.3
SDS	13.7	15.3	19.1	23.6	28.5	33.8	39.2	44.8	47.7
$\frac{1}{2}$ case								
CDC	15.8	17.3	20.3	23.2	26.1	28.9	31.5	34.1	35.3
DEC	11.6	12.2	13.4	14.5	15.7	16.8	17.8	18.8	19.3
SDS	13.7	15.0	17.6	20.3	23.0	25.7	28.2	30.8	31.9
French and British								
2% case								
R								
CII	13.0	14.6	17.7	20.4	22.6	24.6	26.4	28.2	29.0
ICL		13.7	15.4	17.2	18.8	20.4	21.9	23.4	24.2
1.3 × R								
CII	13.0	14.7	18.1	21.0	23.4	25.4	27.3	29.1	30.0
ICL		13.7	15.7	17.7	19.5	21.1	22.8	24.4	25.2
$\Xi(t-1)=1$, R								
CII	0.0	3.9	10.6	15.6	19.4	22.5	25.0	27.2	28.2
ICL		0.0	6.2	11.0	14.7	17.6	20.0	22.2	23.2
3% case								
R								
CII	13.0	14.4	17.4	20.1	22.6	25.1	27.4	29.9	31.1
ICL		13.7	15.2	17.0	18.8	20.7	22.8	25.0	26.2
1.3 × R								
CII	13.0	14.6	17.8	20.7	23.4	25.9	28.3	30.8	32.1
ICL		13.7	15.5	17.5	19.5	21.5	23.7	26.0	27.2

Note: The values in the table are log $\Xi(t)$; the entries for U.S. firms in 1966 are actual values.

13. It is also reasonable to assume that only small research expenditures can be usefully employed at first; in later years the merged operations of these firms will be better coordinated and their research laboratories will have been expanded.

Table 5.4 Projections of Maximum Computer Performance [$\Xi(t)$]
Using Equation (4.14)

Corporations	1966	1967	1969	1971	1973	1975	1977	1979	1980
American									
IBM	15.1	16.1	18.0	19.8	21.5	23.2	24.9	26.6	27.5
Sperry Rand	14.5	15.5	16.9	18.1	19.1	20.0	21.0	21.9	22.4
Burroughs	15.0	15.3	16.5	17.8	19.3	20.7	22.2	23.7	24.4
NCR	11.8	12.0	12.8	13.7	14.7	15.7	16.7	17.7	18.2
CDC	15.8	17.4	20.4	23.4	26.3	29.2	32.1	35.0	36.5
DEC	11.6	12.8	15.9	19.3	22.8	26.3	29.9	33.5	35.3
SDS	13.7	16.8	24.5	33.2	42.4	51.7	61.0	70.4	75.1
½ case									
CDC	15.8	16.6	18.0	19.4	20.7	21.9	23.0	24.2	24.7
DEC	11.6	12.4	14.2	15.9	17.6	19.3	20.9	22.4	23.2
SDS	13.7	15.9	20.3	24.7	29.1	33.4	37.5	41.3	43.0
French and British									
2% case									
R									
CII	13.0	16.0	21.4	25.1	28.0	30.5	32.9	35.4	36.6
ICL		13.7	17.9	21.3	24.0	26.4	28.8	31.2	32.5
1.3 × *R*									
CII	13.0	16.5	22.5	26.4	29.4	32.0	34.5	37.0	38.3
ICL		13.7	18.8	22.5	25.4	27.9	30.4	32.9	34.2
$\Xi(t-1) = 1$, *R*									
CII	0.0	7.8	18.2	23.9	27.4	30.3	32.8	35.3	36.6
ICL		0.0	12.5	19.2	23.1	26.1	28.7	31.2	32.4
3% case									
R									
CII	13.0	15.4	20.5	24.7	28.3	31.9	35.6	39.5	41.4
ICL		13.7	17.3	20.9	24.3	27.7	31.3	35.1	37.0
1.3 × *R*									
CII	13.0	15.9	21.6	26.0	29.8	33.5	37.2	41.2	43.3
ICL		13.7	18.1	22.1	25.7	29.2	32.9	36.8	38.9

Note: The values in the table are log $\Xi(t)$; the entries for U.S. firms in 1966 are actual values.

equations (4.9) and (4.14). They suggest that, under the most favorable assumptions from the European standpoint, CII's machines could be equaling the performance of the most powerful American ones by the late 1970s;[14] ICL's machines would have somewhat lower performance characterizations but would also be among the most powerful in the industry.

14. Although the $\Xi(t)$ predicted in the tables increases year by year, in fact its values will form a step function as they do for U.S. endeavors. The first step (resulting from a newly introduced machine) can hardly occur before 1970, since these combined companies are the results of mergers that took place only a few years earlier. Hence one must conclude that if the European efforts catch up to U.S. machines' performance, it will only be in the 1970s, even if the predicted "crossover" of $\Xi(t)$ occurs somewhat sooner in the tables.

In large measure, this conclusion is the outcome of a much larger commitment by the French government to CII than by the British government to ICL. Even with the assumption that in France the entire R&D costs are covered by the government, while in Britain the company puts up half the funds,[15] the French expenditure for each year is higher. On the other hand, the assumption that CII is the same as SDS in research ability is very generous indeed. The assumption implicit in the "new firms" characterization for ICL, that it is somewhat less able to do research than is CII, is undoubtedly an underestimate.[16] Basing ICL's initial $\Xi(t-1)$ on RCA's with no account of the performance characteristics of its own 1900 series may also lead to an underestimate.

Table 5.3 assumes that all companies have the same research elasticity and indicates that CDC will still be making the most powerful computers in 1980 as it was in 1966 (although the $\frac{1}{2}$ case brings the actual figure for $\Xi(t)$ more in line with the other companies than was the straightforward extrapolation). SDS is in second place, except in the $\frac{1}{2}$ case and with the most expensive plan for CII, in which CII increases its research expenditures at the 3 percent rate and does, in fact, get 30 percent more research for its money in France than it would in the United States.[17] Under the more plausible 2 percent case with research expenditure buying equivalent amounts in both countries, SDS is quite a bit ahead of CII in computer performance and ICL is considerably behind them. Testing the sensitivity of the projections to the choice of initial $\Xi(t-1)$, the $\Xi(t-1) = 1$ case adjusts rather quickly to only slightly lower performance characterization by 1980.

For the varying research elasticities in Table 5.4, the adjustment from the $\Xi(t-1) = 1$ case is even closer to that achieved in the normal R case. In this table, the relatively low elasticity estimate for

15. The British firms have characteristically covered some of the costs of their research in the past, while the scale of research anticipated for CII is considerably above their past experience.

16. In developing the projections set out in Tables 5.3 and 5.4, it was clear that nearly any result could be obtained by suitable readjustments of the hypothesized data after looking at first-round results. Therefore, the approach used here has been to set out all cases for analysis once *before* looking at any results. The cases enumerated above were the ones chosen. It seems more appropriate to comment on possible relative overestimates for CII and underestimates of ICL than to redo the tables with modified assumptions to eliminate possible bias.

17. There is good reason to believe that such a high rate of growth of R&D expenditure is beyond the feasible range for either CII (i.e., through a policy decision of the French government) or ICL. The "3% case" implies annual expenditures by 1979 of four and three times (respectively) the dollar R&D expenditure for 1966 of IBM, the giant of the industry. The "2% case," on the other hand, yields expenditure predictions of about IBM's 1966 level.

CDC in equation (4.14) leads to a second position for it behind SDS within the American firms under the straight extrapolation, and third position behind IBM also under the $\frac{1}{2}$ case. Comparisons using the $\frac{1}{2}$ case assumption for new American firms put CII and ICL in second and third position behind SDS in all cases, except the 3 percent $1.3 \times R$ case in which CII is slightly ahead. It should be emphasized, however, that this comparison not only assumes no "technological gap" between American and foreign firms in the computer field, but even that CII and ICL get better returns from their research efforts than do most American firms.

The assumed expenditure for the research efforts to be undertaken by CII and ICL up to 1979 should be mentioned explicitly, since this prediction period goes beyond any period for which specific plans of expenditure have been stated publicly. These expenditure figures are presented in Table 5.5 for each case of assumed expenditure growth. As can be seen in this table, the difference between 2 and 3 percent cases amounts to over $100 million for CII for the four years to 1975, and to almost 80 million for ICL, which has been assumed throughout to be spending on research at a somewhat lower level than CII. The differences in the final period to 1979 are even more striking. It is also evident that, for both firms and both cases, the method used to extrapolate research expenditure implies at least twice as large an expenditure for the four years after 1971 as for the prior four or five years.

Table 5.5. Required Expenditure for Research and Development by CII and ICL
(millions of dollars)

Firm	Period of public statement	Initial amount	1972–1975		1976–1979		Entire period 1967 or 1968–1979	
			2%	3%	2%	3%	2%	3%
CII	1967–1971	88.0	172.5	274.3	416.9	1119.9	677.4	1482.2
ICL	1968–1971	64.8	144.3	220.1	343.6	874.0	552.6	1158.9

Note: "2%" and "3%" refer to the exponential rates of growth of research funds. The "cases" are described in detail in the beginning of this chapter.

As mentioned above, the elasticities assumed to be relevant to the French and British firm are the same or among the highest prevailing for American firms; this is clearly an upper bound on the elasticities that actually prevail. The assumption could be true only if there were no technology gap in the industry. Thus the estimated

R&D figure for either firm of over half a billion dollars as the price of catching up to the United States in large-sized computer performance by the late 1970s must be viewed as a lower bound on the required expenditure.[18]

Although the prediction results have been presented for equations (4.9) and (4.14), the more accurate representation of the research efforts of the various U.S. corporations is probably equation (4.14). This equation allows for the varying abilities of different research laboratories. It also may account for the extent of diversification of the interests of these laboratories, since, among the older U.S. firms, those most specialized in the computer industry are the ones with the higher elasticities. The basic difference displayed in the tables in comparisons of the domestic industry is the decline in the projected position of Sperry Rand and NCR and the higher ranking of IBM and Burroughs when using the elasticities of equation (4.14).

There are some interesting similarities between these results and the predictions made by M. J. Arachtingi, a Wall Street analyst, on the shares of U.S. firms by 1972 as suppliers of " very large computers and supercomputers."[19] IBM is projected to have 41 percent of this market, CDC is second with 28 percent, UNIVAC is third with 14 percent, and Burroughs is close behind with a little over 12 percent. This ordering conforms precisely to the relative levels of competence of American firms in producing powerful computers projected for 1972 using the $\frac{1}{2}$ case, except that SDS leads all the others. Thus the log $\Xi(t)$ figures for each of these companies for 1972 are: IBM, 20.66; CDC, 20.04; Sperry Rand, 18.58; Burroughs, 18.52; and SDS, 26.94. This comparison should not be interpreted as a prediction that SDS will lead the others in its share of the " supercomputer " market. It does, however, suggest that while Arachtingi's prediction of market shares is roughly consistent with this assessment of innovative achievement, SDS's share of this market may be underestimated.[20] The results in Table 5.4 also indicate that Burroughs will surpass Sperry Rand in the ability to design large computers after 1972.

To conclude, then, the projections for the 1970s for CII and ICL (in the preferred Table 5.4) put their predicted machine performance in the upper end of the ranking of firms, along with SDS, IBM, and CDC, by the end of the period.

18. By early 1969 CII may have decided to trade some future French "independence" for reduced research resource requirements—it extended its license agreement with SDS through 1975.

19. See G. Burck, "The Computer Industry's Great Expectations," *Fortune* 78, no. 2, Aug. 1968, p. 146.

20. The merger of SDS into Xerox could enhance the prospects for SDS's participation in the large-scale computer market.

Effect on Demand from Common Market Expansion

Let us turn now to the other issue mentioned in Chapter 2: an evaluation of the benefit to firms in the industry from a more fully integrated Europe. In Chapter 4, income elasticities of demand for computer installations were estimated, under two different assumptions,[21] for the major company in the international industry, IBM, as well as for some of the other firms. First, the country borders were considered the relevant horizons within which the users of computer services operated. The other case considered the relevant horizons to be large economic areas—still the United States and the United Kingdom, but now the whole European Economic Community combined rather than the individual continental European countries. The latter method produced income elasticities that were somewhat higher for IBM and CDC, but lower for Sperry Rand, than in the former case.

Under either of these formulations, the advantages of a more fully integrated Europe, that is, with the United Kingdom included, can be evaluated.[22] This is done in Table 5.6 for each of the U.S.

Table 5.6 Demand Increase from an Enlarged European Economic Community

Corporation	Elasticity[a]	Percent increase
IBM		
Country	2.103	72
US, EEC, UK	2.418	83
Sperry Rand		
Country	4.235	145
US, EEC, UK	2.422	83
CDC		
Country	3.361	115
US, EEC, UK	3.796	130
Average		
Country	3.233	111
US, EEC, UK	2.879	99

Note: Percent increase is based on the 34.3 percent increase the United Kingdom would have made to total industrial production for the European Economic Community in 1966. For each firm the first line gives the results, based on country data, reported in Table 4.6; the second line gives the results, based on the combined European data, reported in Table 4.7.

[a] Elasticities are based on the second formulation for each company, competitive influence $T(m)$ included.

21. In Chapter 4 these assumptions were stated from the firm's viewpoint; here they are stated from the perspective of the computer users.

22. The increase in size of I_k for the Européan Economic Community in enlarged form still falls within the range of industrial production covered by the estimation analysis. In 1966, the I_{EEC} was $99 billion; with the United Kingdom it would have been $133 billion, while the I_{US} was $271 billion.

companies for which estimates of the income elasticity were obtained under both assumptions. The estimated elasticities faced by the firms imply benefits in increased demand that differ by as much as a factor of two: IBM is estimated to get the least percentage increase in demand with a lower estimate of 72 percent, while Sperry Rand would experience a 145 percent increase in demand according to one of its estimated elasticities. As noted in Chapter 4, there may be an upward bias to these estimates; the conclusion to be drawn from these figures, then, is that although the American firms would certainly benefit from an enlarged, integrated European Economic Community, European firms that are able to participate in the industry could also expect the demand they face to double from such expanded market horizons.

6
Evaluation and Prognosis

From the results of this study, two types of conclusions can be drawn: those concerning the computer industry and, more generally, those concerning the adequacy of the model for new industries.

The model elaborated in Chapter 3 is based on the hypothesis that a country may have a comparative advantage in a particular industry because of the ability of firms in that industry to innovate. After a brief review of the facts known about the ingredients needed for innovation, a structural model was hypothesized in which the cumulative value of innovations by a firm are embodied in the characteristics of the product. The products are then produced, and they are marketed internationally in a setting in which each firm faces a demand curve with finite price-elasticity. The specific formulations chosen for the functions set out in general terms in Chapter 3 are identified in Chapter 4. It seems reasonable to conclude that the relations of the model that were explored empirically in Chapter 4 produced a good explanation of activities of the firms investigated; thus the model provides a useful framework for analyzing one new industry.

This industry, made up of the manufacturers of general-purpose digital computers, is classified as "new" because the technology necessary for production is available in only a limited number of countries. The domestic and foreign operations of the main American firms in the industry have been described and confirmed as compatible with the Kravis-Posner innovation/imitation approach, which provides the basis for the international aspects of the theoretical model. The comparative advantage held by the United States in this industry was also clearly established by that discussion.[1]

Following the model, the implementation of innovations in computers was studied measuring innovative achievement of firms by their maximum achievement in computer performance up to a specified year. It was firmly established by this analysis that, although the

1. Although the "industry" composed of general-purpose digital computer manufacturers considered in this study is by far the largest segment of the broader computer industry, there are firms actively developing other varieties. For example, in process-control computers American predominance is not as decisive; West Germany's Siemens (including Zuse) and Britain's ICL (including English Electric computers) are quite active in computer developments in this area.

elasticities of response in computer performance from research expenditure may vary across firms, all firms get increasing returns in potential improvement of computer performance from their research expenditures. However, through caution in implementing innovations, the effective response in actual computer performance may be inelastic.

Analysis of the demand curves faced by several of the American computer manufacturers not only confirmed the widely observed fact that there is greater demand (in terms of number of machines) for the machines of lower performance characteristics, it also determined that after this shift in demand is taken into account the price elasticities are negative and greater than one, whereas income elasticities are positive and often greater than two. There is reasonable evidence that American firms find stiffer competition in marketing computers at home than they do abroad.

IBM has made effective use of direct investment as a means of participating on a large scale in every major geographic market for computers.[2] Since computers are capital goods providing services over an extended period, and since they are new, relatively unfamiliar tools for many potential users, local support facilities for servicing and consulting as well as marketing are essential. Thus direct investment not only protects the company's latest developments in technology, it also provides the necessary presence of support facilities close to the users. IBM's operations have managed to combine coordinated worldwide efforts in research with foreign manufacturing subsidiaries that attempt to be responsive to the local country's national goals and interests.[3]

RCA, on the other hand, has depended on foreign firms—through license agreements—for the necessary local support for machines it has designed. Although it has used this method rather successfully in the past, the experience gained by foreign firms through these arrangements could be sufficient for them to begin independent participation in the industry.

Several foreign firms are making significant efforts. The Japanese government has for some time encouraged domestic activity by

2. Except, perhaps, for its participation in the developing Eastern European market. See "Toward the Computer Age," *East Europe* 16, no. 6, June 1967, pp. 9–12. This market is discussed further below.

3. Although these points were made in reviewing IBM's operations in Chapter 2, they were also emphasized by the vice president of IBM's World Trade Corporation during a symposium on Technology and World Trade; see E. S. Groo, "The Transfer of Technology Through Enterprise-to-Enterprise Arrangements," Washington, D.C., National Bureau of Standards Miscellaneous Publication 284, 1967.

allowing relatively little direct foreign investment; the industry has acquired new technology quite successfully through licensing agreements. Several of Japan's firms have had over a decade of experience in computer development and one, Fujitsu, is a completely independent computer designer and manufacturer.

In Europe, where such policies have not been used, the only important national efforts are those of France's CII and Britain's ICL. Their capabilities for developing a large-scale computer have been evaluated. The elasticities estimated for the innovative activity of the major U.S. firms were applied to obtain projections of future computer performance for the French and British, as well as the American companies. Although the indications are that the project of developing very powerful computers would be quite expensive, either of these two companies could expect to achieve this objective by the late 1970s if there were no "technological gap" between their countries and the United States in this industry.[4] But is there such a gap?

As noted in the introductory chapter, the wide-ranging discussions that have been directed toward this question seem to have confused the issue. Some people have claimed that there is a technological gap between the United States and particularly Europe, while others have responded that the gap is really one of sophistication in the use of management techniques. In the computer industry both gaps seem to be present,[5] but is the relevant gap one of technological prowess or one of ability to achieve commercial success in the industry?

The question of technological achievement can be viewed both as the ability to explore problems in new technologies and as the outcomes of these explorations. Chapter 5 assumed that the former

4. The analysis of Chapter 5, on which these statements are based, assumed that CII and ICL began their development programs in 1966 and 1967, respectively, and that both will be able to continue to finance R & D activities at the prescribed *increasing* levels. If either of these conditions has not held, or does not at some time in the future, the timetable for developing these very powerful machines will be lengthened.

It is interesting to view C. Layton's appraisal of the industry in the light of that analysis. He asserts that "the development of ... a European-based industry is becoming easier now that computer technology has stabilized. The hard place to catch up is not in the construction of central processors but in software" (*European Advanced Technology; A Programme for Integration*, London, Allen & Unwin, 1969, p. 198). Although his emphasis on software requirements is quite appropriate, minimizing the extent to which computer technology is still evolving and the difficulty (i.e., cost) of catching up in hardware development may be premature.

5. This point has also been made, for example, by M. A. Charguéraud, head of Diebold, Europe, S.A., "Abstract of Remarks at Meeting of Diebold Research Program," New York, The Diebold Group, Inc., Press Release, Oct. 18, 1967; and A. T. Knoppers, "The Technostructure Gap," *Interplay* 1, no. 9, Apr. 1968, p. 26.

ability for CII and ICL was no less than that existing in American firms in the computer industry.[6] With this assumption, the European firms were predicted to take about a decade, not to mention considerable resources, to catch up in the latter ability—to produce computers with superior performance characteristics. In the case of France's CII, there is little to support the contention of equal ability to explore problems in computer technology.[7] For Britain's ICL, the ability to explore such problems seems to be adequate[8]—both within the company and within the scientific community in general, which has been concerned with computer development at least as long as have American scientists.

Some firms have lagged behind in extending the maximum performance of their line of computers; this technical competence may have little to do with the ability to achieve commercial success. The establishment of public utilities, based on time-sharing by many users on a very large computer, has often been pictured as the predominant use for computers in the future;[9] such giant time-sharing facilities will undoubtedly materialize eventually and will require very powerful machines. But it is not at all clear now whether "eventually" is 10 or 50 years away; the former figure may be the closer.[10] In the meantime the European market for computers has particularly emphasized the smaller systems, and European technological ability to design such systems is well-established by the cases of European research by IBM (Germany), GE (Italy),[11] and ICT's

6. C. Freeman concluded in his 1965 survey of electronic capital goods that "taking the whole spectrum from applied research through development to final production and manufacturing, American firms probably enjoy little or no productivity advantage at the research stage; but their advantage grows the closer they get to manufacture, where productivity in most American industries is two or three times as high as in Europe," "Research and Development in Electronic Capital Goods," *National Institute Economic Review* 34, Nov. 1965, p. 68.

7. Also, France's high priority for financing such efforts was probably revised along with its postponement of the nuclear development program as an after-effect of the mid-1968 country-wide upheavals.

8. Its competence in electronic component technology may be lacking, however. See C. Freeman, "Research and Development in Electronic Capital Goods," pp. 63–67.

9. See, for example, G. Burck, "The Computer Industry's Great Expectations," *Fortune* 78, no. 2, Aug. 1968, pp. 142, 145.

10. Sales of time-sharing services doubled in the United States from 1967's $50 million level to $100 million in 1968. See W. D. Smith, "Computer Business Races On," *New York Times*, Jan. 6, 1969, p. 85.

11. To some extent, foreign subsidiaries can be directly beneficial to the "host" country when they undertake R & D locally. They may provide valuable experience for the domestic researchers who can keep in touch with the latest technology without emigrating, and may later join a national firm. A related point is made in the OECD report, *Gaps in Technology: General Report*, p. 41.

British designers (who are now part of ICL). Even when the "computer utility" is finally achieved, many small systems will still be needed as "terminals" for the central facility.

Thus, for commercial success, technological constraints are decreasing in their relevance. Management and marketing techniques may need improvement, and increased provision of servicing and software support seems essential. ICT's success, the acceptance of its 1900 series, is attributed in large part to its increased efforts in these areas. Changes in IBM marketing policies that may result from the 1969 antitrust suit initiated by the U.S. Justice Department would undoubtedly benefit foreign as well as domestic competitors. The possibility of commercial success would probably also be enhanced by the elimination of some of the problems of mergers between firms of different European countries. The present system actually makes it more convenient for an American firm to set up coordinated European operations than for European firms to merge.[12]

As a final aspect of the potential for commercial success of any of the foreign firms, the rapidly developing Eastern European market should not be overlooked. Within the framework of the model, most of these countries must be characterized as less technologically advanced in computer development than are Great Britain, Japan, France, or even West Germany. The Soviet Union and Poland are the only two countries producing modern computers.[13] Although the Soviet Union clearly has very good hardware in military and space applications, it has lagged behind in industrial applications; the last five-year plan was aimed at beginning to close the gap, but as of 1966

12. The system has, for example, given inadequate double taxation relief, thus hindering participation in companies across national boundaries. Although discussions of Common Market plans for encouraging larger corporate units have gone on for some time now, they have not yet produced major revisions of legal obstacles. See also Servan-Schreiber, *The American Challenge*, p. 108; and the discussion between E. W. Stone and J. J. Servan-Schreiber in *New York Times*, "Discussion: Europe Ponders Ways to Meet U.S. Challenge," Jan. 13, 1969, p. 65.

13. F. Brodski, "Electronic Computer Technology in the Polish People's Republic," trans. I. Agnew and reported in D. McDonald, ed., *Soviet Cybernetics: Recent News Items*, no. 22 (The Rand Corporation, P-3600/22) Oct. 1968, p. 49. While these two countries are the only ones producing digital computers, the East Germans, Czechs, and Rumanians have also displayed "increasing interest— and competence—in the field" (W. Holland, "Computer Production in Poland— Analysis," *Soviet Cybernetics: Recent News Items*, no. 22, p. 51). See also A. Galek, "Czechoslovakian Computer Technology," trans. I. Agnew and reported in D. McDonald, ed., *Soviet Cybernetics: Recent News Items*, no. 24, Dec. 1968, pp. 53–55; G. Rudins, "Soviet Computers: A Historical Survey," in W. B. Holland, ed., *Soviet Cybernetics Review*, RM-6200/1-PR, The Rand Corporation, Jan. 1970, pp. 6–44; and *East Europe*, "Toward the Computer Age."

their fastest computer was said to be only about one-fourth as fast as CDC's fastest system.[14]

Britain's ICL is continuing to develop a leading position in exports to this market, with encouragement from the British government; it has already been quite successful.[15] This contrasts with American expertise—U.S. firms are discouraged from participating in the Eastern European market by the requirement that individual licenses must be issued to firms for each sale made.[16] French firms have been pursuing licensing arrangements with two of the countries—by 1969, Bull-GE already had established arrangements with Tesla (the Czech manufacturing organization) and CII was in the process of negotiating one (for a machine based on SDS's technology) with the Hungarian government.[17]

The potential markets for computers in Eastern Europe combined, for European firms, with increased demand generated by a more fully integrated European Economic Community[18] suggest that technologically competent foreign firms will be able to participate successfully in the computer industry. Such participation may even contribute to European and Japanese ability to use computers in other technological endeavors.

14. "Russia Bets Its Future on Computer Know-How," *Business Week*, Aug. 13, 1966, pp. 92, 94. See also "Soviet Union: The Computer Gap," *Electronics* 39, no. 2, Jan. 24, 1966, pp. 92, 94; and R. W. Judy, "The Measure of the Technological Gap Between the Soviet Union, Eastern Europe and the West: The Case of Computer Technology," presented at the Conference on Trade and Technology Transfer to Eastern Europe, Washington, D.C., October 10–11, 1968.

15. T. Schoeters, "Soviet £2½ m. Order for ICL Computers," *Financial Times*, Jan. 3, 1969, p. 1; "West Pursues Fat Eastern Market," *Electronic News* 12, Mar. 21, 1967, p. 45; "Computers' British Jackpot," *Economist* 221, Dec. 24, 1966, p. 1347.

16. U.S. House of Representatives (Committee on Foreign Affairs, Subcommittee on Europe), *Basic Documents on East-West Trade*, Washington, D.C., 1968, p. 36; W. D. Smith, "Computer Makers and U.S. Government Agencies Debate Effects of Sales to Soviet Bloc," *New York Times*, May 26, 1968, pp. F1, F9. IBM's chairman, Thomas J. Watson, Jr., noted during the corporation's 1969 annual meeting that his company considered its products bound by this requirement regardless of the country in which they were produced. He also noted that the British have about 75 percent of this market.

17. International Newsletter, "Hungary May Build 'French' Computer," *Electronics* 42, Jan. 20, 1969, p. 196.

18. The income elasticity estimates from the demand analysis have been used to determine the extent of increase—a doubling of demand—that would result from the acceptance and integration of the United Kingdom into the European Economic Community; see Chapter 5.

Bibliography
Index

Bibliography

General

Abel, M. E. and F. V. Waugh, "Measuring Changes in International Trade," *Journal of Farm Economics* 48, no. 1, Part 1 (Nov. 1966) 847–861.

Abott, L., *Quality and Competition*, Columbia University Press, New York, 1955.

Ahmad, S., "On the International Supply of Capital Goods," *Indian Economic Review* 5, no. 1 (Feb. 1960) 1–12.

Ames, E., "Research, Inventions, Development and Innovation," *American Economic Review* 60, no. 3 (June 1961) 370–381.

Arrow, K., "The Economic Implications of Learning by Doing," *Review of Economic Studies* 29, no. 3 (June 1962) 155–173.

———, H. Chenery, B. Minhas, and R. Solow, "Capital-Labor Substitution and Economic Efficiency," *Review of Economics and Statistics* 43, no. 3 (Aug. 1961) 225–250.

Awad, F. H., "The Structure of World Export Trade, 1926–1953," *Yorkshire Bulletin* 11, no. 1 (July 1959) 19–37.

Balassa, B., "An Empirical Demonstration of Classical Comparative Cost Theory," *Review of Economics and Statistics* 45, no. 3 (Aug. 1963) 231–238.

———, "Tariff Reductions and Trade in Manufactures among the Industrial Countries," *American Economic Review* 56, no. 3 (June 1966) 466–473.

Baldwin, R. E., "The Commodity Composition of Trade; Selected Industrial Countries, 1900–1954," *Review of Economics and Statistics* 40, supplement (Feb. 1958) 50–71.

———, "The Role of Capital-Goods Trade in the Theory of International Trade," *American Economic Review* 56, no. 4 (Sept. 1966) 841–848.

Balogh, T., *The Dollar Crisis—Causes and Cures*, Oxford University Press, London, 1949.

———, "Factor Intensities of American Foreign Trade and Technical Progress," *Review of Economics and Statistics* 37, no. 4, (Nov. 1955) 425–427.

Bardhan, P. K., "On Factor Accumulation and the Pattern of International Specialization," *The Review of Economic Studies* 33, no. 1 (Jan. 1966) 39–44.

Barr, J. L. and K. E. Knight, "Technological Change and Learning in the Computer Industry," *Management Science: Theory* 14, no. 11 (July 1968) 661–681.

Bhagwati, J., "The Pure Theory of International Trade: A Survey," *Economic Journal* 74, no. 293 (Mar. 1964) 1–84.

———, "Some Recent Trends in the Pure Theory of International Trade," in R. Harrod, ed., *International Trade Theory in a Developing World*, St. Martin's Press, New York, 1963.

——— and H. G. Johnson, "Notes on Some Controversies in the Theory of International Trade," *Economic Journal* 70, no. 277 (Mar. 1960) 74–93.

Bickel, G. W., "Factor Proportions and Relative Prices under C.E.S. Production Functions: An Empirical Study of Japanese–U.S. Comparative Advantages," Institute for Mathematical Studies in the Social Sciences (Technical Report no. 148), Stanford, Calif., 1966.

Blondel, D., "Transmission Internationale des Innovations," *Revue Economique* 17, no. 3 (May 1966) 434–466.

Brozen, Y., "Invention, Innovation, and Imitation," *American Economic Review* 41, supplement (May 1951) 239–257.

———, "Trends in Industrial Research and Development," *Journal of Business* 33, no. 3 (July 1960) 204–217.

Brunner, E. D., *The Cost of Basic Scientific Research in Europe: Department of Defense Experience, 1956–1966*, The Rand Corporation, Santa Monica, Calif., RM-5275-PR, Apr. 1967.

Buchan, A., "Battening Down Vauban's Hatches," *Interplay* 1, no. 10 (May 1968) 4–7.

Cairncross, A. K., "World Trade in Manufactures since 1900," *Economia Internazionale* 8 (Nov. 1955) 715–738.

Carter, C. F. and B. R. Williams, *Industry and Technical Progress*, Oxford University Press, New York, 1957.

Caves, R. E., *Trade and Economic Structure, Models and Methods*, Harvard University Press, Cambridge, 1960.

Chenery, H., "Patterns of Industrial Growth," *American Economic Review* 50, no. 4 (Sept. 1960) 624–654.

Chipman, J. S., "A Survey of the Theory of International Trade: Part 1, The Classical Theory," *Econometrica* 33, no. 3 (July 1965) 477–520.

———, "A Survey of the Theory of International Trade: Part 2, The Neoclassical Theory," *Econometrica* 33, no. 4 (Oct. 1965) 685–760.

———, "A Survey of the Theory of International Trade: Part 3, The Modern Theory," *Econometrica* 34, no. 1 (Jan. 1966) 18–76.

Chow, G. C., "Technological Change and the Demand for Computers," *American Economic Review* 57, no. 5 (Dec. 1967) 1117–1130.

———, "Tests of Equality Between Sets of Coefficients in Two Linear Regressions," *Econometrica* 28, no. 3 (July 1960) 591–605.

Cochrane, D. and G. Orcutt, "Application of Least Squares Regression to Relationships Containing Autocorrelated Error Terms," *Journal of the American Statistical Association* 44, no. 245 (Mar. 1949) 32–61.

Denison, E. F., *Why Growth Rates Differ*, The Brookings Institution, Washington, D.C., 1967.

Devons, E., "World Trade in Invisibles," *Lloyd's Bank Review* 60, no. 60 (Apr. 1961) 37–50.

Douglass, G. K., "Product Variation and International Trade in Motion Pictures," Ph.D. thesis, Department of Economics, Massachusetts Institute of Technology, Cambridge, 1963.

Fei, J. C. H. and G. Ranis, "Innovation, Capital Accumulation and Economic Development," *American Economic Review* 53, no. 3 (June 1963) 283–313.

Fellner, W. J., "The Influence of Market Structure on Technological Progress," *Quarterly Journal of Economics* 65, no. 4 (Nov. 1951) 556–577.

Fisher, F. M., *A Priori Information and Time Series Analysis; Essays in Economic Theory and Measurement*, North-Holland Publishing Co., Amsterdam, 1962.

———, "Embodied Technology and the Existence of Labor and Output Aggregates," *Review of Economic Studies* 35, no. 4 (Oct. 1968) 391–412.

———, "Tests of Equality Between Sets of Coefficients in Two Linear Regressions," *Econometrica* 38, no. 2 (March 1970) 361–366.,

Freeman, C., "Research and Development in Electronic Capital Goods," *National Institute Economic Review*, no. 34 (Nov. 1965) 40–91.

——— and A. Young, *The Research and Development Effort in Western Europe, North America, and the Soviet Union*, Organization for Economic Cooperation and Development, Paris, 1965.

——— et al., *An Experimental International Comparison of Research Expenditures and Manpower in 1962*, Organization for Economic Cooperation and Development, Paris, 1965.

Friedman, M., *Essays in Positive Economics*, University of Chicago Press, Chicago, 1963.

Gilbert, M. and I. Kravis, *An International Comparison of National Products and the Purchasing Power of Currencies*, Organization for European Economic Cooperation, Paris, 1954.

Gilpin, R., *France in the Age of the Scientific State*, Princeton University Press, Princeton, 1968.

Grubel, H. G., "Intra-industry Specialization and the Pattern of Trade," *The Canadian Journal of Economics and Political Science* 33, no. 3 (Aug. 1967) 374–388.

——— and A. D. Scott, "The Immigration of Scientists and Engineers to the United States, 1949–1961," *The Journal of Political Economy* 74, no. 4 (Aug, 1966) 368–378.

Gruber, W., D. Mehta, and R. Vernon, "The R & D Factor in International Trade and International Investment of United States Industries," *Journal of Political Economy* 75, no. 1 (Feb. 1967) 20–37.

——— and R. Vernon, "The R & D Factor in a World Trade Matrix," presented at the Conference on Technology and Competition in International Trade, Oct. 11–12, 1968; Universities–National Bureau Committee for Economic Research volume, forthcoming.

Gustafson, W. E., "Research and Development, New Products, and Productivity Change," *American Economic Review, Papers and Proceedings* 52, no. 2 (May 1962) 177–185.

Haavelmo, T., *A Study in the Theory of Economic Evolution*, 2nd ed., North-Holland Publishing Co., Amsterdam, 1956.

Haberler, G., "The Relevance of the Classical Theory under Modern Conditions," *American Economic Review, Papers and Proceedings* 44, no. 2 (May 1954) 543–551.

Hamberg, D., *R & D: Essays on the Economics of Research and Development*, Random House, New York, 1966.

Hanover, N., "An Analysis of the Electronic Computing Industry," unpublished.

——, "Economic Aspects of Computer Use," Ph.D. thesis, Department of Economics, Massachusetts Institute of Technology, Cambridge, forthcoming.

Harman, A. J., "Innovations, Technology and the Pure Theory of International Trade," Ph.D. thesis, Department of Economics, Massachusetts Institute of Technology, Cambridge, 1968.

Heckscher, E., "The Effect of Foreign Trade on the Distribution of Income," *Ekonomisk Tidskrift* 21 (1919) 497–512. Reprinted in translation in *Readings in the Theory of International Trade*, Blakiston Press, Philadelphia, 1949.

Hicks, J. R., "An Inaugural Lecture," *Oxford Economic Papers*, NS 5, no. 2 (June 1953) 117–135. Abridged and with supplementary notes in his *Essays in World Economics*, Clarendon Press, Oxford, 1959.

Hildreth, C. and J. Lu, "Demand Relations with Autocorrelated Disturbances," Technical Bulletin no. 276, Michigan State University Agricultural Experimental Station, East Lansing, Nov. 1960.

Hilgerdt, F., *Industrialization and Foreign Trade*, League of Nations, Geneva, 1945.

Hirsch, S., *Location of Industry and International Competitiveness*, Oxford University Press, London, 1967.

——, "The United States Electronics Industry in International Trade," *National Institute Economic Review*, no. 34 (Nov. 1965) 92–97.

Hirschman, A. O., *National Power and the Structure of Foreign Trade*, University of California Press, Berkeley, 1945.

Hoch, I., "Estimation of Production Function Parameters Combining Time-series and Cross-section Data," *Econometrica* 30, no. 1 (1962) 34–53.

Hodd, M., "An Empirical Investigation of the Heckscher-Ohlin Theory," *Economica* 34, no. 133 (Feb. 1967) 20–29.

Hodjera, Z., "Technical Progress and International Trade," Ph.D. thesis, Columbia University, New York, 1964.

——, "Unbiased Productivity Growth and Increasing Returns," *Oxford Economic Papers*, NS 15, no. 3 (Nov. 1963) 244–265.

Hoffmeyer, E., *Dollar Shortage and the Structure of the U.S. Foreign Trade*, North-Holland Publishing Co., Amsterdam, 1958.

Hufbauer, G. C., "The Commodity Composition of Trade in Manufactured Goods," presented at the Conference on Technology and Competition in International Trade, Oct. 11–12, 1968; Universities National Bureau Committee for Economic Research volume, forthcoming.

——, *Synthetic Materials and the Theory of International Trade*, Gerald Duckworth, London, 1965.

Hume, D., "Of Money" in T. H. Green and T. H. Grose, eds., *Essays: Moral, Political, and Literary*, Longman's, Green, and Co., London, 1875.

Hymer, S. H., "The International Operations of National Firms, A Study of Direct Foreign Investment," Ph.D. thesis, Department of Economics, Massachusetts Institute of Technology, Cambridge, 1960.

Jewkes, J., D. Sawers, and R. Stillerman, *The Sources of Invention*, Macmillan and Co., London, 1962.

Johnson, H. G., "Factor Endowments, International Trade and Factor Prices," *Manchester School of Economic and Social Studies* 25, no. 3 (Sept. 1957) 270–283.

Johnston, R. E., "Technical Progress and Innovation," *Oxford Economic Papers* 18, no. 2 (July 1966) 158–176.

Jones, R. W., "Factor Proportions and the Heckscher-Ohlin Model," *Review of Economic Studies* 24, no. 1 (Oct. 1956) 1–10.

———, "The Role of Technology in the Theory of International Trade," presented at the Conference on Technology and Competition in International Trade, Oct. 11–12, 1968; Universities–National Bureau Committee for Economic Research volume, forthcoming.

Judy, R. W., "The Measure of the Technological Gap Between the Soviet Union, Eastern Europe and the West: The Case of Computer Technology," presented at the Conference on Trade and Technology Transfer to Eastern Europe, Washington, D.C., Oct. 10–11, 1968.

Keesing, D. B., "The Impact of Research and Development on United States Trade," *Journal of Political Economy* 75, no. 1 (Feb. 1967) 38–48.

———, "Labor Skills and Comparative Advantage," *American Economic Review, Papers and Proceedings* 56, no. 2 (May 1966) 249–258.

———, "Labor Skills and International Trade: Evaluating Many Trade Flows with a Single Measuring Device," *Review of Economics and Statistics* 47, no. 3 (Aug. 1965) 287–294.

Kenen, P. B., "Nature, Capital and Trade," *Journal of Political Economy* 73, no. 5 (Oct. 1965) 437–460.

Kindleberger, C. P., "Anciens et Nouveaux Produits en Commerce International," *Economie Appliquée* 7, no. 3 (1954) 281–297.

———, "*The American Challenge* by J.-J. Servan-Schreiber," *Journal of Economic Literature* 7, no. 1 (Mar. 1969) 113–114.

———, "Balance-of-Payments Deficits and the International Market for Liquidity," *Essays in International Finance*, no. 46, International Finance Section, Department of Economics, Princeton University, Princeton, May 1965.

———, *Europe's Postwar Growth; the Role of Labor Supply*, Harvard University Press, Cambridge, Mass., 1967.

———, *Foreign Trade and the National Economy*, Yale University Press, New Haven, 1962.

———, "International Trade and United States Experience: 1870–1955," in R. E. Freeman, ed., *Postwar Economic Trends in the United States*, Harper & Brothers, New York, 1960, pp. 337–373.

Knoppers, A. T., "The 'Technostructure' Gap," *Interplay* 1, no. 9 (Apr. 1968) 26–34.

Kravis, I. B., "'Availability' and Other Influences on the Commodity Composition of Trade," *Journal of Political Economy* 64, no. 2 (Apr. 1956) 143–155.

Kuznets, S., *Economic Change*, W. W. Norton, New York, 1953.

——, *Modern Economic Growth; Rate, Structure and Spread*, Yale University Press, New Haven, 1966.

——, "IX. Level and Structure of Foreign Trade: Comparisons for Recent Years," of the series "Quantitative Aspects of the Economic Growth of Nations," in *Economic Development and Cultural Change* 13, no. 1, Part 2 (Oct. 1964).

Lange, O., "A Note on Innovation," *Review of Economics and Statistics* 25, no. 1 (Feb. 1943) 19–25.

Layton, C., *European Advanced Technology; A Programme for Integration*, George Allen & Unwin, London, 1969.

——, *Trans-Atlantic Investments*, Atlantic Institute, Boulogne-sur-Seine, France, 1966.

Leontief, W., "Domestic Production and Foreign Trade: The American Capital Position Re-examined," *Proceedings of the American Philosophical Society*, Sept. 1953, pp. 331–349; *Economia Internazionale* 7, no. 1 (Feb. 1954) 9–38.

——, "Factor Proportion and the Structure of American Trade: Further Theoretical and Empirical Analysis," *Review of Economics and Statistics* 38, no. 4 (Nov. 1956) 386–407.

——, "An International Comparison of Factor Costs and Factor Use: A Review Article," *American Economic Review* 54, no. 3 (June 1964) 335–346.

Lewis, W. A., "International Competition in Manufactures," *American Economic Review*, Supplement 47, no. 2 (May 1957) 578–587.

Linder, S. Burenstam, *An Essay on Trade and Transformation*, Almquist and Wiksells, Stockholm, 1961.

McCreary, E. A., *The Americanization of Europe: The Impact of Americans and American Business on the Uncommon Market*, Doubleday and Co., Garden City, N.Y., 1964.

MacDougall, G. D. A., "British and American Exports: A Study Suggested by the Theory of Comparative Costs," *Economic Journal* (Part 1) 61, no. 244 (Dec. 1951) 697–724; (Part 2) 62, no. 247 (Sept. 1952) 487–521.

——, "India's Balance of Payments Problem," in P. N. Rosenstein-Rodan, ed., *Pricing and Fiscal Policies, A Study in Method*, M.I.T. Press, Cambridge, Mass., 1964.

——, *The World Dollar Problem*, Macmillan & Co., London, 1957.

Maddala G. S. and P. T. Knight, "International Diffusion of Technical Change—A Case Study of the Oxygen Steel Making Process," *The Economic Journal* 77, no. 307 (Sept. 1967) 531–558.

Maizels, A., *Industrial Growth and World Trade*, Cambridge University Press, Cambridge, England, 1963.

Mansfield, E., *The Economics of Technological Change*, W. W. Norton, New York, 1968.

——, "Entry, Gibrat's Law, Innovation, and the Growth of Firms," *American Economic Review* 52, no. 5 (Dec. 1962) 1023–1051.

——, "Industrial Research and Development Expenditures—Determinants, Prospects, and Relation to Size of Firm and Inventive Output," *The Journal of Political Economy* 72, no. 4 (Aug. 1964) 319–340.

————, *Industrial Research and Technological Innovation*, W. W. Norton, New York, 1968.

————, "Research and Technological Change," *Industrial Research* 6, no. 2 (Feb. 1964) 25–28.

————, "Size of Firm, Market Structure, and Innovation," *The Journal of Political Economy* 71, no. 6 (Dec. 1963) 556–576.

————, "Technical Change and the Rate of Imitation," *Econometrica* 29, no. 4 (Oct. 1961) 741–766.

———— and R. Brandenburg, "The Allocation, Characteristics, and Outcome of the Firm's Research and Development Portfolio," *Journal of Business—University of Chicago* 39, no. 4 (Oct. 1966) 447–464.

Marschak, J. and W. H. Andrews, Jr., "Random Simultaneous Equations and the Theory of Production," *Econometrica* 12, nos. 3 and 4 (1944) 143–205.

Michaely, M., "Factor Proportions in International Trade: Current State of the Theory," *Kyklos* 17, no. 4 (1964) 529–550.

Minabe, N., "The Heckscher-Ohlin Theorem, the Leontief Paradox, and Patterns of Economic Growth," *American Economic Review* 56, no. 5 (Dec. 1966) 1193–1211.

————, "The Stolper-Samuelson Theorem, the Rybczynski Effect, and the Heckscher-Ohlin Theory of Trade Pattern and Factor Price Equilization: The Case of a Many-Commodity, Many-Factor Country," *Canadian Journal of Economics and Political Science* 33, no. 3 (Aug. 1967) 401–419.

Minhas, B. S., "The Homohypallagic Production Function, Factor-Intensity Reversals, and the Heckscher-Ohlin Theorem," *Journal of Political Economy* 70, no. 2 (Apr. 1962) 138–156.

————, *An International Comparison of Factor Costs and Factor Use*, North-Holland Publishing Co., Amsterdam, 1963.

Moody's Industrial Manual; American and Foreign, Moody's Investors Service, New York, Annual.

Moody's Investment Handbook; Part One, Industrial Trustee Companies, Moody's Services, London, Apr. 1968.

Mookerjee, S., *Factor Endowments and International Trade: A Statement and Appraisal of the Heckscher-Ohlin Theory*, Asia Publishing House, New Delhi, 1958.

Moroney, J. R. and J. M. Walker, "A Regional Test of the Heckscher-Ohlin Hypothesis," *Journal of Political Economy* 74, no. 6 (Dec. 1966) 573–586.

Mundlak, Y., "Empirical Production Function Free of Management Bias," *Journal of Farm Economics* 43, no. 1 (Feb. 1961) 44–56.

National Science Foundation, *Research and Development in Industry, 1960*, NSF 63–7, Washington, D.C., 1963.

————, *Scientific and Technical Personnel in Industry*, NSF 63-32, Washington, D.C., 1963.

Nelson, R. R., "Big Technology, the Technology Gap, and a Dangerous Policy Pitfall," The Rand Corporation, Santa Monica, Calif., P-3795, Mar. 1968.

————, "The Link Between Science and Invention: The Case of the Transistor," *The Rate and Direction of Inventive Activity: Economic and*

Social Factors, in Universities–National Bureau of Economic Research, Princeton University Press, Princeton, pp. 549–587.

——, "The Technology Gap: Analysis and Appraisal," presented at a Conference in Turin, Italy (Nov. 1967), and published as P-3694-1, The Rand Corporation, Santa Monica, Calif., Dec. 1967.

——, M. J. Peck and E. D. Kalachek, *Technology, Economic Growth, and Public Policy*, The Brookings Institution, Washington, D.C., 1967.

Nerlove, M., *Estimation and Identification of Cobb-Douglas Production Functions*, Rand McNally, Chicago, 1965.

——, "Further Evidence on the Estimation of Dynamic Economic Relations from a Time Series of Cross-Sections," Cowles Foundation for Research in Economics at Yale University, New Haven, Discussion Paper no. 257, Nov. 1968.

Ohlin, B., *Interregional and International Trade*, Harvard University Press, Cambridge, Mass., 1933.

Okita, S. and T. Miki, "Treatment of Foreign Capital—A Case Study for Japan," in J. Adler, ed., *Capital Movement and Economic Development*, St. Martin's Press, New York, 1967.

Organization for Economic Cooperation and Development, *Gaps in Technology: General Report*, OECD, Paris, 1968.

——, *Gaps in Technology: Electronic Components*, OECD, Paris, 1968.

——, *Gaps in Technology: Electronic Computers*, OECD, Paris, 1969.

Ozawa, T., "Imitation, Innovation, and Trade: A Study of Foreign Licensing Operations in Japan," Ph.D. thesis, Faculty of Political Science, Columbia University, New York, 1966.

Polk, J., I. W. Meister, and L. A. Veit, *U.S. Production Abroad and the Balance of Payments*, National Industrial Conference Board, New York, 1966.

Pontryagin, L. S. et al., *The Mathematical Theory of Optimal Processes*, Interscience, New York, 1962.

Posner, M. V., "International Trade and Technical Change," *Oxford Economic Papers*, NS 13, no. 3 (Oct. 1961) 323–341.

Quinn, J. B., "National Planning of Science and Technology in France," *Science* 150, no. 3699 (Nov. 19, 1965) 993.

——, "Technological Competition: Europe vs. U.S.," *Harvard Business Review* 44, no. 4 (July–Aug. 1966) 113–130.

Robinson, R., "Factor Proportions and Comparative Advantage," (Parts 1–2), *Quarterly Journal of Economics* 70, nos. 2 and 3 (May, Aug. 1956) 169–192, 346–363.

Roesti, R. M., "The American Semiconductor Industry in World Trade," *Quarterly Review of Economics and Business* 3, no. 4 (1963) 49–58.

Ruff, L. E., "The Optimal Program of Research and Its Achievement in a Cournot Economy," Econometric Society Meetings, Dec. 1967.

Samuelson, P. A., *Foundations of Economic Analysis*, Harvard University Press, Cambridge, Mass., 1947.

Satler, W. E. G., *Productivity and Technical Change*, Cambridge University Press, London, 1960.

Scherer, F M., "Firm Size, Market Structure, Opportunity, and the Output of Patented Inventions," *American Economic Review* 55, no. 5 (Dec. 1965) 1097–1125.

Schmookler, J., "Bigness, Fewness, and Research," *Journal of Political Economy* 67, no. 6 (Dec. 1959) 628–632.

——, *Invention and Economic Growth*, Harvard University Press, Cambridge, Mass., 1966.

Schumpeter, J. A., *Business Cycles*, McGraw-Hill, New York, 1939.

——, *Capitalism, Socialism, and Democracy*, 3rd ed., Harper & Brothers, New York, 1950.

——, *History of Economic Analysis*, Oxford University Press, New York, 1952.

——, *The Theory of Economic Development*, trans. R. Opie, Harvard University Press, Cambridge, Mass., 1949.

Schweitzer, P. R., "Usher and Schumpeter on Invention, Innovation, and Technological Change: Comment," *Quarterly Journal of Economics* 75, no. 1 (Feb. 1961) 152–156.

Scitovsky, T., "Economic Theory and the Measurement of Concentration," in Universities–National Bureau Committee for Economic Research, *Business Concentration and Price Policy*, Princeton University Press, Princeton, 1955.

Scott, J. T., Jr., "The Measurement of Technology," *Journal of Farm Economics* 46, no. 3 (Aug. 1964) 657–661.

Servan-Schreiber, J. J., *The American Challenge*, trans. R. Steel, Atheneum, New York, 1968.

Shapley, L. and M. Shubik, "Price Strategy Oligopoly with Product Variation," *Kyklos*, 22, no. 1 (1969) 30–44.

Sharpe, W. F., *The Economics of Computers*, Columbia University Press, New York, 1969.

Sheshinski, E., "Tests of the 'Learning by Doing' Hypothesis," *Review of Economics and Statistics* 49, no. 4 (Nov. 1967) 568–578.

Simpson, D. and J. Tsukui, "The Fundamental Structure of Input-Output Tables: An International Comparison," *Review of Economics and Statistics* 48, no. 4 (Nov. 1965) 434–446.

Sohmen, E., "Notes on Some Controversies in the Theory of International Trade: A Comment," *Economic Journal* 71, no. 282 (June 1961) 423–430.

Solow, R. M., "Research and Development in the Synthetic Rubber Industry," *Quarterly Journal of Economics* 68, no. 1 (Feb. 1954) 61–82.

——, "Technical Change and Aggregate Production Function," *Review of Economics and Statistics* 34, no. 3 (Aug. 1957) 312–320.

Spoegelglas, S., "The Commodity Structure of World Trade: Comment," *Quarterly Journal of Economics* 75, no. 1 (Feb. 1961) 157–166.

Stobaugh, R. B., Jr., "The Product Life Cycle, U.S. Exports, and International Investment," D.B.A. thesis, Graduate School of Business Administration, Harvard University, Cambridge, Mass., 1968.

Suranyi-Unger, T., Jr., "What Is the Technology Gap?" *Interplay* 2, no. 1 (June–July 1968) pp. 22–25.

Svennilson, I., *Growth and Stagnation in the European Economy*, United Nations, Geneva 1954.

Time, "The Technology Gap," Jan. 13, 1967, pp. 18–19.

Tyszynski, H., "World Trade in Manufactured Commodities, 1899–1950,"

Manchester School of Economics and Social Studies 19, no. 3 (Sept. 1951) 272–304.

United Nations, *Standard International Trade Classification, Revised*, Statistical Office, Department of Economic and Social Affairs, New York, 1961.

————, *Yearbook of International Trade Statistics, 1963* and *1965*, Statistical Office, Department of Economic and Social Affairs, New York, 1965 and 1967.

U.S. Department of Commerce, *Technological Innovation: Its Environment and Management*, Washington, D.C., 1967.

————, *Technology and World Trade: Proceedings of a Symposium, November 16–17, 1966*, National Bureau of Standards Miscellaneous Publication 284, Washington, D.C., 1967.

U.S. House of Representatives (Committee on Foreign Affairs, Subcommittee on Europe), *Basic Documents on East-West Trade*, Washington, D.C., 1968.

Universities–National Bureau of Economic Research. *The Rate and Direction of Inventive Activity: Economic and Social Factors*, Princeton University Press, Princeton, 1962.

Uribe, P., H. Theil, and C. G. deLeeuw, "The Information Approach to the Prediction of Interregional Trade Flows," *Review of Economic Studies* 33, no. 3 (July 1966) 209–220.

Vanek, J., "The Natural Resource Content of Foreign Trade, 1870–1955, and the Relative Abundance of Natural Resources in the United States," *Review of Economics and Statistics* 41, no. 2 (May 1959) 146–153.

————, *The Natural Resource Content of United States Foreign Trade, 1870–1955*, M.I.T. Press, Cambridge, Mass., 1963.

Vernon, R., "International Investment and International Trade in the Product Cycle," *Quarterly Journal of Economics* 80, no. 2 (May 1966) 190–207.

Walters, A. A., "Production and Cost Functions: An Econometric Survey," *Econometrica* 31, nos. 1 and 2 (Jan.–Apr. 1963) 1–66.

Wells, L. T., Jr., "Product Innovation and Directions of International Trade," Doctoral thesis, Harvard Business School, Cambridge, Mass., 1966.

Yance, J., "Investment Behavior in the Railroad Industry," Ph.D. thesis, Harvard University, Cambridge, Mass., 1955.

Yates, P. L., *Forty Years of Foreign Trade*, George Allen & Unwin, London, 1959.

Zarembka, P., "Manufacturing and Agricultural Production Functions and International Trade: United States and Northern Europe," *Journal of Farm Economics* 48, no. 4, Part 1 (Nov. 1966) 952–966.

Zellner, A., J. Kmenta, and J. Drèze, "Specification and Estimation of Cobb-Douglas Production Function Models," *Econometrica* 34, no. 4 (Oct. 1966) 784–795.

Computer Industry

Amdahl, G. M. and L. D. Amdahl, "Fourth-Generation Hardware: A View from the Third," *Datamation* 13, no. 1 (Jan. 1967) 25–26.

Ash, L. P., "American and European Firms in the Third Generation of Computer Production," 1967, unpublished.

Barsamian, H., "Soviet Cybernetics Technology: XI Homogeneous, General-Purpose, High-Productivity Computer Systems—A Review," RM-5551-PR, The Rand Corporation, Santa Monica, Calif., Apr. 1968.

Belden, T. G. and M. R. Belden, *The Lengthening Shadow: The Life of Thomas J. Watson*, Little, Brown and Co., Boston, 1962.

Biffen, J., "I.B.M.: Strategy for France," *Statist* 190 (July 8, 1966) 113.

Boston Globe (Evening ed.), "IBM Too Big? U.S. Is Asking the Competition" (Nov. 22, 1967) 15.

———, "Laser Memory" (Nov. 13, 1967) 33.

Bourne, C. P. and D. F. Ford, "The Historical Development and Predicted State-of-the-Art of the General Purpose Digital Computer," *Proceedings of the Western Joint Computer Conference*, May 3–5, 1960, pp. 1–21.

Brodski, F., "Elektronnaya vychislitel'naya tekhnika v Pol'skoj narodnoj respublike" ("Electronic Computer Technology in the Polish People's Republic"), *Kibernetika* (*Cybernetics*) No. 3 (May/June 1968) 103; translated from the Russian by I. Agnew with analysis by W. Holland and reported in D. McDonald, ed., *Soviet Cybernetics: Recent News Items*, no. 22 (The Rand Corporation, P-3600/22), Oct. 1968, pp. 49–51.

Burck, G., "The Computer Industry's Great Expectations," *Fortune* 78, no. 2 (Aug. 1968) 93–97.

"Burroughs Corporation: 1967 Annual Report," Burroughs Corp., Detroit, Mich., 1968.

Business Automation, "Reference Issue" 16, no. 9 (Sept. 1969).

Business Week, "IBM Buys Its Own Sales Pitch" (Oct. 30, 1965) 140–146.

———, "Russia Bets Its Future on Computer Knowhow" (Aug. 13, 1966) 92–94.

Cattani, J., "Peripherals Growth Keys R & D at Philco," *Electronic News* Sec. 2 (Nov. 13, 1967) 50.

Charguéraud, M. A., "Abstract of Remarks at Meeting of Diebold Research Program," Diebold Group Press Release, New York, Oct. 18, 1967 (see also: *New York Times* (Nov. 29, 1967) 67, 76).

Computer Characteristics Quarterly, Charles Adams and Associates, Bedford, Mass.

Computer Consultants, *British Commercial Computer Digest 1966*, Enfield, England (1966).

Computers and Automation, "Impact of Integrated Circuits on the Computer Field" 14, no. 7 (July 1965) 9–10.

———, "The Computer Directory and Buyer's Guide" 17, no. 7 (June 30, 1968); 18, no. 7 (June 30, 1969).

Control Data Corp., "Annual Report, 1967," Minneapolis, Minn. (1967).

Dakin, T., "Marketing: Computer Colossus Expands in Europe," *British Industry Week* (Oct. 1967), 14–16.

Dale, E. L., Jr., "U.S. Accuses I.B.M. of Monopolizing Computer Market," *New York Times* (Jan. 18, 1969), 1, 15.

Datamation, "World Report; Germany Strengthens Computer Facilities" 13, no. 3 (Mar. 1967), 91.

———, "World Report: Philips Announces New GP Computer" 11, no. 6 (June 1965), 71.

de Bruijn, W., "Automation in Europe," *Datamation* 12, no. 9 (Sept. 1966) 25–27.

Desmonde, W. H. and K. J. Berkling, "The Zuse Z3; German Predecessor of the Mark I," *Datamation* 12, no. 9 (Sept. 1966) 30–31.

Diebold, J. and Associates, *Automatic Data Processing Newsletter*, Management Science Publishing, New York, "Census of European Computer Installations" 6, no. 24 (Apr. 30, 1962); 8, no. 14 (Dec. 9, 1963); 9, no. 14 (Dec. 7, 1964); 9, no. 24 (Apr. 26, 1965); 10, no. 10 (Oct. 11, 1965); 11, no. 1 (June 6, 1966); 11, no. 12 (Nov. 14, 1966); 11, no. 23 (Apr. 17, 1967); 13, no. 11 (Dec. 30, 1968).

———, "The French National Computer Effort," *Automatic Data Processing Service Newsletter* 11, no. 25 (May 15, 1967).

———, "Industry Notes—G.E.," *Automatic Data Processing Service Newsletter* 12, no. 11 (Feb. 5, 1968) 2.

———, "Japanese Computers—A Threat?" *Automatic Data Processing Service Newsletter* 8, no. 3 (July 8, 1963).

Digital Equipment Corp., *Prospectus* (Preliminary—July 18, 1966) for sale of 375,000 shares of common stock, Lehman Brothers, New York, 1966.

Dougherty, P. H., "Advertising: A Story behind I.B.M.'s Story," *New York Times* (Jan. 23, 1969) 77.

DP Focus, "A Report on the European Market: N. V. Philips' Computer Industrie Netherlands" 2, no. 5 (Feb. 1969) 106–108, 111; DP Data Publishing Co., Marlboro, Mass.

East Europe, "Toward the Computer Age" 16, no. 6 (June 1967) 9–12.

Economist, "Any Old Computers?" 215 (June 12, 1965) 1309.

———, "Approaching Multiple Access" 222 (Mar. 4, 1967) 850.

———, "Are You Making Micro-Circuits?" 217 (Nov. 27, 1965) 978–979.

———, "Aux Armes Citoyens!" 218 (Mar. 19, 1966) 1149–1151.

———, "Beeching-the-Brain?" 226 (Mar. 16, 1968) 87–88.

———, "Britain's New Computer Group" 226 (Mar. 30, 1968) 72–75.

———, "Burroughs: Very British" 220 (Sept. 10, 1966) 1058.

———, "Cash and Computers" 223 (Apr. 22, 1967) 368–369.

———, "Computers: British Jackpot" 221 (Dec. 24, 1966) 1347.

———, "Computers: Deuxième Affaire Bull" 222 (Jan. 7, 1967) 56–58.

———, "Computers: Eastern Question" 218 (Feb. 26, 1966) 824.

———, "Computers: Enough Cash for Now" 230 (Jan. 18, 1969) 78.

———, "Computers: Europe Fights Back" 219 (June 11, 1966) 1209–1210. (Correction letter: 219 (June 24, 1966) 1375.)

———, "Computers: GEC Opts Out" 222 (Feb. 25, 1967) 754.

———, "Computers: Green Light for Plan Calcul" 223 (Apr. 22, 1967) 379. (Correction: 223 (Apr. 29, 1967, 492.)

———, "Computers: Here Comes GE" 220 (July 16, 1966) 283.

————, "Computers: I.B.M. on the Brink?" 218 (Jan. 8, 1966) 122.

————, "Computers: On the Defensive" 214 (Jan. 9, 1965) 142.

————, "Computers: Rationalising" 224 (June 24, 1967) 1376.

————, "Computers: Why the Reticence?" 230 (Jan. 4, 1969) 46.

————, "Computers: World's Fourth" 226 (Feb. 3, 1968) 56–58.

————, "Europe's Electricals: Fighting Off Westinghouse" 229 (Dec. 21, 1968) 58.

————, "European Computers: The Money Runs Out on Philips" 220 (Sept. 10, 1966) 1048.

————, "£40m for French Computers" 220 (Aug. 13, 1966) 659, 662.

————, "French Computers: Independence Too Costly?" 229 (Oct. 26, 1968) 92.

————, "Micro-Electronics: American Challenge" 224 (Sept. 2, 1967) 807–808.

————, "Olivetti: A Choice of Strategies" 227 (Apr. 27, 1968) 78–79.

————, "Olivettis' Return" 222 (Feb. 25, 1967) 744.

————, "Sperry Rand: Univacuum?" 216 (Aug. 7, 1965) 556.

————, "The Technological Gap—in Russia" 230 (Feb. 8, 1969) 64–65.

————, "That's My Software!" 229 (Dec. 21, 1968) 32.

————, "Towards the European Company" 227 (June 15, 1968) 60–61.

————, "Who Exports Computers?" 271 (Oct. 16, 1965) 304.

————, "Who Leads Computers?" 216 (Sept. 25, 1965) 1228.

————, "Xerox-SDS: To the Rescue" 230 (Feb. 15, 1969) 79–80.

————, "Yapping Around IBM at Bay" 230 (Jan. 25, 1969) 67.

Electronic News, "French AEC Unit to Buy CDC 6600 and IBM 360" 11 (Dec. 26, 1966) 29.

————, "Honeywell Figures Indicate $910 Million World-wide Sales" 12 (Jan. 16, 1967) 52.

————, "Tokyo Subsidiary of Control Data Seeks Japan OK" 11 (Dec. 26, 1966) 30.

————, "West Pursues Fat Eastern Market" 12 (Mar. 21, 1967) 45.

Electronics, "Government: IBM and Antitrust" 42, no. 2 (Jan. 20, 1969) 54.

————, "International Newsletter: Addenda" 42, no. 2 (Jan. 20, 1969) 196.

————, "International Newsletter: Hungary May Build 'French' Computer" 42, no. 2 (Jan. 20, 1969) 196.

————, "Soviet Union: The Computer Gap" 39, no. 2 (Jan. 24, 1966) 187–188.

Evans, D., "Computer Logic and Memory," *Scientific American* 215, no. 3 (Sept. 1966) 75–85.

Fairchild, R. F., "French EDP Independence Leans Heavily on U.S. Support," *Electronic News* 11 (Dec. 26, 1966) 29.

Farnsworth, C. H., "Computer Builders in Europe Pressed to Challenge IBM," *New York Times* (Feb. 1, 1969) 37, 41.

Finke, W. W., "Computers: Yesterday, Today, and Tomorrow," *Credit and Financial Management* 68 (Jan. 1966) 18–20.

Forbes, "Anatomy of a Turnaround" 102, no. 9 (Nov. 1, 1968) 25–30.

————, "GE's Edsel?" and "GE's Computer Troubles—How They Happened" 99 (Apr. 1967) 21–23, 23–26.

Fortune, "The Battle of the Computer Marketeers" 71, no. 1 (Jan. 1965) 171–172.

France, Boyd, *I.B.M. in France,* National Planning Association, Washington, D.C., 1961.

Galek, A., "Vychislitel'naya tekhnika Chekhoslouakii," ("Czechoslovakian Computer Technology"), *Radio,* no. 9 (Sept. 1968) 9; translated by I. Agnew with analysis by W. Holland and reported in D. McDonald, ed., *Soviet Cybernetics: Recent News Items,* no. 24, P-3600/24, The Rand Corporation, Santa Monica, Calif., Dec. 1968, 53–56.

Garrison, L., "France Is Alarmed over the Inroads of U.S. Computers," *New York Times* (Mar. 30, 1968) 43, 53.

Gee-Smyth, S., "Computer Companies Fight for EEC Market," *European Community,* no. 97 (Oct. 1966) 12–13.

Glinski, G. S., "Computing in Canada," *Datamation* 11, no. 5 (May 1965) 38–39.

Groo, E. S., "The Transfer of Technology through Enterprise-to-Enterprise Arrangements," in R. L. Stern, ed., *Technology and World Trade; Proceedings of a Symposium,* National Bureau of Standards Miscellaneous Publication 284, Washington, D.C., 1967.

Gruenberger, F., "Editors' Readout—.06 Idea per Kilo Man Year, A Guest Editorial," *Datamation* 8, no. 9 (Sept. 1962) 23.

Gunton, M., "Industry in Britain Growing Despite Step-child Treatment," *Electronic News* 12 (Mar 21, 1967) 46.

———, "Peripheral Trends in the U.K.," *Electronic News,* Section 2 (Nov. 13, 1967) 52.

Hayden Stone, Inc., "A Report on Scientific Data Systems, Inc. "Investment Research Department, Boston, 1965.

Hirsch, P., "Software Patent Future Murky Despite Recent Count Decision," *Datamation* 15, no. 1 (Jan. 1969) 78.

Knight, K. E., "Changes in Computer Performance: A Historical View," *Datamation* 12, no. 9 (Sept. 1966) 40–54.

———, "Evolving Computer Performance 1963–1967," 14, no. 1 (Jan. 1968) 31–35.

———, "A Study of Technological Innovation—The Evolution of Digital Computers," Ph.D. dissertation, Carnegie Institute of Technology, Pittsburgh, 1963.

Lee, J. M., "Britain to Finance Computer Merger," *New York Times* (June 12, 1968) 61, 72.

———, "Europeans Weigh Bigger Mergers," *New York Times* (Mar. 11, 1968) 59, 64.

London Stock Exchange, *The Stock Exchange Official Year-Book* 2, Thomas Skinner and Co., London, 1967.

Los Angeles Times, "Business & Finance; Briefly Told—Burroughs," Part 3 (Jan. 16, 1969) 13.

———, "Business & Finance; Briefly Told—Honeywell," Part 3 (Jan. 13, 1969) 11.

———, "Company Formed," Part 3 (Jan. 25, 1969) 9.

McCarthy, J., "Information," *Scientific American* 215, no. 3 (Sept. 1966) 65–72.

McInnes, N., "No Monopoly on Brains; Competition Has Sharpened in the Fast-Growing Foreign Market for Computers," *Barrons* 46 (Oct. 31, 1966) 9, 14–15.

Main, J., "Computer Time-Sharing—Every Man at the Console," *Fortune* 76, no. 2 (Aug. 1967) 88–91ff.

Merrill Lynch, Pierce, Fenner and Smith, Inc., "Investing in the Computer Industry," Securities Research Division, Boston, 1967.

Mooney, R., "France Entering Computer Battle," *New York Times* (Apr. 15, 1967) 55–56.

————, "U.S. to Drop Ban on Sale of Computers to France," *New York Times* (Oct. 22, 1966) 37, 47.

New York Times, "Common Market Plans Action to Spur Big Corporate Units" (Feb. 6, 1967) 41.

————, "Companies Slate Merger in France" (Sept. 14, 1967).

————, "Computers: The Ink Is Now Black" (Jan. 8, 1968) 78.

————, "Discussion: Europe Ponders Way to Meet U.S. Challenge" (Jan. 13, 1969) 65–66.

———— "Former G.E. Chief Tells How I.B.M. Won on Computers" (Oct. 14, 1967) 31, 36.

————, "G.E. Gets Control of Machines Bull" (May 30, 1967) 25–26.

————, "Has IBM Spoiled the Computer Business for Others? Let's Look at the Record ..." [advertisement] (Jan. 22, 1969) 20–21.

Newsweek, "Where the Brains Are" (Jan. 29, 1968) 57.

Pantages, A., "Control Data Puts Legal Money Where Its Mouth Was ... Sues IBM," *Datamation* 15, no. 1 (Jan. 1969) 78–79.

Reckert, C. M., "Burroughs Profit at Record in 1968," *New York Times* (Jan. 16, 1969) 55, 81.

————, "I.B.M. Earnings up 43.7% in Year," *New York Times* (Jan. 17, 1969) 37, 43.

Reveillon, P., "A Comparison of the Approach to E.D.P. Systems in America and in Europe,": in OEEC, *Integrated Data Processing and Computers*, EPA Project 6/02B, Paris, 1961.

Rudins, G., "Soviet Computers: A Historical Survey," in W. B. Holland, ed., *Soviet Cybernetics Review*, RM-6200/1-PR, The Rand Corporation, Santa Monica, Calif. (Jan. 1970) 6–44.

Schoeters, T., "Soviet £21½ m Order for ICL Computers," *Financial Times* (Jan. 3, 1969) 1.

Schonberger, E. A., "Xerox-SDS: Marriage That Was Meant to Be?" *Los Angeles Times*, Part 3 (Feb. 11, 1969) 13.

Schussel, G., "IBM vs. REMRAND (Part 1—The Early Struggle; Part 2)," *Datamation* 11 (Part 1) no. 5 (May 1965) 54–57; (Part 2) no. 6 (June 1965) 58–66.

"Scientific Data Systems 1968 Annual Report," Scientific Data Systems, El Segundo, Calif., 1969

Shuster, A., "British Will Create a Computer Giant to Assist Exports," *New York Times* (Mar. 22, 1968) 69, 79.

Siekman, P., "In Electronics, the Big Stakes Ride on Tiny Chips," *Fortune* 73, no. 6 (June 1966) 120–125 ff.

Smith, G., "N.C.R. Unveils New Data Series," *New York Times* (Mar. 6, 1968) 61, 72.

———, "Xerox Joins Computer Industry," *New York Times* (Mar. 16, 1969) 67, 72.

Smith, W. D., "Britain Presses Drive to Develop Her Own Data Industry," *New York Times* (Oct. 22, 1966) 37, 43.

———, "Competitors Unsure I.B.M. Should be Split," *New York Times* (Jan. 26, 1969 Sunday ed.) 1F, 5F.

———, "Computer Business Races On," *New York Times* (Jan. 6, 1969) 85.

———, "Computer Makers and U.S. Government Agencies Debate Effects of Sales to Soviet Bloc," *New York Times* (May 26, 1968 Sunday ed.), F1, F9.

———, "Computers: Instruments for Change," *New York Times* (Jan. 9, 1967) 135, 137.

———, "Honeywell Plans Data Servicing," *New York Times* (Jan. 29, 1969) 49.

———, "I.B.M. Battle Is Joined; Antitrust Suit Challenges the Giant in World's Fastest Growing Industry," *New York Times* (Jan. 21, 1969) 61, 68.

———, "I.B.M. Confirms Antitrust Unit Is Studying Computer Industry," *New York Times* (Feb. 1, 1967) 47, 51.

———, "New Team at G.E. Is Optimistic," *New York Times* (Jan. 23, 1969) 65, 67.

———, "R.C.A. to Sell Large Computers," *New York Times* (Feb. 26, 1969) 61.

Standard and Poor's Corp., "Scientific Data Systems," *Standard Listed Stock Reports* 35, no. 123, section 2 (June 26, 1968) 1987.

Statist. "Computers; Groundwork for the Seventies" 190 (Aug. 26, 1966) 532.

——— "Computers; Keeping Japan's Own Industry Going" 190, Supplement (Dec. 30, 1966) 11–13.

———, "Honeywell Controls; Changing Gear in Europe" 191 (Mar. 3, 1967) 414.

———, "Unilever; Almost a Double First" 191 (Mar. 3, 1967) 414.

Steiger, P. E., "Xerox to Pay $930 Million for Scientific Data Systems," *Los Angeles Times*, Part 3 (Feb. 8, 1969) 8–9.

Stiefel, R. C., "Computers Large or Small? In Which Direction Will They Go?" *Computers and Automation* 15, no. 11 (Nov. 1966) 18–19.

Time, "Computers; Down to the Corner Store" (Mar. 15, 1968) 85A-B.

———, "Computers: Successful Stripling" (May 17, 1968) 91–92.

———, "Computers: Tackling IBM" (Dec. 20, 1968) 77–78.

———, "Industry: The Long-Term View from the 29th Floor" (Dec. 29, 1967) 56–59.

Tomaszewski, W., "Color Memory in Computers?" *New York Times*, Business and Financial Section (Nov. 26, 1967) 1, 9.

Trumbull, R., "Mergers Reshaping Japanese Industry," *New York Times* (May 2, 1968), 67.

Tugendhat, C., "IBM's World-Wide Research Organization: Wary Eye on the Problems of National Pride," *Financial Times* (Jan. 3, 1969) 14.

Value Line Selection and Opinion, "E.D.P. Industry" 23, no. 12 (Jan. 5, 1968) 164.

Vichnevetsky, R., "For Easy Rapport between Man and Machine, There's Nothing Quite Like an Analog Computer," *New York Times* (Jan. 9, 1967) 140.

Wall Street Journal, "Former Bank of England Head Named Chairman of IBM Unit" (Sept. 19, 1967).

———, "GE, Japanese Firms Deadlocked on Plans for Computer Concern" (Aug. 24, 1967) 18.

Western, J., "With Computers, Sales Pitch is for 'Software'," *National Observer* (Feb. 6, 1967) 1, 20.

White, C., "European EDP: The View from England," *Datamation* 12, no. 9 (Sept. 1966) 22–24.

Wierzynski, G. H., "GE's $200 Million Ticket to France," *Fortune* 15, no. 6 (June 1, 1967) 92–95 ff.

Wise, T. A., "Control Data's Magnificent Fumble," *Fortune* 74, no. 4 (Apr. 1966) 165ff.

———, "I: I.B.M.'s $5,000,000,000 Gamble," and "II: The Rocky Road to the Marketplace," *Fortune* 74, nos. 4 and 5 (Sept. and Oct. 1966) 118ff., 138ff.

Wood, R. E., "Control Data Sues IBM on Antitrust Violation Charges," *Los Angeles Times* (Dec. 12, 1968) 15, 17.

Index

Acquisition and mergers of
  computer companies
Burroughs, 15
CDC, 11, 14
El-Tronics, 9
General Electric, 22–25
Honeywell, 13–14, 25
Litton, 11
NCR, 15
problems for European
  companies, 37n, 38, 149 and n
Sperry Rand, 6–7, 13
Underwood, 9
See also Compagnie
  Internationale de
  l'Informatique; Direct
  investment; International
  Computers, Ltd.; Philips;
  Siemens and Halske
Aiken, H. H., 6
Allgemeine Elektrizitäts-Ges
  (AEG), 24, 31
See also General Electric;
  Telefunken
Alwac Corporation, 9
Arachtingi, M. J., 142
Argentina, 61t, 62n
Arrow, K., on learning by doing,
  44n, 91, 92t, 93
Baring, G. R. S., 22
Barr, J. L., 70n
Bendix Corporation
  component of "Miscellaneous
    Corps." demand equations,
    99t, 101
  computer division acquired by
    CDC, 11, 14
  demand analysis data, 128t
Benelux countries
  computer firm activities in
    Dutch firms, 30–31, 61t
    U.S. firms, 20, 27
  computer use in, 19
  demand analysis data
    computer installations,
      121–129t
    industrial production, 119t, 120
  See also Philips
Blondel, D., 59n
"Brain drain," 21, 136 and n, 148n

British General Electric, *see*
  General Electric Co.—British
  (GEC)
Brunner, E. D., 136n
Bull, *see* Compagnie des Machines
  Bull; General Electric Co.
  (GE)
Bunker Ramo, 29
Burroughs Corporation
  background
    computer producer, 8n, 15
    foreign operations, 27
  computer performance
    (maximum)
    achievements, 91f, 110t
    projections, 138–139t, 142
  demand analysis
    data, 128t
    equations (component of
      "Miscellaneous Corps."),
      99t, 101
  innovative activity analysis
    data, 106, 110t, 114
    discussion, 76–93 *passim*
    equations, 76–77, 78t, 81t, 82,
      84t, 86–89t, 90, 92t
    time period of analysis, 75t
  projected share of
    "supercomputer" market,
    142
  R & D expenditures
    data, 104, 106, 110t
    elasticity of performance, 83,
      86t, 88–89t, 90
    growth projection, 133–134, 134t
  retained earnings
    data, 110t
    elasticity of performance,
      80–81, 86t
    proportion, 68, 133
CAE, *see* Compagnie Européene
  d'Automatisme Electronique
Cairncross, A. K., 2n
Canada, 19 and n, 61t
Caves, R. E., 39n
CDC, *see* Control Data Corp.
CEIR, 14
  See also Control Data Corp.
Century series, *see* National Cash
  Register

Selected Rand Books

Arrow, Kenneth J., and Marvin Hoffenberg, *A Time Series Analysis of Interindustry Demands*, North-Holland Publishing Co., Amsterdam, 1959.

Baum, Warren C., *The French Economy and The State*, Princeton University Press, Princeton, New Jersey, 1958.

Becker, Abraham S., *Soviet National Income 1958–1964*, University of California Press, Berkeley and Los Angeles, 1969.

Bellman, Richard E., *Adaptive Control Processes: A Guided Tour*, Princeton University Press, Princeton, New Jersey, 1961.

———(ed.), *Mathematical Optimization Techniques*, University of California Press, Los Angeles, 1963.

———, Robert E. Kalaba, and Jo Ann Lockett, *Numerical Inversion of the Laplace Transform*, Volume 4, American Elsevier Publishing Co., New York, 1966.

Bergson, Abram, *The Real National Income of Soviet Russia Since 1928*, Harvard University Press, Cambridge, Massachusetts, 1961.

———, and Hans Heymann, Jr., *Soviet National Income and Product, 1940–48*, Columbia University Press, New York, 1954.

Chapman, Janet G., *Real Wages in Soviet Russia Since 1928*, Harvard University Press, Cambridge, Massachusetts, 1963.

Dole, Stephen H., and Isaac Asimov, *Planets for Man*, Random House, Inc., New York, 1964.

Dorfman, Robert, Paul A. Samuelson, and Robert M. Solow, *Linear Programming and Economic Analysis*, McGraw-Hill Book Co., Inc., New York, 1958.

Downs, Anthony, *Inside Bureaucracy*, Little Brown and Co., Boston, 1967.

Dresher, Melvin, *Games of Strategy: Theory and Applications*, Prentice-Hall Inc., Englewood Cliffs, New Jersey, 1961.

Dreyfus, Stuart, *Dynamic Programming and the Calculus of Variations*, Academic Press Inc., New York, 1965.

Fishman, George S., *Spectral Methods in Econometrics*, Harvard University Press, Cambridge, Massachusetts, 1969.

Gale, David, *The Theory of Linear Economic Models*, McGraw-Hill Book Co., Inc., New York, 1960.

Hearle, Edward F. R., and Raymond J. Mason, *A Data Processing System for State and Local Governments*, Prentice-Hall, Inc., Englewood Cliffs, New Jersey, 1963.

Hirshleifer, Jack, James C. DeHaven, and Jerome W. Milliman, *Water Supply: Economics, Technology, and Policy*, University of Chicago, Chicago, 1960.

Hitch, Charles J., and Roland McKean, *The Economics of Defense in the Nuclear Age*, Harvard University Press, Cambridge, Massachusetts, 1960 [also available in paperback].

Hoeffding, Oleg, *Soviet National Income and Product in 1928*, Columbia University Press, New York, 1954.

Johnson, William A., *The Steel Industry of India*, Harvard University Press, Cambridge, Massachusetts, 1966.

Jorgenson, D. W., J. J. McCall, and R. Radner, *Optimal Replacement Policy*, North-Holland Publishing Co., Amsterdam, and Rand McNally, Chicago, 1967.

Kershaw, Joseph A., and Roland N. McKean, *Teacher Shortages and Salary Schedules*, McGraw-Hill Book Company, Inc., New York, 1962 [also available in paperback].

Kiviat, Philip J., Richard Villanueva, and Harry M. Markowitz, *The Simscript II Programming Language*, Prentice-Hall, Inc., Englewood Cliffs, New Jersey, 1969.

Leites, Nathan, and Charles Wolf, Jr., *Rebellion and Authority*, Markham Publishing Co., Chicago, 1970.

Liu, Ta-Chung, and King-Chia Yeh, *The Economy of the Chinese Mainland: National Income and Economic Development, 1933–1959*, Princeton University Press, Princeton, New Jersey, 1965.

Lubell, Harold, *Middle East Oil Crises and Western Europe's Energy Supplies*, Johns Hopkins Press, Baltimore, Maryland, 1963.

McKean, Roland N., *Efficiency in Government Through Systems Analysis: With Emphasis on Water Resource Development*, John Wiley & Sons, Inc., New York, 1958.

Marschak, Thomas, Thomas K. Glennan, Jr., and Robert Summers, *Strategy for R & D*, Springer-Verlag New York Inc., New York, 1967.

Meyer, John R., John F. Kain, and Martin Wohl, *The Urban Transportation Problem*, Harvard University Press, Cambridge, Massachusetts, 1965.

Moorsteen, Richard, *Prices and Production of Machinery in the Soviet Union, 1928–1958*, Harvard University Press, Cambridge, Massachusetts, 1962.

Nelson, Richard R., Merton J. Peck, and Edward D. Kalachek, *Technology, Economic Growth and Public Policy*, Brookings Institution, Washington, D. C., 1967.

Novick, David (ed.), *Program Budgeting: Program Analysis and the Federal Budget*, Harvard University Press, Cambridge, Massachusetts, 1965.

Pascal, Anthony (ed.), *Thinking About Cities: New Perspectives on Urban Problems*, Dickenson Publishing Co., Belmont, California, 1970 [paperback].

Quade, Edward S., and Wayne I. Boucher, *Systems Analysis and Policy Planning Applications in Defense*, American Elsevier Publishing Co., New York, 1968.

Rosen, George, *Democracy and Economic Change in India*, University of California Press, Berkeley and Los Angeles, 1966.

Sharpe, William F., *The Economics of Computers*, Columbia University Press, New York, 1969.

Williams, J. D., *The Compleat Strategyst: Being a Primer on the Theory of Games of Strategy*, McGraw-Hill Book Co., Inc., New York, 1954.

Wolf, Charles, Jr., *Foreign Aid: Theory and Practice in Southern Asia*, Princeton University Press, Princeton, New Jersey, 1960.

TEXAS A&M UNIVERSITY-TEXARKANA